DON'T LET
JERKS
GET THE BEST
OF YOU

Other Books by the Author

The Third Millennium
Free to Forgive
    with Dr. Frank Minirth
The Path to Serenity
    with Dr. Robert Hemfelt, Dr. Frank Minirth, and Dr. Richard
    Fowler
A Walk with the Serenity Prayer
    with Dr. Frank Minirth, Dr. David Congo, and Janet Congo
Love Is a Choice
    with Dr. Frank Minirth, Dr. Robert Hemfelt, and Don
    Hawkins
Love Is a Choice Workbook
    with Dr. Frank Minirth, Dr. Robert Hemfelt, Dr. Brian
    Newman, and Dr. Deborah Newman
Love Hunger
    with Dr. Frank Minirth, Dr. Robert Hemfelt, and Dr. Sharon
    Sneed
Worry-Free Living
    with Dr. Frank Minirth and Don Hawkins

For general information about other Minirth Meier New Life Clinic branch offices, counsling services, educational resources and hospital programs, call toll-free 1-800-NEW-LIFE. National Headquarters: (214)669-1733 (800)229-3000

DON'T LET JERKS

GET THE BEST OF YOU

Dr. Paul Meier

THOMAS NELSON PUBLISHERS

Published in Nashville, Tennessee, by Thomas Nelson, Inc., and distrib-
uted in Canada by Word Communications, Ltd., Richmond, British Co-
lumbia, and in the United Kingdom by Word (UK), Ltd., Milton Keynes,
England.

ISBN 0-8407-7596-2 (CB)

CONTENTS

PART I:

Welcome To a World of Jerks—and Masochists

Chapter One: 3
 It's a Jungle Out There, and It's Full of Jerks!

Chapter Two: 16
 What Does a First-Degree Jerk Look Like?

Chapter Three: 30
 Careful! Second-Degree Jerks Can Be Anywhere!

Chapter Four: 55
 Society's Sociopaths—Nth-Degree Jerks

Chapter Five: 78
 But Why Are We Such Pushovers for the Predatory Jerks?

PART II:

Six Steps Out of Masochism to Maturity

Chapter Six: 101
 Meet the Enemy—He Is Definitely Us
 STEP ONE: *Take a Good Look at the Jerk Within*

Chapter Seven: 126
Are Mom and Dad Still Parenting You?
STEP TWO: *Finish Leaving Home Psychologically*

Chapter Eight: 147
Why Not Sing Your Own Song?
STEP THREE: *Break the Jerk Addiction Cycle*

Chapter Nine: 168
You Can't Stuff Your Anger Forever
STEP FOUR: *Bury the Hatchet, Handle, and All*

Chapter Ten: 188
Why Keep Running the Rat Race?
STEP FIVE: *Become Your Own Best Friend*

Chapter Eleven: 216
Moving on Toward Maturity
STEP SIX: *Be Accountable All Your Life*

APPENDIX: Thirty-Two Other Defense
Mechanisms   239

NOTES   247

About the Author   250

PART
I

WELCOME TO A WORLD OF JERKS— AND MASOCHISTS

CHAPTER
1

It's a Jungle Out There, and It's Full of Jerks!

I felt a little like Rodney Dangerfield ("I can't get no respect") when an editor from the Thomas Nelson Publishing Company called and said:

"Remember our conversation about new book projects at dinner the other night? You were talking about how everyone has to contend with jerks in this life—in fact, we are all jerks to some degree, and you sort of joked that what this world needs is a good book on how to live in a world filled with jerks."

"Yes, I remember," I said. "We all laughed because I was really just sort of joking."

"Well, we *aren't*. We think the world *is* ready for a book on how to survive in a world of jerks, and that you are just the jerk who can write it! In fact, your wife agrees. One of our editors chatted with Jan after dinner, and she said that she could easily recall several hundred jerky things you've done throughout your marriage. We know you're good at being vulnerable, plus you're a psychiatrist and an established author, so we can see you being a major example in the book!"

I told the editor that it was an intriguing idea and that I'd talk it over with Jan and see what she thought. As I hung up I turned to my sweet wife and told her about the call. It *did* sound like an interesting book because it would be fun to recount the progress I had made in becoming more mature and less of a jerk in our twenty-seven years of marriage.

Then, remembering the slightly slanderous remark Jan had made to the editor, I decided to call her bluff: "You told someone at the publishing house that you had several hundred examples of my jerky behavior in your head. Why don't you 'wrack your brain' and give me just a few of them right now?"

Whenever Jan smiles patiently, I know I'm in for trouble, and this was no exception: "Well, let's see now. How about the time you had the entire family in the van with you and those girls in that Volkswagen convertible wouldn't let anybody pass? Do you remember what you did with your giant cup of soda when you finally did get around them?"

I winced. Yes, I did remember (a story I'll share later when defining various kinds of jerk behavior), but I decided to press my luck. Surely she couldn't remember anything else. I was wrong.

"Well, speaking of your driving, for years whenever we went anywhere, you usually did the driving and you would tell us that the car had to be at the temperature *you* liked, and the music on the radio had to be the kind *you* wanted to listen to—all because *you* were the driver. I remember the kids and I froze a lot because you liked the window down so much.

"And speaking of your likes and dislikes, ever since we've been married you've always wanted to choose what restaurant we go to. You've gotten a little bit better about that, and, while now you ask my opinion, you still sometimes finagle things around so we go where you want to go anyway.

"And what about when we moved into our very first apartment after we got back from our honeymoon? We had all the wedding gifts, our clothes, and boxes of other stuff to start life in our first little love nest, and, on moving day, where were you? You went out to find a part-time job and left me to do *all* the moving. Not only *that*, but you capped it all off by coming home after I had put away practically everything, and telling me you had stopped off at a grocery store and had been very attracted to a beautiful redhead you saw shopping in the meat department!

"Oh, yes, here's another quick example. Remember when I went into labor with Dan? It was our first baby, and I was scared to death. It was 4:00 in the morning and my water had just broken. I was trying to get everything together to go to the hospital, and where were you? In the bedroom getting dressed, and you came out and asked me what *tie* you should wear with your brown sport coat! I said, 'I don't care what tie you wear, Paul. Let's go, get me to the hospital, please!' "

"Okay, I give, I give," I said, throwing up my hands in more than mock surrender. "It's obvious you had better help me with this book—to improve my memory, if for no other reason."

Jan did make many contributions to this book, and her help was invaluable. Not only did she remember numerous examples of my jerkiness, but, probably even more important, Jan has her own marriage and family counseling practice. She has seen hundreds of examples of jerky behavior in the marriages she has helped salvage over the years.

Although this book is designed to protect readers against all kinds of jerks, one of its major goals is to help those who are married to jerks, of one degree or another, learn how to survive—and, if possible, live with their jerky spouses more happily. And another major goal is to help jerky spouses learn how to become less jerky and more loving. (I've made some real strides there, but I still like to choose what music is played on the car radio!)

Just What Is a Jerk?

Before we go any further, we need a good working definition for the word *jerk*. In its simplest form, being a jerk means "being selfish." Taking that brief concept a bit further, being a jerk means "exhibiting any selfish thoughts or behavior that are ultimately harmful to someone."

And for an even more encompassing definition, a jerk is

"anyone of any race, creed, sex, or color who selfishly uses or abuses human beings, animals, or the environment in any way, shape, or form."

The root cause of jerkiness is a sense of selfish "entitlement" that is both inborn and learned. "Entitlement" simply says "I deserve to act, be, or have what I want."

Entitlement is embodied by the Tenth Commandment: "Thou shalt not covet." When entitlement goes to seed, it starts saying, "My friend's wife is mine, I deserve her. I also deserve his car, his house—in fact, I deserve *everything.*"

Another definition of jerkiness is good, old-fashioned narcissism. Narcissus, as you may recall from Greek mythology, sat gazing at his reflection in a pool for so long that he fell in love with himself and became so enthralled with his own image that he was eventually transformed into the flower that bears his name. Simply put, narcissism is self-centeredness.

While we are all born with the capacity to love and be loved and do good, that capacity is overshadowed during our first few years of life by our sense of narcissistic entitlement. According to the best research studies on how little children think, from birth to eighteen months the infant believes his mother is literally an extension of him. If Mom leaves the room he cries because part of him has just left, and after all, he is entitled to always have all of him there.

At about eighteen months, children figure out that Mom is a separate person, and they spend the next eighteen months—up to age three—thinking that the world revolves around them. Mom may be a separate person, but she is now the child's total slave, and he wants her there to do every single thing he wants when he wants it.

The term *terrible twos* is a lot more than just a cute label. Two-year-olds need a lot of loving discipline. They need to learn boundaries and limits because they think they rule the roost. They think they should be able to decide what they'll do or not do, and they also believe they can decide what Mother and Dad should do or not do. When their little desires are not met, they can get angry—*very* angry. Their sense of entitlement is at its height.

Around age three, children start developing a conscience.

If they are getting any discipline at all, along with plenty of love, they start feeling some good, legitimate, healthy guilt when they do something wrong. And they start accepting limitations and learning how to get along in a world where there are limits. In short, they learn they are not entitled to everything.

So, while we are all born narcissists, most of us manage to conquer these tendencies as we grow up and learn that there are limits. Some of us obviously conquer our narcissistic sense of entitlement better than others, but, and here's the important point, none of us conquer that sense of entitlement completely. The first premise of this book is: *Jerkism is unavoidable.* None of us is perfect, or, to put it another way, completely mature.

If I am willing to admit my lack of perfection, then I must go on to admit that part of me is a jerk, just as part of everyone that I'm going to love or be loved by, deal with or work with, or even go to church with, is going to be a jerk, *at least to some degree.* Reality says I'm going to be a jerk to some people, and they're going to be jerks to me. That's not necessarily okay, but it *is* reality, and we are all going to have to live with this jerky reality until we get to heaven.

There Are Three Kinds of Jerks

In our work at the Minirth-Meier clinics, we have dealt with literally thousands of examples of jerky behavior. Roughly speaking, we see our patients breaking down into three categories:

- Mild to moderate selfishness (hereafter referred to as First-Degree Jerk).
- Serious to acute selfishness (hereafter referred to as Second-Degree Jerk).
- Severe to sociopathic selfishness (hereafter referred to as Nth-Degree Jerk).

Roughly speaking, we see the general population breaking down this way:

40 percent First-Degree Jerks,
40 percent Second-Degree Jerks,
10 percent Nth-Degree Jerks.

If you bother to do a bit of quick addition, you will see that that adds up to only 90 percent. Because we do not deal with every living person on Planet Earth, we have left one other category open. Somewhere out there are folk who have practically conquered all their jerky tendencies. We call these people Mature Adults. To become a totally mature, loving, caring adult should be everyone's goal, and we'll be discussing how this is done in later chapters.

First-Degree Jerks Are the "Good Guys"

Actually, First-Degree Jerk behavior is really not that bad. To put it simply, we could call the First-Degree Jerks "good guys" who mean well, try to be honest, fair, and trustworthy for the most part, but who may be a bit selfish now and then or take advantage of others without meaning real harm. In other words, by definition, a First-Degree Jerk is your ordinary, run-of-the-mill individual who believes in "live and let live" and "do unto others as you want them to do unto you."

If everyone in the world were a First-Degree Jerk, most of our serious problems would be solved. Oh, we'd still have some pollution, disagreements, and rule-breaking, but crime would be markedly reduced, wars would be infrequent, and divorces much less common. It wouldn't be a "perfect world," but it would be a lot nicer one.

Trouble is, a goodly number—about 50 percent of the inhabitants of Planet Earth—are jerks of a much different color. While First-Degree Jerks act selfishly at times, they usually are unaware that they are doing so and they don't mean any harm. Second-Degree Jerks, however, purposefully and willfully manipulate, control, and abuse their fellowman. And, while they usually feel some guilt afterward, they are likely to do it again.

For example, a First-Degree Jerk would not have an affair. A Second-Degree Jerk *would* have an affair and feel bad later, but possibly have another affair, depending on circumstances.

Nth-Degree Jerks are far more dangerous than Second-Degree Jerks. They are the real sickos of society who truly enjoy controlling, abusing, and dominating their fellowman and not feeling *any* guilt about the pain and suffering they cause. A clinical name for an Nth-Degree Jerk is someone with a sociopathic personality disorder. The Nth-Degree Jerk has no conscience. For example, Nth-Degree Jerks can have multiple affairs without even blinking.

The Pendulum Has Swung Too Far

There have always been First-Degree, Second-Degree, and Nth-Degree Jerks down through history. We aren't sure if the percentages have always been the same. Chances are around 10 percent of society has always fallen into the Nth-Degree category. But we are wondering if the 1970s, 1980s, and early 1990s (the "Me Generation") have possibly produced more than the usual crop of Second-Degree Jerks.

The past two decades or so have brought on some welcome and unwelcome changes. One of the welcome developments has been a widespread move toward healthy assertiveness. There has been slow but steady improvement in the fair treatment of women, minorities, and the environment.

The good news of the "Me Generation" is that it brought a lot of people out of their passivity, low self-esteem, and self-defeating behavior into a healthy assertiveness that helped them improve and succeed, mentally, emotionally, and financially. The bad news, however, is that for a large number of people, the pendulum swing kept right on going past healthy assertiveness, right into narcissistic jerkiness— feeling that it's okay if I use and abuse others. After all, "I have to look out for Number One."

How far will the pendulum swing? I believe it has already swung too far. In our clinics, we have observed the enormous grief and human suffering that have occurred due to the tragic emotional fallout of the Me Generation. We have seen an increase in abuse, in compulsions, in addictions of all kinds, and in existential despair over potential failure and/or abandonment.

Are Men More Jerky Than Women?

We all know certain individuals who are much bigger jerks than others. But we have also observed that no nation, race, creed, color, or sex has an exclusive corner on jerkiness. If you generalize this trait to large groups or races of people, you become a "prejudiced jerk" yourself.

Contrary to popular opinion, men (as a group) are *not* more jerky than women. I realize that my use of the word *jerk* for the general population may be difficult for some women readers to swallow, because a few may think only men are jerks. A woman may have had an Nth-Degree Jerk for a father, or she may now have one for a husband. So she falls victim to black-and-white thinking that all men are Nth-Degree or at least Second-Degree Jerks and all women are innocent victims. It's true enough, I guess, that the term *jerk* is usually applied to men, but some of our most dependable psychological tests show there are an equal number of women who are jerks as well—or, if you prefer, "jerkettes."

The most popular personality test used throughout the world is the *Minnesota Multiphasic Personality Inventory* (MMPI). At least ten million people have taken this test. Colleges, graduate schools, psychology clinics, and even seminaries give it. I was required to take it to get into medical school. It's not gospel—no psychology test is perfect—but it's basically a *very* good test.

One of the traits the MMPI tests for is sociopathy, the tendency to selfishly use and abuse others, knowingly or unknowingly. None of us is totally devoid of sociopathy. We all have some, but according to records kept on the MMPI, the millions of males and millions of females who have taken the test have scored quite equally. The MMPI is fairly irrefutable proof that men and women are equally selfish. There is no significant statistical difference between the sexes in over-all sociopathy, only in the ways the men and women demonstrate it in their daily lives.

In our work with thousands of patients in Minirth-Meier Clinics throughout the nation, we see the findings of the MMPI borne out daily. Jerky husbands abuse their wives, and jerky wives abuse their husbands. I have a great deal of compassion and empathy for sufferers of both sexes. Many of them have been innocent victims of physical, sexual, or verbal abuse while growing up, and they have developed some "extra baggage"—repressed hostility, a fear of not being in control, and lowered self-esteem, just to name a few of dozens of problems. Ironically, it is very common for these abused individuals to marry someone who is like the parent of the opposite sex, no matter how much of a jerk that parent might have been.

So while men may seem to fit the jerk description better than women, it is quite true that women are equally jerky (i.e., "selfish").

I realize, however, that a lot of women reading this book are still thinking, *Okay, Dr. Meier, I guess I fit the jerkette category, but my husband can really be a jerk—not to mention my boss. If I start admitting I'm a little jerky at times, how do I learn to handle the people who can be really jerky to me?*

A good question deserves a good answer, and I'll try to give it: In learning about our own jerkiness, we will be better equipped to handle the jerks who are more powerful, controlling, and assertive. Basic military strategy says, "Know your enemy." And as Pogo, a military genius without peer, once stated, "We have met the enemy, and he is us!" The more clearly we can see our own tendencies toward a narcissistic sense of entitlement, the better we will be able to identify what is happening when our spouse, boss, pastor, or friend really starts jerking us around.

Talk to just about anyone today, and they will tell you that they know people who think they have a right to place excessive demands on our time, our money, our willingness to help others, and even on our bodies.

Narcissistic drivers on the highways of life speed up to

prevent us from entering obvious openings in their lanes or else ride our bumpers rather than switching lanes themselves.

Supposed "friends" who have a strong sense of entitlement invite us out to eat at nice restaurants, flirt with our mates, then leave us to pick up the tab.

Our workaholic bosses try to feel important by laying guilt trips on us when we make our families a higher priority than our jobs. Yes, the pendulum has definitely swung too far! Second-Degree and Nth-Degree Jerks, in particular, are having a field day at the expense of the rest of us.

Maybe, Just Maybe, You're a Masochist

Unfortunately, many of us set ourselves up to be abused by the jerks who are predators. In fact, as I will show later, there is a direct link between being First-Degree Jerks and being unwitting "masochists" who follow a kind of failure script that allows the Second-Degree and Nth-Degree Jerks to take us for a ride, con us, cheat us, lie to us, and in some cases, hurt us badly in emotional and even physical ways.

When I use the word *masochist* here, I'm not talking about whips and chains. In this book, *masochism* simply means "the tendency to set yourself up to get hurt, victimized, or taken advantage of." Masochism is self-defeating behavior that we may indulge in consciously or unconsciously. Masochism is a failure script that we follow when we have a hard time saying no. In short, masochism is the tendency to allow ourselves to be used or abused by jerky people.

Perhaps you fit this description of the kind of person who gets taken advantage of all too often. Perhaps you've been thinking that your problem has simply been bad luck, but lately you're not so sure. Probably one of the major reasons you picked up this book in the first place was to learn how to deal with the people who are unfairly getting the best of you, one way or another. You have been looking for instructions on the art of psychological self-defense against jerk abuse. You are fed up with being the fall guy and the doormat, and you aren't going to take it anymore!

From the many thousands of patients we have treated at our Minirth-Meier Clinics throughout the country, we have learned that much of the emotional pain humans go through is unnecessary and avoidable with proper education and counseling. The rest is *unavoidable* pain, which can eventually benefit us, because it helps us learn valuable lessons about life and survival. As the "Serenity Prayer"—used by Alcoholics Anonymous for many years—teaches, we can ask God for the *serenity* to accept the unavoidable pains we cannot change, the *courage* to change the pains we can, and the *wisdom* to know the difference.

In his best-selling book *Inside Out,* Dr. Larry Crabb states that authors and leaders who teach us that we can go from painful reality to a life of constant joy and bliss are phoney, and I agree with him! We can improve our lives dramatically, but we still have that "necessary pain" to prepare for, deal with, and learn from. It's part of the real world.

This book will offer *real solutions* to *real problems* by thoroughly evaluating the real pain that we all suffer because of the jerks who hurt us, as well as the narcissism we sometimes painfully discover in our mates and ourselves! We have to make painful changes on the inside before we can see behavioral changes on the outside. As Dr. Larry Crabb states, however, "This kind of change—change from the inside out—is worth the pain."[1]

This book is written in the hope that it will help you gain the wisdom to tell necessary and unnecessary pain apart. Of course, we want success in life—physically, emotionally, and spiritually. Yes, we want significance, love, and meaning in what we do and how we live. But at the same time, we are living in a jungle and it's full of hungry jerks. How far do we let them push us? How much is enough? And how much is too much?

Sometimes I run into nice people who are tempted to allow the predators of society to use or abuse them in certain ways, because they think this is how they can get ahead in life. My answer is always the same: Please, don't do it. Don't sell your soul for a sense of significance! The Me Generation may want to punch you in the nose or run roughshod over you, but their rights end where your nose begins!

What This Book Can Do for You

In the following chapters, I want to show you:

- How to recover from jerk abuse that you may have already suffered in the past.
- How to prevent or at least strongly curtail abuse from jerks, particularly Second-Degree or Nth Degree Jerks who may be in a position to affect you and your family adversely.
- How to deal with your masochistic tendencies and their roots, such as false guilt, and a certain sense of pervading shame that you probably aren't even aware of, but it all sets you up for jerk abuse, just the same.

I want to teach you some simple psychological judo holds and throws that will allow you to face predatory jerks with confidence, gain the advantage, and deal with them lovingly, or at least in a civil manner that lets them know you will not be manipulated, controlled, or abused anymore.

As I have already alluded to above, the best way for you to gain all these insights is by learning more about your own jerkiness—your own tendency to take advantage, be a little selfish, and put yourself ahead of others—all without meaning any harm, of course. I feel I can write this book not simply because I'm a psychiatrist, but because I have personal experience in being at least a First-Degree Jerk who at times used to slide over the line into Second-Degree Jerk behavior.

In addition, I also know quite a bit about being the fall guy for clever or seemingly sincere Second-Degree Jerks who took advantage of my masochistic, self-destructive tendencies, which I thought were just "good guy characteristics."

In short, I'm your typical First-Degree Jerk who has been taken to the cleaners by experts—the more selfish and ruthless jerks of the world because far too often I have put myself in a position where I could be abused. Today, I'm still at work on preventing jerk abuse of myself and my family, being less open to self-destruction, less gullible, less of a patsy, and more of a mature adult.

At the same time, however, as I guard against being abused by Second-Degree and Nth-Degree Jerks, I don't want to overreact and become selfish, uncaring, and unloving. So, I'm still working on some First-Degree Jerk traits that stubbornly refuse to go away completely.

In a word, to fight off predatory jerks of this world, we need balance. And the first step toward getting that balance is to know a little bit more about what it means to be a First-Degree Jerk. Why do I say that we are all jerks of at least the First-Degree at some time or another? Personally, I don't want to be a jerk! I don't like being a jerk, but it comes automatically, like breathing and sleeping. What does a First-Degree Jerk look like? Are some First-Degree Jerks more jerky than others? We'll look at all these questions and more in the next chapter.

CHAPTER
2

What Does a First-Degree Jerk Look Like?

Since my publisher agrees that I am the most qualified jerk to write this book, and because you've already read several of my wife's recollections of my jerkiness, I'll begin sketching a portrait of the First-Degree Jerk by giving one more personal example of what a First-Degree Jerk really looks like.

As you might have guessed, Jan also helped me remember a lot of the following true account. I admit that I can be oblivious at times, lost in my world of thoughts, theories, and book writing. I have worked on "tuning in" to Jan and the kids for years, but earlier in our marriage I was in my own world a lot of the time, much to Jan's frustration.

When we got married, Jan was a teacher, holding a degree in early childhood education. Her lifelong dream had been to work in a counseling capacity of some kind and, after she had helped me get through medical school and when our four children had arrived, she decided that it was now or never if she wanted to do any additional graduate work toward a marriage and family counseling degree. At the time, our youngest child was around two and our oldest was somewhere near ten. Because this story may be more interesting from a mother's perspective, I'll let Jan take over at this point.

When I reentered graduate school, Paul sounded very supportive. "It's a great idea," he told me, "I know you've always wanted to do this, and don't worry about the kids. I can take care of them, or, if necessary, we can get a sitter sometimes."

It turned out that one of my first courses was offered on Monday nights from 7:00 to 10:00 P.M. After getting everyone fed and our two-year-old bathed and in bed, I'd leave for school, reminding Paul that the older kids needed to get their baths and be in bed by a reasonable time.

"Sure, sure," he'd mutter. "Don't worry. I've got it all under control."

Off to school I would go, always calling in around 9:00 during a break in my schedule to check on things and ask the usual questions: How were the kids? Have they had their baths? Had Dan done his spelling homework? Paul was always rather vague. He'd say things like: "The kids? . . . Well, I don't know, I haven't seen them for a while . . ." And then he'd always add the clincher: "Say, where *are* you anyway?"

"I'm where I always am on Monday nights," I would reply, "at school."

"Well, everything's okay here, I guess," he would say. And then I would hear him shouting to the kids in the next room: "Okay, kids, get your baths now!"

Every Monday night we went through the same phone routine, and Paul always asked the same question: "Where *are* you? When will you be *home*?"

I'm not sure how I got through grad school or how the kids survived to grow up. I can still recall coming in one night and finding water trickling down the stairs from an overflowing bathtub on the second floor. Paul meant well, and his outward verbal message was, "Yes, I want you to go to school." But his nonverbal message was really this: "I'm really not tuned in to what you're doing, and besides you really should be home watching your kids as a good mother should."

I'm happy to have Jan share this account of one example of what a First-Degree Jerk looks like because I'm sure it's a familiar one to many wives. Husbands do have a way of tuning things out, not paying attention, really wanting their wives to be sure they take care of the kids and keep the home running. While I really was all for Jan going to grad school, deep down in my First-Degree Jerk heart, I didn't want to be bothered with some of the inconveniences that were involved. In other words, I was a little selfish—maybe more than a little.

Lest you think that I hold a monopoly on jerkiness in our family, I'd like to share a couple examples of how Jan can be a "jerkette" at times. When I'd fade off into my typical state of oblivion, Jan had her own devious ways of getting revenge. She seldom got openly angry with me about my jerkiness, but instead she would manage to be late getting home from late-night graduate school classes, and she would "forget" to call to let me know she wouldn't be home on time. This, of course, left me wondering if something had happened to her.

Or when I'd duck out on chores and go play golf instead of taking care of a "honey-do" project for Jan, she would pout, withdraw, forget to pick up my shirts at the laundry, or "have a headache" at inconvenient times.

All these behaviors are called "passive aggressiveness," a defense mechanism we'll look at more closely in Chapter 6. Suffice it to say, passive aggressiveness is a good way to unconsciously get back at your jerky husband with little jerkette ploys of your own and not even be aware you're doing it!

First-Degree Jerks Can Be Very Controlling

The examples we have just given you of First-Degree Jerk tendencies in the Meier family are only a small part of the total picture of what a First-Degree Jerk looks like. Let's look for a moment at a typical businessperson—your boss, perhaps, who, as a First-Degree Jerk is a very fine, moral, upstanding citizen. He's a good husband, father, and, for the most part, not a bad guy to work for—except for one thing. Your boss is very controlling. *Everything* has to go through him, even the simplest tasks by the maintenance people pass his inspection first. As a result, his employees suffer loss of self-esteem and the company loses time and money.

A major characteristic of many First-Degree Jerks is that they are controllers. I identify because, as a reformed high-level First-Degree Jerk who is working on becoming a mature adult, I am still struggling with wanting to control others, particularly my own family. As Jan often points out, I do tend to pick which restaurant we go to, or at least I heavily influence our choice. I am improving, though. At least I no longer order my meal first, as I used to. Now I go last on purpose.

Actually, I've come a long way from the early days of our marriage. Not long after we got back from our honeymoon, Jan went to the refrigerator to get herself an ice cream bar. Because I had been raised in a very strict German home where my father was "the boss," I let Jan know, "I didn't give you permission to get that ice cream bar out of the refrigerator."

Jan is a very peaceful sort by nature, but with this Neanderthal remark I went past her line. She let me know in no uncertain terms that she would get an ice cream bar when she felt like it, and if I didn't like it, I knew what I could do! Jan enjoyed her ice cream bar, and for the rest of the evening it was cold enough in the apartment to make ice cream without a machine.

First-Degree Jerks can be wonderful people. They can work with the homeless, give hours of their time to serve their church or their community, but they still have blind spots. I know of a man who loves God and people, and people genuinely love him, too. His Bible study classes are always packed out and he has a wide reputation for being able to apply biblical principles to real life situations.

But in a small dinner party setting, this man's jerky Achilles' tendon shows through. If he is with two or three other couples, and the entire group spends four hours together, he dominates the conversation for at least three of those hours. Whenever anyone shares something personal, this man has a favorite response: "That reminds me of . . ." Although this man is a truly wonderful person, he is still a First-Degree Jerk, at least in this one area.

First-Degree Jerk Parents Are Common

An obvious place for First-Degree Jerk characteristics to show up is in parenting. It has often been said that children are a crystal-clear mirror of their parents' attitudes and actions. They can also be their parents' severest critics. Our children, who are all teenagers at present, offered to write an entire chapter for this book on the jerky tendencies of their parents, but we declined their offer. While we're willing to be vulnerable, we aren't crazy! Besides, maybe I'm afraid the kids will zero in on me more than their mom.

One thing that I'm guilty of quite often is wanting my children to succeed, not for what it does for them, but for what it does for me. I want them to impress people to show what a good father I am. Oh, yes, I want them to succeed for their own sakes, but I also want to look good, too. In short, I want it both ways.

Another jerky parent habit I have comes out of a "tape" that has been played in my head ever since I was a child: "You're not quite good enough." Directly and indirectly, I have communicated this same tape to my kids, and they hear the "you're not quite good enough" message playing in their ears and minds a lot of the time.

When one of our daughters turned fourteen, the pressure she felt from having to "look good enough" became too great. She got very depressed and decided to run away from home. When she came back, she went to a counselor several times, and then he decided he would also like to talk to both of her parents.

Jan thought it would be a painful but insightful experience, but I was embarrassed because I'm a psychiatrist and a supposed "expert" on relationships in family matters. The first book I ever wrote dealt with child-rearing and personality development, and featured a bibliography of 450 books and research articles on "how to raise perfect kids." Running away is a distress signal from a hurting child, and here I was, a supposed authority on how to parent children, being called in by a counselor to find out what I was doing wrong with my own daughter.

Our counseling session was set for 9:00 on Saturday morning, but after going to bed about 10:00 on Friday night, I woke up about 2:00 A.M. and couldn't get back to sleep. I knew God was speaking to me because I couldn't get my mind off the passage in Matthew 7:3-5, which talks about seeing the toothpick in your brother's eye instead of seeing the log in your own eye.

I became obsessed with this passage, and finally I had to get up, get out my Bible, and read the entire chapter for context. As I read, God showed me that there were things about my daughter—jerky behavior, so to speak—that irritated me and that these very same behaviors were similar to behaviors in myself that I had not yet recognized.

In a sense, I had been tough on my daughter because she reminded me of myself. I wondered if my daughter wasn't doing exactly the same thing. She was having a hard time accepting me because she wasn't yet aware of certain jerky behaviors in herself, but she saw them in me. In a sense, then, she was mad at me for reminding her of herself, and I was mad at her for reminding me of myself!

After almost two hours of praying and reading the passage over and over, I went back to bed and finally got to sleep. I got up around 7:30 and never told Jan about my 2:00 A.M. devotions. At 9:00 we appeared at the counselor's office, and, as soon as introductions were complete, an amazing thing happened. We all sat down and the first thing the counselor did was open his Bible to Matthew 7:3-5, and read it aloud:

Why do you look at the speck of sawdust in your brother's eye and pay no attention to the plank in your own eye? How can you say to your brother, "Let me take the speck out of your eye," when all the time there is a plank in your own eye? You hypocrite, first take the plank out of your own eye, and then you will see clearly to remove the speck from your brother's eye. (NIV)

As the counselor finished reading, I started to weep. He said, "Why are you crying?" He had wanted to show me what he thought might be going on between me and my daughter, but he never dreamed that it would have this effect!

"I'm bawling because the chances of this happening are one in 100,000," I said. "It really makes me realize that God does love me and He loves my daughter. He wants healing in all of this." Then I told the counselor, as well as Jan and my daughter, how I had awakened the night before with that same passage in mind and how I had pondered it for almost two hours.

It turned out that this passage of Scripture—Matthew 7:3–5—was the one thing that really broke the ice. It helped me and my daughter see that we had been judging each other for jerky behavior, while failing to see our own jerkiness. Both of us had been inconsiderate, sarcastic, and guilty of putting the other down. We also played a "passive aggressive waiting game" in carpool situations. I'd show up late to pick her up, and that meant she'd have to wait for me; or she would show up late when I came to pick her up, and I would have to wait for her.

But one of my major jerky mistakes was not giving my daughter enough "complimentary empowerment." The key to parenting well is to empower your kids, and you do this by complimenting them for the things they do well. When they come up with a good insight or make a good decision, that is the moment to compliment them for their good thinking or capable actions.

Unfortunately, as the "all-wise psychiatrist," I would correct my daughter's insights just a bit in order to make them my own. Instead of empowering her by saying, "That's a great idea!" I would say, "That's not bad, but let's also think about this and this . . ." Or if she would do something well, I would tell her to "do it a little bit better next time."

I meant well—I really wanted to be a great dad—but my First-Degree Jerk kept getting in the way. As counseling with my daughter progressed, her low self-esteem and perfectionism showed up, as I knew they would, because they are the same basic problems Jan and I have. Too many times I accept and praise my children only for conforming to what I consider important, for instance, achieving success in sports, an area where I have never shone much at all.

I'm nearly 6'5", a great size for sports, and as a kid I loved trying to play baseball, basketball, and football, but I had one problem: I couldn't walk and chew gum at the same time! The only basketball team I ever won a position on was my sixth grade squad, and we got creamed in every game. Once we lost 22–2 with our only points coming because a really tall kid on the other team, who grew up, by the way, to play for the University of Michigan, accidentally made a basket for us!

Mom and Dad Meier learned a lot from going to counseling with their daughter, especially Dad. But the breakthrough began with Matthew 7:3–5. Once I got the log out of my own eye, we were able to deal with the issues and heal some wounds.

Are You a Jerky Driver?

Another obvious area where jerky traits emerge is in the way people drive a car. Some typical First-Degree Jerk practices include:

- Driving ten miles or more above whatever the speed limit might be, "just keeping up with traffic."
- Driving slowly and holding up traffic, oblivious to the people who are going crazy behind you.
- Driving so absentmindedly it scares your mate or other passengers.
- Tailgating the car ahead of you, or cutting off the guy in the next lane when you try to pass.

The First-Degree Jerk driver doesn't really mean any harm. He just does his own thing without thinking too much, leaving a trail of frustrated, angry fellow motorists behind him.

Jerkiness Includes the Opposite Sex

As you may have suspected, we engage in a lot of jerky behavior regarding the opposite sex. A typical First-Degree Jerk practice is finding ways to help and/or protect attractive members of the opposite sex so you can win their approval. Perhaps you simply flirt in subtle ways with popular or powerful members of the opposite sex. You may feel a little guilty afterward, but you realize you'll do it again anyway.

Keep in mind that all this attracting and flirting is not done with the intent of being overtly unfaithful to your mate. When you're a First-Degree Jerk, you're committed to being sexually faithful, but there are those moments when you wish you didn't have to be. During sex with your mate, you may have fleeting moments when you fantasize about other people. While you give verbal assent to wanting to please your mate, you are primarily concerned with your own sexual enjoyment.

How Jerky Are You?

The examples could go on and on. To be a First-Degree Jerk means that you are a fairly normal person who is basically trying to live a good life, but who has weaknesses and imperfections. Following is my official "First-Degree Jerk Test," which I devised from studying my own behavior as well as that of numerous patients.

The test questions reflect certain attitudes and behaviors of the mild to moderate First-Degree Jerk—which is, by the way, about as good as most of us humans ever get. Note that I have left two scoring columns, one for yourself and one for a significant other (for example, your mate or your boss). Take the test yourself first, scoring yourself as follows: 1,

Seldom (you have been guilty of the statement at least once in your life); 2, Sometimes (guilty of this statement at least several times); 3, Often (guilty of this statement on a fairly regular basis). If the statement does not pertain to you at all, give yourself a 0.

First-Degree Jerk

	Myself	Mate (or other)
1. I may act or think selfishly, putting my own interests and needs ahead of others.	_____	_____
2. When in a group of people, I talk more than most of the others in the group.	_____	_____
3. In social situations (such as a conversation or while out to dinner) I am more comfortable if I can feel I am in control of what's being said.	_____	_____
4. I boast about my talents or accomplishments.	_____	_____
5. When someone gets angry with me, my first inclination is to be angry back rather than to analyze why that person is angry.	_____	_____
6. In social situations, my goal is to be successful and well liked, rather than be interested in others for their own sake.	_____	_____
7. When in an argument, I am more concerned about presenting my point of view than in finding the so-called truth.	_____	_____
8. When things go wrong, I blame others.	_____	_____
9. Even though I want to be a responsible person, I may still act		

	Myself	**Mate** *(or other)*

irresponsibly or in an immature
manner.

10. When someone offends me, I
find a way to get even, subtly or
openly.

11. When my rights are violated, I
tend to lose my temper.

12. I tend to give myself too many
rights (be selfish).

13. Even though I am unusually
honest, I will tell white lies to
avoid making trouble for myself
or others.

14. I enjoy "exchanging news"
(gossiping) about certain people
or types of people.

15. I have a certain dislike, distrust,
or resentment for authority
figures (such as police, teachers,
pastors).

16. I like reading or hearing news
stories about authority figures
who have gotten into trouble,
arguments, or fights.

17. I enjoy helping others, if they
are people who are attractive,
powerful, or popular.

18. Although I feel sorry for orphans
or the poor and homeless, I avoid
thinking about, reading about, or
helping them.

19. When I participate in athletics
(such as tennis, softball, golf),
winning is more important than
just having fun.

20. I may shut out my own loved
ones with too much TV, video

	Myself	**Mate** *(or other)*

games, or some other hobby or
interest that distracts me.   _____ _____

21. When I have the opportunity, I
may pressure or manipulate
others into doing what I want to
do.   _____ _____

22. I may feel guilty about taking
advantage of wealthy friends in
various ways, but I tend to do it
anyway.   _____ _____

23. When going out to a restaurant
with associates, friends, or family,
I tend to choose where we will all
eat rather than asking for other
opinions.   _____ _____

24. When ordering in a restaurant, I
tend to order my meal before
any others at the table order
theirs.   _____ _____

25. In general, I feel I deserve (am
entitled to) more privileges than I
have now.   _____ _____

Now, add up your score and see in which category of
First-Degree Jerk you fall:

> 56-75—high-level First-Degree Jerk
> 36-55—mid-level First-Degree Jerk
> 16-35—mild, low-level First-Degree Jerk
> 15 or below—Lying is probably one of your jerky prob-
> lems. On the other hand, if you swear you are telling
> the truth, be sure to check with your mate because you
> may be suffering from delusions of sainthood, which
> she or he can probably correct in a hurry!

In fact, you and your spouse may want to both take this
First-Degree Jerk Test to score yourselves and then take it

again to score each other. If you are communicating fairly well, this could lead to some very meaningful dialogue. On the other hand, if communication is a problem, or there are other tensions in your marriage, you may want to go slowly pointing out each other's jerkiness. Instead of leading to meaningful dialogue, it could result in a knock-down, drag-out fight, and in extreme cases, a divorce!

After taking this test, I hope you can see why I say almost all of us are First-Degree Jerks, *at least to some degree.* After working on my own jerkiness for years, I still score in the high 30s, which qualifies me as a "mid-level First-Degree Jerk." (As you might suspect, Jan scores in the high teens, just barely making it into the low-level First-Degree Jerk classification.)

If you haven't taken the First-Degree Jerk test yet, I hope you'll stop reading and take it right now. Not only will it give you insights into your own behavior, but it will help you understand your wife, children, Uncle Harry, or even the next door neighbor better. When you see First-Degree jerkiness in your loved ones, you can be more tolerant of what they're doing because you realize that they're just doing the same kind of things *you* do, in their own particular way. We all have our own approach to being jerks. We all have logs, branches, or toothpicks in our eyes that keep us from seeing the whole truth.

Keep in mind that it's no disgrace to be a First-Degree Jerk. First-degree jerks are generally pretty decent folks, but not perfect. As a typical First-Degree Jerk, you probably had a decent upbringing, but you still have a few faults, shortcomings, and weaknesses. First-Degree Jerks are jerky at times, but usually they are unaware of just how jerky they actually are.

Remember the definition of *jerkiness* that we started with: "a bit of self-centered narcissism mixed with a strong sense of entitlement." Ironically, many First-Degree Jerks often have masochistic tendencies (to be discussed thoroughly in Chapter 5). To put it another way, if you're a typical "good guy" First-Degree Jerk, you may be unconsciously putting yourself in a position to be abused by a formidable group of predators—Second-Degree Jerks, who can really do you in. In the next chapter, we'll take a look at Second-Degree Jerks to learn more about how they operate and what you can do to defend yourself from their wily ways.

CHAPTER
3

Careful! Second-Degree Jerks Can Be Anywhere!

As a young husband and father, I was a rather high-level First-Degree Jerk, but I could occasionally cross the line into Second-Degree Jerk behavior. One such incident occurred while Jan and I were driving home from a vacation with all four of our kids in the family van. We were on a divided highway, with two lanes on our side, a rather wide island in the middle, and two lanes for oncoming traffic.

The speed limit was 55, and a big truck was in the slow lane going about 45. Up ahead, four girls in a Volkswagen convertible with the top down had decided to play their own little passive-aggressive game and began going exactly 45 miles an hour right next to the truck. Soon the girls had a line of about twenty cars behind them, which began tooting with frustration because the girls wouldn't speed up and get ahead of the truck, or slow down behind the truck to let others pass them.

I came up behind this parade of vehicles and, after being patient for maybe two or three minutes, began to get angry. Finally, I noticed a long stretch ahead where the shoulder was wide enough to pass, and I took off on the shoulder, passing all twenty or so cars and the truck. I should have driven on, satisfied to have gotten around the snarl, but then I decided, *I'm going to teach those girls a lesson.*

I had been drinking a huge soda, which I had placed on the dashboard caddy while I made my maneuver around the twenty cars and the truck. Taking the almost full cup of soda out of the caddy, I slowed down to about 35 miles an hour, which meant the truck had to slow down as well. Unaware of my strategy, the girls pulled up beside me for a few seconds, which was all the time I needed.

Reaching out the open window, I threw the huge cup of soda all over them and then took off. Our children, who were all rather young at the time, cheered, but Jan just groaned. Obviously, the girls "deserved" some kind of comeuppance, but what I did was certainly jerky, not to mention stupid. I could have easily gotten into an accident, trying to pass so many vehicles on the righthand shoulder, and the soda could have temporarily blinded the driver of the Volkswagen and caused her to run off the road.

I drove on in smug triumph—for at least half a mile. Then Jan's disapproval and my own natural First-Degree Jerk nature caught up with me, and I felt guilty the rest of the trip for having such a Second-Degree Jerk reaction.

Tossing the soda all over the girls in the VW convertible was definitely Second-Degree Jerk behavior. I felt rather good (vindicated) at the time, but doing something that hostile was not my usual nature. A genuine Second-Degree Jerk tries to control, bully, dominate, and even abuse most of the time, and is often well aware of what he or she is doing. A Second-Degree Jerk would have laughed all the way home.

Setting Prisoners Free Is Our Business

Second-Degree Jerk behavior is often involved in the hundreds of cases we treat at Minirth-Meier Clinics each year. I recall driving down to our Dallas Psychiatry Unit on a hot Fourth of July morning with the phrase "set the prisoners free!" running through my mind. I was a prisoner of my own profession that day. Being a psychiatrist has far more advantages than disadvantages, but one disadvantage is having to work on holidays, if you have a hospital practice.

But whatever I felt about being a prisoner of my hospital practice on the Fourth of July was offset by one great advantage, the rewarding experience of setting our patients free from the emotional scars of past abuses, free from addictions, free from anxiety and depression, or free from the bondage of jerk abuse in marriage.

In addition, I had the normal patriotic surges of being an American that well up in me every July 4. My parents had escaped as children from the Communist revolution in Russia, after seeing some of their uncles shot to death for refusing to "enlist." Their joy of living in freedom in the great country of America was passed on to me and my siblings.

Mixed with all these thoughts were memories of the sermon I had heard my pastor, Dr. Stanley Toussaint, deliver on the previous Sunday. He had spoken of how Jesus came to earth to set all kinds of prisoners free, including those who were haunted by mental and emotional problems.

When I arrived at the Minirth-Meier Behavioral Medicine Unit in Dallas, Texas, my first task was to evaluate two new patients who had checked in the evening before. I saw both as being prisoners of sorts, as we all are from time to time.

Tom was the prisoner of a very controlling, verbally abusive, "castrating wife," who cut him down at every opportunity in order to keep him under her thumb.

Tom's wife was a highly regarded head nurse in the surgical unit at a big name hospital in an Eastern city. She had been sexually unfaithful to him on more than one occasion, usually with doctors she worked with. She did her surgical nurse work with precision, and she was also adept at surgically destroying Tom's ego, self-esteem, and any desires he might have toward developing a sense of self-determination.

Our therapists do not recommend divorce. Our job is to be a mirror to our patients, helping them to see the truth about what is happening. We point out conscious and unconscious conflicts through intensive, insight-oriented therapy. The decisions are left up to each patient, as they should be.

After a month of therapy, Tom decided to stand up to "Nurse Ratchet." He laid down some boundaries and told her he would separate from her if she didn't honor those boundaries. He wanted to give her the chance to choose: repent and get conjoint therapy with him for a couple of years, or else not have Tom at home to kick around anymore.

Much to everyone's pleasant surprise, "Nurse Ratchet" chose to get long-term therapy. She developed insights into how her own parents had taught her terrible values and perspectives. She repented of her Second-Degree Jerkiness, stopped having affairs, and gradually became a mid-level First-Degree Jerk, which was fine with Tom.

Jim Was a Prisoner of Perfectionism

The other patient I evaluated that Fourth of July was Jim. He was also a prisoner—of his own perfectionism. He had married Sally a dozen years earlier because she was a beautiful college cheerleader and junior class president. At first Jim had enjoyed showing Sally off to his friends and business associates. But now, a dozen years later, she had put on fifteen pounds and wasn't able to keep their two children under perfect control every second.

"Another thing, she takes way too long to get her makeup on whenever we go out," Jim complained, "and she's always moaning about her aches and pains. She's turned into a hypochondriac!"

We learned later, while talking to Sally, that her aches and pains were directly linked to her repressed rage toward Jim for having such unrealistic expectations of her. But an even more serious result of Jim's expectations of his wife was that he had become so bitter that it had caused him to go into a serious biochemical, clinical depression. He was even feeling suicidal, and he blamed it all on Sally.

Sally wasn't perfect, but she was a long way from being a "Nurse Ratchet." We drilled away at Jim's expectations, which he had learned from overindulgent parents, who made him feel that whatever he wanted was exactly what he should get. Unfortunately, Jim's story didn't turn out as well as Tom's. After six weeks of treatment, his suicidal urges left him, but Jim didn't appreciate our insights into what was really causing his problems. He checked out of our voluntary unit, divorced his good wife, and married his younger, beautiful-but-co-dependent secretary, and they both lived miserably together thereafter!

Sally continued in outpatient therapy with my brother, Dr. Richard Meier, and improved greatly. In fact, by some "amazing coincidence," when Jim remarried and dashed all hopes of reconciliation with Sally, her aches and pains vanished for the most part.

Sally's real problem, however, which we had to work with at length during the rest of her therapy, was her attraction to perfectionists, which she developed during childhood as she tried to get the attention of her workaholic, perfectionistic father. There is an old saying about people not learning from experience, and this is very true of those who get divorced. The divorce rate in the United States is roughly 40 percent for first marriages, 60 percent for second marriages, 80 percent for third marriages, and 90 percent for fourth marriages. Without proper therapy, Sally would have been in danger of going right back to a Second-Degree Jerk perfectionist who would have abused her all over again.

Why do we call Jim a Second-Degree Jerk? Because he *willfully* engaged in an affair with his secretary and *continued* to hold cruel and unrealistic expectations of his wife, even when his errors were clearly pointed out to him. In fact, Jim became so angry at his wife that his rage turned inward and caused the chemical imbalance that drove him into a suicidal depression.

A key characteristic of the Second-Degree Jerk is that he almost always blames others completely for his problems, and that's what Jim was doing—blaming Sally for not measuring up to what he thought he wanted in a wife. Although he had a considerable degree of awareness of what he was doing, Jim willfully destroyed his marriage and, at one point, was ready to destroy himself.

Second-Degree Jerks Love to Control

A major difference between the First- and Second-Degree Jerk is that the First-Degree Jerk manipulates people and sometimes controls them without really meaning to. Second-Degree Jerks are more overt controllers who deliberately jerk people around because they enjoy the sense of power and control it gives them.

You may recall our look at a First-Degree Jerk boss in Chapter 2. Basically a very fine fellow, this First-Degree Jerk employer had to have everything go through him. He wanted to be in control, but only because he honestly thought he needed to be of help to everyone else. He didn't realize that he was being a pain in the neck to many of his employees, as well as a chief cause of his company losing precious time and money.

A Second-Degree Jerk boss, however, would be controlling in a far different way. He would be more apt to ask people to work overtime on short notice for no extra pay, or to pressure or criticize people who wanted to put their families ahead of long hours at the office. The Second-Degree Jerk boss would *willfully* push his employees to unrealistic limits, always trying to get more than what was reasonable out of them, not for their benefit, but purely for his own. He might feel a little guilty after delivering one of his shape-up-or-ship-out tirades, but he'd soon do it again in order to get production up.

Now let's look at a man who plays a pretty fair game of golf. He's popular in his country club and is even known for his charitable work in the community. The truth is, however, he is a Second-Degree Jerk, and those who watch him carefully while he plays golf can testify to that fact. He loves to tee up a foot or two ahead of the proper line, and he frequently uses his "foot wedge" when his ball has a bad lie. While playing friends in a friendly game of "a buck a hole," he will often "forget" a stroke here or there to keep his score low. In a word, he purposely cheats, because he loves to win at any cost.

If somebody catches him cheating, he might feel guilty for

a while and play one or two honest rounds, but sooner rather than later he'll go back to his cheating ways. He may also have a tendency to let God know in no uncertain terms how he feels about his ball going where he hit it, rather than where he felt it ought to go!

Unfortunately, Second-Degree Jerk parents are all too common. There is always the classic Second-Degree Jerk father, for example, who wants his child to excel in some area where the father didn't make it himself when he was younger. For example, a father might want his son to excel in math because he wants his son to become an engineer. The boy doesn't like math, and only gets average grades, so the father rejects his son. The rejection may be very subtle or very willful and obvious, depending on the father's degree of jerkiness. In some cases, the father may just plain state his rejection, accusing the boy of being lazy because "he doesn't want to be an engineer."

When Daughters Have a Jerky Dad

A common syndrome we often treat is the daughter who has been rejected or neglected by a Second-Degree Jerk father. Numerous books have been written in recent years concerning the importance of the relationship between daddies and their daughters, and what happens when Daddy isn't there for his little girl when she grows up.

I remember talking with Sylvia, a former patient who told me, "Dr. Meier, I'm twenty-five years old and I want very badly to save sex until marriage. I'm a Christian and I know that's what would be best, but if any good-looking guy comes along who is selfish and demanding, it seems that I immediately get a crush on him, go out with him, and I always give in and have sex as soon as he asks me. I've been doing this over and over. I keep telling myself I will say no to these guys, but I can't. I hate myself for my hypocrisy and I think I'm suicidal. Why do I keep falling in love with guys like this, and what can I do about it?"

I asked Sylvia if she remembered a top-forty song Tina Turner sang a few years back: "What's Love Got to Do with

It?'' Sylvia could recall the song, and then I told her, "What's happening to you has nothing to do with love. It's my guess that you grew up with what we call 'a hole in your soul.' Tell me, did your father give you a lot of attention when you were younger?''

Sylvia looked at me and burst into tears. She couldn't stop crying for quite some time, but when she was finally able to talk, the description she gave of her dad fit a Second-Degree Jerk to a "T." He had been a traveling salesman and had engaged in several affairs over the years. When he wasn't gone on a trip he was out with the boys at one of the bars near home. Sylvia had craved his love, but the only time he paid her any attention was to make suggestive, sexual remarks. She had never given up, however, and was still trying to connect with her dad by making phone calls and by sending him cards and letters. Dad remained polite but superficial.

Sylvia had a "father-vacuum," which is very common in today's society, especially when Daddy is a Second-Degree Jerk. The emotions Sylvia had attached to her father were extremely powerful, and she *switched* those emotions to every jerk she met who had a similar personality. Unconsciously, Sylvia was still trying to get her dad's attention, and even fulfill the subtle, incestuous flirtations he had made toward her in the past by having affairs with similar men now that she was a grown woman. Sylvia was also punishing herself for not being "good enough" to deserve her father's loving attention. Her father-vacuum was a bottomless pit, and she was looking for "love" in all the wrong places.

This complex phenomenon of switching emotions from one person to another was coined "transference" by Sigmund Freud, and, while Freud was off on a lot of things, his writings on transference were very accurate. In brief form, transference works like this:

In psychology we speak of "object relations," a good example of which is the strong attachment a little baby has for its mother. In fact, as a little baby, you actually think your mother is *you*. When you are wet or soiled, your mom changes you; when you are hungry, she feeds you; when you are lonely and afraid, she hugs you to her breast and says kind, loving words to make you feel warm all over.

The attachments that the typical person makes first to Mother and then later to Dad form a great deal of that person's self-concept and sense of self-worth. The parents' opinion of the child becomes the child's opinion of herself. Then the child grows up and many of these same strong attachments to the parents are still operating in her unconscious mind.

In Sylvia's case, her strong attachments to Daddy were still there, and when someone just like her dad came along, ZAP! Her unconscious antenna locked in, and she felt attracted. From there it was all down hill and straight into bed, but Sylvia could never figure out why she couldn't say no to these jerks who didn't love her but only wanted to use her. The explanation was really not that difficult. Sylvia simply transferred her feelings for her dad to the boyfriends who reminded her of her dad. She thought she was in love, but, as Tina Turner pointed out, love really had nothing to do with it.

I have seen the effects of transference in thousands of patients across the country. In fact, if pastors and counselors across America understood transference better and recognized counter-transference feelings in themselves, a great number of them could avoid falling into impulsive affairs with people they are counseling, erroneously thinking themselves, as Sylvia did, to have fallen in love. No wonder they say love is blind. Unfortunately, even trained counselors can be blinded when a certain client stirs their unconscious and they are victims of transference themselves.

And Sons Can Have Jerky Moms

While the relationship between father and daughter is crucial, the relationship between son and mother is equally powerful. The morning I began writing this chapter, I saw a new male patient at the hospital. We'll call him Jack. He had a wonderful father who was fun, kind, loving, and who spent lots of time with him. Jack's mother, however, was something else. She was critical, cold, controlling, and accepted Jack only according to her very stringent standards. She also ran her own business and spent very little positive time with Jack as he was growing up. In a word, Jack's mother was a Second-Degree Jerk.

In college, guess who Jack fell in love with? That's right, a beautiful, but cold, critical, and controlling, Second-Degree Jerk, just like Mom. They went together all four years of college, and were planning on getting married. The transference phenomenon was again at work, and Jack was trying to find in his jerky fiancée the love he'd never gotten from his mother. Deep down inside, however, Jack could sense something was really wrong.

During a period when Jack's steady girlfriend was gone on a lengthy vacation with her parents, he had a chance to have a casual date with a really nice young lady who was kind, loving, humble, and sweet. When his controlling girlfriend got back, she found out about it and ditched Jack immediately, no discussion. Jack felt hurt, but instead of getting angry with the cold, calculating girlfriend, he got angry with himself for dating a nice young lady and losing the girl he thought was going to give him the love he needed.

Jack stuffed his feelings, however, and went on with life. He kept dating the sweet, loving young lady for a year, and his friendship with her grew and grew. The romantic feelings came very slowly, because it was real love, not transference. Jack eventually got engaged to the sweet, loving girl, but the moment he slipped the diamond on her finger, strange things started happening to Jack's mind. He still had a huge hole in his soul that his mother's treatment of him had left there. He committed himself to a girl who was really not at all like his mother. "World War II" erupted as his conscious thoughts, feelings, and motives engaged in an all-out battle with his unconscious thoughts, feelings, and motives.

In the three months following the announcement of his engagement, Jack attempted suicide twice. Nonetheless, his loving fiancée stuck with him. After his first suicide attempt, he spent two months in a psychiatric hospital unit, which only medicated him and dealt with superficial issues, so he didn't get better. Within a few weeks of leaving that hospital, he attempted suicide again. Fortunately, he pulled through and came to a Minirth-Meier hospital where our therapists began digging and probing immediately into his transference problems.

Soon we were able to offer him hope, if he would be willing to cooperate and look at the painful truth about his mother and his subconscious yearnings to continue a sick kind of relationship. In time, we were able to defuse the powerful drives of Jack's unconscious mother-vacuum. We observed Jack's fear of intimacy dissipate as he learned to love and be loved by the emotionally healthy young lady who had stuck by him throughout his ordeal.

Jack gave up on his mother ever loving him, forgave her, grieved her loss, and moved on with life by truly loving and being loved by a warm, supportive woman who was nothing like the "girl who married dear old Dad."

"Second-Degree" Driving, Sex, Money Management

Remember the First-Degree Jerk driver described in Chapter 2? He or she drives carelessly and sometimes dangerously without thinking much about it. When other drivers honk or make unseemly gestures, the First-Degree Jerk motorist shrugs and wonders, What gets into some people anyway?

Second-Degree Jerk drivers, however, are much more aggressive. They willfully drive well over the speed limit, leading the pack, so to speak. They dart in and out of traffic and deliberately speed up in order not to let someone in ahead of them in their lane. Second-Degree Jerk drivers also have no qualms about using a fuzz buster. As a rule, they feel as if they own the road and wonder why other drivers keep trying to "borrow" it from them.

When the Second-Degree Jerk driver gets a ticket or has someone roll down the window and scream nasty comments about his pedigree, he may feel a twinge of guilt for a few moments, but he is soon back to his same old tricks.

As one might suppose, other problem areas for many Second-Degree Jerks are sex and money. Second-Degree Jerks use sex to control others and may demand sexual acts from their partners that make them feel like gods or goddesses, but they don't think of asking their partners if these acts are objectionable to them. As for money, they tend to be impulsive spenders and compulsive shoppers. They buy extravagant gifts for people they want to impress or manipulate. Paradoxically, however, when they go to a restaurant, they often wait for other people at the table to pay the tab. Second-Degree Jerks frequently become compulsive gamblers because their sense of entitlement developed into false expectations that got out of control.

Second-Degree Jerks are also known for cheating the IRS by exaggerating deductions or not reporting some of their income. Many Second-Degree Jerks will cheat or lie in business dealings if they feel fairly certain they won't get caught.

Ever Have a Jerky Teacher?

Most of us didn't get through school without having at least one Second-Degree Jerk for a teacher, and maybe more. The Second-Degree Jerk teacher would be critical of the character of the students and not be afraid to say so right in front of the class. He would reward those who flattered him and his opinions while severely punishing those who refused to butter him up or those who would dare to have an independent opinion.

Second-Degree Jerk teachers would expect their students to make them look good in front of the principal, so they would push hard for everyone to get high test scores. For Second-Degree Jerk teachers, getting their students to "really learn" is everything (because this way *they* look good). Developing the character of their students, however, is less important.

I had a patient—we can call him Burt—who was a college boy and basically a good kid. He came to me for counseling because he had been so depressed that he hadn't been able to go back to his college classes for the past two years. He just sort of lay around the house, depressed, unmotivated, not sleeping—the classic signs of clinical depression. After he described what had been happening, I said, "Okay, let's figure this out. It came on two years ago?"

"Yeah, just about two years ago when I was a sophomore in college."

"Do you have any idea what brought it on?"

"No, not really . . ."

"Think about what happened a week or two before you got really depressed for the first time. Did something make you very angry, for example?"

"Well, I had this history teacher who was really tough. She loved to make digs about how 'historically ignorant' we all were. I was taking the big final at the end of the term when she walked up to me right in the middle of the test, jerked my paper away from me, ripped it up, and accused me of cheating right in front of the rest of the class."

"Had you cheated?"

"I hadn't cheated one lick. I don't know what in the world made her think so, but she humiliated me, and then she flunked me to boot. I'm still so angry at her today, I can hardly stand it."

"So you recognize that you're hanging on to a lot of your anger toward this teacher?"

"Yeah, I sure do."

"And you'd like to get even with her perhaps?"

"Would I? What do you think?"

"So in your mind you're even punishing her right now," I commented. "I think we've found your problem. You need to forgive this teacher or you'll never get over your depression."

"Forgive her? I'll never forgive that witch because she doesn't deserve it."

"You're right, she doesn't deserve it. But all you're doing is punishing yourself because she acted like a jerk toward you. You've *got* to forgive her so that you can go on with your life. Look at what you've done for the last two years— moping around in heavy depression because you're hanging on to your desire to get revenge against someone who treated you unfairly."

"But I don't think I can forgive her."

"I think you can. Face it, she's not worth it. She's just not worth all the pain you're putting yourself through. Forgive her and get on with your life."

That conversation changed Burt's perspective. While forgiveness didn't come to Burt automatically, I helped him learn how to forgive his teacher by using a Gestalt technique. I placed an empty chair before Burt and had him imagine his teacher was sitting there. First, I had Burt verbalize his anger toward his teacher; then I instructed him to tell her that he had forgiven her, even though she didn't deserve it.

Although doing his Gestalt work helped, Burt still had to "re-forgive" his teacher several more times when she came back to his mind. At one point he prayed, "God, You deal with my teacher in any way You think is fair. But the best I know how, I forgive her and leave vengeance to You."

While it took a considerable amount of effort, Burt was able to forgive his Second-Degree Jerk teacher, and by the time the next fall term rolled around, he was back in school.

Second-Degree Jerks in the Church?

An interesting thing about many Second-Degree Jerks is that they have charisma. They can be popular in their neighborhood, their community, or their church. I have been in counseling situations that involved Second-Degree Jerks who are pastors or elders, or other kinds of Christian leaders. They are extremely charming and appear to be very godly, but they are people-users who love to manipulate, control, or dominate and be praised for their godliness at the same time.

For example, I have known of missionaries who were experts in raising money for their own support, but once they got out to the field, they lived well, hiring local people as servants, but did very little missionary work to speak of.

In other cases I have treated pastors who have had a series of extramarital affairs, which left them feeling some guilt, but they seemed powerless to change without therapy. And I have worked with numerous people who have had psychological problems because they were members of a church where the pastor was an overcontrolling, hostile dictator who shoved his brand of legalism down their throats.

Such pastors are not hard to spot. When my parents moved to Dallas a few years ago, they began looking for a church home and dropped in one Sunday at a church not too far from where they lived. Just before he was to preach his sermon, the pastor arose and asked the congregation: "If you were not here for calling last Thursday night, would you please stand up."

Over half the congregation rose to its feet, including my parents.

"You are all fools!" the pastor chided. "The Bible says he that winneth souls is wise, and if you weren't here to go calling last Thursday on our soul-winning night, then you are a fool. Sit back down!"

Despite their strict German background and having been in many legalistic churches in the past, my parents drew the line with being called fools by the pastor. They did not make a return visit to that church and wound up members in another one, where the doctrine was sound and the pastor was a kind, well-adjusted person, who was practically in the category of "mature adult."

How to Spot Second-Degree Jerks

Following is a list of Second-Degree Jerk attitudes and practices. If you want to use it to test yourself, that is your prerogative, but its primary purpose is to help you identify Second-Degree Jerks who may be part of your life. Go through the list with someone in mind you suspect could very well be a Second-Degree Jerk and see how many of these attitudes and practices apply to this person.

You may note that the attitudes and practices listed are sometimes similar to First-Degree Jerk tendencies, but more acute or extensive. This is done to dramatize that the Second-Degree Jerk is more overt and deliberate in controlling, deceiving, dominating, or abusing others. As a rule, First-Degree Jerks do jerky things without realizing it or meaning to. Second-Degree Jerks cross over a crucial line, however, and become predators by *willfully* controlling, deceiving, dominating, or abusing others. They usually feel guilt afterward, but seldom do they feel guilty enough to change their ways.

Attitudes and Practices of The Second-Degree Jerk

(Male and Female Pronouns Can Be Used Interchangeably)

_____ 1. Controls the conversation and focuses attention on herself most of the time.

_____ 2. Freely lets others know how good, fast, or successful he is, with the obvious intention of making a good impression.

_____ 3. Remembers nearly every offense against her and has lifelong intention to get a certain degree of vengeance.

_____ 4. Gets angry and waits to get even with those who get angry toward him for any reason.

_____ 5. Spreads gossip freely but tries to make it look as if she's "really concerned" about the party being discussed.

_____ 6. Seldom if ever says, "I was wrong; I'm sorry." Almost always has an explanation that puts the cause (blame) elsewhere.

_____ 7. Has open dislike and disrespect for authority figures because they threaten his own ability to control what he says or does.

_____ 8. Will help the poor, homeless, or hungry, but only if she gets attention and credit for doing so.

_____ 9. Enjoys helping and protecting powerful, popular, or sexy people, if it is understood "you owe me one and will pay back the favor someday."

_____ 10. Denounces chauvinism or bigotry, but practices both in subtle, "acceptable" ways, such as telling slightly off-color jokes, or making condescending remarks.

_____ 11. Breaks traffic laws when he won't be caught, but doesn't intend to do any harm.

_____ 12. Relatively honest, but tells lies with little, if any, guilt whenever it is more convenient to do so.

_____ 13. Pays lip service to the importance of his family, but engages in workaholism or other acceptable compulsions to shut out or ignore family members.

_____ 14. Keeps most thoughts private. Not very vulnerable, especially about personal shortcomings.

_____ 15. In athletic events, winning to prove personal significance is more important than enjoying the play.

_____ 16. Seldom, if ever, gives in at any point during an argument. Her opinion is always "right."

_____ 17. Sees self as very attractive to the opposite sex. Enjoys gaining their attention.

_____ 18. Flirts with others often, even if they are married, with little guilt.

_____ 19. Intends to stay married for life, but justifies an occasional affair or one-night stand. May have remorse afterward, but not enough to prevent it from happening again.

_____ 20. Sex with mate is mostly for personal gratification.

_____ 21. May speak openly about how attractive members of the opposite sex are and wonders about "how good they would be in bed."

_____ 22. Enjoys reading soft porn magazines and seeing erotic R-rated movies. Likes to appear "sexually sophisticated."

_____ 23. Seldom saves any money. Likes to spend, especially to impress others.

_____ 24. If given too much change, he says nothing. If he happens upon lost money, his motto is "finders keepers."

_____ 25. Borrows frequently from friends, but seldom pays it back or takes an inordinately long time to repay the loan by using rationalization or excuses.

_____ 26. Is stingy with family members, sees the money she makes as "mine."

_____ 27. Forgives others only if they apologize and/or there is something to gain by doing so.

_____ 28. Has difficulty controlling anger, but usually feels some guilt when his temper hurts someone badly.

_____ 29. Complains about being part of the "rat race" but devotes a great deal of time to career interests in order to look and feel "significant."

_____ 30. Feels guilty about certain behaviors or attitudes but refuses to work on trying to change.

_____ 31. Will go to a professional therapist, but only to straighten out his mate or children so he can manipulate or control them better. Gets angry at any honest therapist or pastoral counselor who tells him the truth about his narcissistic behavior and attitudes.

_____ 32. Freely disobeys all the "unfair" laws of the land (such as posted speed limits, paying income tax) and feels "above the law" unless punishment is feared.

_____ 33. Will use his personal interpretation of the Bible to control and manipulate others. (Sometimes true of pastors, priests, and televangelists.)

If you have gone over these characteristics with a certain person in mind, you may wonder how many checks that person would need to have before qualifying as a "Second-Degree Jerk." *There is no particular number.* Even as few as one or two of these characteristics can mean a person is a Second-Degree Jerk *in that area of life,* and therefore someone who is out to prey on others.

Protecting Yourself from Second-Degree Jerks

Ideally, you don't want to have any Second-Degree Jerks in your life, but it is highly unlikely that you are that fortunate. Following are some basic suggestions for what you can do to protect yourself from Second-Degree Jerk abuse without becoming abusive yourself. Obvious as these suggestions are, many people continue to fall victim to Second-Degree Jerks because they don't think about simple changes they could make to avoid this abuse.

1. *Study your life, particularly your schedule of daily activities.* Ask yourself, "When and where have I been jerked around in the past month and by whom?" If you have trouble remembering details like this, try keeping a journal for a month and see if any patterns of jerk abuse emerge. Write down even the slightest examples of what you might call being "jerked around." Don't worry about being paranoic or touchy. All you're trying to do with this kind of inventory is identify habits that you have or certain patterns to the way your life is going.

If you do find some patterns that include jerk abuse, ask yourself, "How many of these situations can I avoid?" It's likely you can't avoid all of them, particularly if you are married to a Second-Degree Jerk or work for one. But you can probably avoid some of them, which means less stress and hassle for you.

In the past month, I have been "jerked around" in the following ways (e.g., suggestive remarks or other sexual harassment at work; treated disrespectfully by clerks; habitually cheated in golf, tennis, or some other sport):

_____

_____

People who usually jerk me around in this way are (list names and/or occupations such as spouse, father, mother, boss): _____

_____

Steps I can take to eliminate or cut down this abuse (e.g., confront the abuser, shop elsewhere, get a new playing partner): _____

_____

2. *Don't let the comments, opinions, or behavior of Second-Degree Jerks affect your self-concept.* Make up your mind to base your sense of self-worth on what God says about you, as well as what loving, supportive people say. Predatory jerks will willfully try to put you down or treat you as if you are nothing and worth even less. God says you are of great significance and worth (see, for example, Ps. 139, which is discussed in Chapter 10). Who are you going to believe?

Jerky people who put me down on a regular basis include (names, relationship, occupation):

_____

_____

Specific comments, criticisms, or opinions that really erode my self-worth include (e.g., "When are you going to get some new clothes?" "Do you have to wear *that* shirt again?" "You really aren't going to try to take on *that* job, are you?"): _____

_____

The next time I hear a derogatory put-down of my self-worth, I will stop and tell myself:

_____ My self-worth does not depend on his/her opinion.
_____ My self-worth does not depend on being perfect or pleasing everyone.
_____ "God don't make no junk!"
_____ Choose your own comment: _____

_____
_____

3. *Monitor your own self-talk to see what you may be doing to undermine your sense of self-worth and make you more susceptible to remarks made by jerky predators.* Self-talk simply means your thoughts, which can run through your brain at up to 1,500 words per minute. What do you tell yourself all day long that could make you jerk bait? Following are some typical examples of negative self-talk that can erode self-worth and give a person a poor self-concept.

Check off any of the following examples of negative self-talk that you may be using:

_____ "I'm just no good at remembering names."
_____ "What's the use, I always screw it up!"
_____ "This isn't working, I'll never be able to do this."
_____ "Just my luck . . . I always have rotten luck."
_____ "I'm a clutz, born clumsy, I guess."
_____ "I'm never organized—I've got to get organized."
_____ "I'm always running late."
_____ "Why did I say that? I'm such a jerk."
_____ "Nothing ever goes right for me."
_____ "I never seem to have any money."
_____ "That was really stupid of me!"
_____ "If only I didn't have to work such long hours."
_____ "If only I had a job that paid a decent wage."

Fill in below some other typical self-talk remarks you might be using on yourself. For example, put down other "if only" comments you may frequently come up with:

_____

_____

_____

After you identify the negative self-talk you are using on yourself, think about how you can change this into positive self-talk. For more on changing negative self-talk to positive self-talk, see Chapter 10.

4. *Think about your strengths and weaknesses.* Then identify weak areas where a Second-Degree Jerk might be able to manipulate or abuse you most easily.

For example, you may be very susceptible to flattery. Or, possibly, you are easily made to feel guilty when you're hit with a sob story or accused of being unfair or uncaring. Become alert to these kinds of manipulations and think of ways to resist them, instead of caving in as you usually do.

My strengths are: _____

_____

My weaknesses are: _____

_____

The next time a Second-Degree Jerk tries to manipulate me by using such weapons as flattery, unfair accusations, or deceptions, I will fight back by: _____

_____

5. *Confront all jerk abuse when it happens.* Tell the jerk who has tried to manipulate, control, dominate, or abuse

you how you feel about his or her behavior. Don't speak in terms of "You should or shouldn't do that." Simply tell this person how you feel, tactfully but directly, lovingly but firmly. Remember, *it's your responsibility to make sure you aren't abused.*

Don't expect the jerks to be concerned for your welfare. Don't sit around thinking, "They shouldn't do that," or "I don't know why they do that." Why they do that is very simple. They are Second-Degree Jerks, and you are somebody they can victimize. They will continue to do so until you speak up and take steps not to allow this to happen.

The next time I am abused by (name jerky person) _____, I will confront him or her and say:

_____

_____

_____

If you are a fairly confident and assertive person, the above suggestions may be all you need to learn how to handle Second-Degree Jerks in a much more effective way. There is a strong possibility, however, that you need help with some deeper causes of why jerks abuse you. It may be that you have a strong shame base (strong guilt feelings from the past for any number of reasons) that needs to be resolved. Or you may have what we call "holes in your soul" that are there for any number of reasons. Perhaps you have a father- or mother-vacuum and you're trying to fill this hole in your soul by allowing jerks to abuse you in various ways.

It is quite possible that you are a masochist, or at least have some masochistic tendencies (discussed in detail in Chapter 5). In Part II of this book, Chapters 6 through 11, we will look at a plan for dealing with deeper problems, such as the "holes in your soul" that may be the real underlying reasons why you let Second-Degree Jerks push you around.

As irritating and abusive as Second-Degree Jerks are, there are a small number of people out there who are even more dangerous predators—the Nth-Degree Jerks. In Chapter 4, we'll look at Nth-Degree Jerks to see what makes them tick, why they are so dangerous, and how you can avoid being hurt by them.

Dealing with a Second-Degree Jerk Friend

A friend keeps borrowing small amounts of money for such things as coffee, newspapers, or phone calls and does not pay it back. Instead of continuing to put up with this jerky behavior, you can say: "No, Bill, I just don't want to loan you any more money. You're into my pocket for several bucks already, and it's not the money as much as it is the principle. I feel I'm being taken advantage of."

*

Or suppose your neighbor calls and wants you to baby-sit her children so she can go shopping. You work full-time and have two children of your own, while she does not work out of the home. You can say: "No, Mary, I really can't do that. I have a very busy schedule today, and it will be all I can do to take care of my own kids and get everything done."

- **Note:** When you no longer allow people to take advantage of you, relatively mature First-Degree Jerks will respect you more for standing up for yourself, but Second-Degree Jerks may reject you. But don't feel bad; instead, celebrate, because another harmful jerk has been graciously removed from your life.

Dealing with a Second-Degree Jerk Boss

If he says: "I need you to work overtime this weekend. These orders must go out . . ."
You can say: "I'm sorry, but I have several things planned with my family. Have you asked Jim or John? They haven't worked overtime for at least a month."

*

If she says: "Jane, I have an assignment I know you can handle along with the rest of your responsibilities, can you take it on?"
You can say: "I really feel I have enough to do, and if I'm going to handle my present work load well, taking on anything else at this time just won't work."

*

If your boss says: "I've always put the company first. The family comes second—besides, why am I working so hard if not for my family?"
You can say: "I appreciate how you feel, but I don't agree. I believe in giving the company my best, but I also believe in making my family a top priority."

CHAPTER
4

Society's Sociopaths—Nth-Degree Jerks

In Minirth-Meier Clinics across the country, we treat a lot of First- and Second-Degree Jerks in the course of doing marriage and family counseling. Indeed, Second-Degree Jerk behavior is usually the cause of serious marital difficulties; for example, the mate who is a Second-Degree Jerk often has an affair or affairs as a way of getting vengeance on his or her spouse. Second-Degree Jerk parents can also mess up their children in numerous ways.

Every now and then, however, we come across people who go beyond the Second-Degree Jerk level into what we label a Sociopathic Personality Disorder. These are the Nth-Degree Jerks who comprise possibly 10 percent of society as a whole. What sets the Nth-Degree Jerk apart is his or her ability to abuse others selfishly and feel *no real guilt* in doing so. In this chapter I will use two examples of Nth-Degree Jerk behavior, one of whom is a household name in recent years. The other, while a real person, must remain anonymous for obvious reasons.

The Abused Little Boy Became a Monster

This is a true story about a little baby boy whose father
died just before he was born. His mother was left poverty
stricken and soon married her dead husband's brother, who
turned out to be an abusive Second-Degree Jerk. The little
boy hated his stepfather, and his relationship to his mother
wasn't much better. Both parents used him as soon as possible to work or beg for money.

At the age of ten the boy's parents made him quit school
to work full-time, so the boy ran away and moved in with his
maternal uncle. Unfortunately, it was a case of "out of the
frying pan into the fire." The maternal uncle turned out to
be a pro-Nazi rageaholic who lost his job after he attempted
to assassinate a political leader. Again, the boy ran away.

By now the boy was in his early teens, filled with years of
abuse, loneliness, sadness, and rage. He lived alone, fending
for himself by selling chewing gum and other trinkets on the
streets of a large city. He managed to attend school and soon
became the school bully, frequently carrying a pistol to class
for protection, as well as to bully other students into submis-
sion.

As he grew older, he transferred his rage from abusive
family members to significant authority figures in his imme-
diate environment. His insecurity and inferiority feelings
drove him into a frenzied rat race for significance, and he
became addicted to power and gaining vengeance on his enemies, real or imagined.

Have you guessed who this little boy is today? If this poor
little fellow had been properly loved and nurtured by his
mother and stepfather, hundreds of thousands of deaths
would have been prevented and the Persian Gulf War
avoided. This innocent little baby, whose main caretakers
were severe Second-Degree Jerks, grew up to become Saddam Hussein, an Nth-Degree Jerk if the world has ever seen
one.

Like his uncle, Saddam became a political assassin and
later rose to become president of Iraq. Within days of as-

suming power, he had assassinated anyone who represented any kind of opposition.

When a man confronted him about what he was doing, Saddam stuck his cigar butt in the man's eye. And when a woman confronted him on the streets of Baghdad, he gouged her eye out with his thumb!

When a general at Saddam's cabinet meeting disagreed with a decision Saddam had made, the Iraqi president pulled out a pistol and shot the man in the head. Then he coolly asked if anyone else disagreed (no one did).

On another occasion, Saddam took a cancer-stricken relative to the best doctor in Baghdad, expecting a cure. When the doctor couldn't help him, Saddam tied the doctor to a ceiling fan and had him tortured with electrical shocks for ten days. That doctor eventually escaped and now resides in England.[1]

Thousands of years ago, Moses observed that the sins of the parents tend to be visited upon three or four generations in the family. The sins of Saddam Hussein's family definitely bear out this wise observation. Another little boy whose father beat him regularly was Adolf Hitler, and we all know what little Adolf grew up to be.

Saddam Hussein and Adolf Hitler are rather obvious examples of Nth-Degree Jerks, but there are literally hundreds of thousands of them running around loose in society today, and they range from drug dealers in the ghetto to "respectable leaders" in high political office. Some are powerful financial magnates or chief executive officers in large corporations. And some are pastors and evangelists. You may even be related to an Nth-Degree Jerk. I doubt that you are one yourself, however, because you would not be taking the time to read a book like this one.

The Sickly Saga of Edward and Jane

Let's turn our attention to a wealthy lawyer and his wife, who are still functioning right here in America. I treated their daughter, a victim of their terrible abuse. As you read the following true story about this family, you will understand why I cannot even hint at anyone's real identity. In this account, I will take you back to the 1960s, and bring you up to the present time, using false names, details, and locations. The story itself, however, is unfortunately true, and this lawyer was still exerting his clout at the time of this book's publication.

The 1960s were a time of turmoil—political unrest, protest movements of all kinds, and the Vietnam war. But on a lovely June day, Edward and Jane took a break from one of their protest demonstrations and got married. The wedding reception was at an exclusive country club where both sets of in-laws were members. The sun glistened through the trees, and robins sang their hearts out as they played tag among apple blossoms in full glory. All of the big wigs and wealthy of the area attended. Everyone was smiling. After all, no one wanted to hurt his chances in the rat race of life.

Edward and Jane smiled and pretended that they had no problems with their wealthy, ultraconservative parents. In reality, they detested them. And while the in-laws were smiling on the outside and giving everyone big hugs, on the inside they ached with pain that comes from emptiness and guilt.

Jane's pretty blue eyes met Edward's as they whispered words of encouragement to each other. They had each graduated from an Ivy League college, and Edward had completed law school. They had jumped through all the hoops to get what they wanted in life—to be out on their own where they could rebel against the sick values of their parents, but live comfortably while doing so. One more hour and they would be out of this phony high-society crowd. It was worth the pretense to get a financial boost from both sets of parents, which would give them the head start they needed.

But Jane and Edward felt like screaming the truth to the crowd at the top of their voices. Jane could have shrieked: "My parents are both phony jerks! My father sexually abused me for years, and my mother let it happen."

And Edward wanted to shout: "My parents are jerks, too! They both sexually abused me as I was growing up and convinced me for a long time that it was normal among the 'successful' people. And to top it all off, my mother was selfish, manipulative, and controlling, and my father was always beating me up and slapping my face! I hate them!''

Finally it was over and the young couple glanced triumphantly at each other as they climbed into their Jaguar, rice flying everywhere. They sped off to begin a brand new life in law, and eventually politics, where they believed they would fight injustice in their terrible world. Neither had ever told the other about being sexually abused during childhood. It was a secret that was just too horrible to share.

Edward and Jane Used Their Daughter

Family traditions are hard to break, and most abusive parents were abused themselves. Rage, insecurity, and vengeance are powerful emotions and only massive denial convinces people they can control these emotions without therapy and supernatural help. It wasn't long before Edward and Jane were seeing a secular psychiatrist for their own sexual dysfunctions. He recommended pornography and the occasional use of male and female prostitutes, with protection, of course. Later, they progressed into mate-swapping with another couple from their law firm.

By the time the couple had their first daughter, Jennifer, they were as busy as their parents had been. The only difference was that conservative organizations were replaced by liberal ones. Jane and Edward placed Jennifer in day-care while they pursued making money and protesting their parents' "false values."

Pornography is an addiction. What thrills one day soon becomes boring, and Edward and Jane soon became bored. They had holes in their souls left by how they had been parented, and they were foolishly trying to fill these holes with lust instead of love.

By the time Jennifer reached elementary school, her parents rationalized that it would be fine to include her in their sexual activities. After all, they were liberal minded, intelligent people, and Jennifer was a "consenting" child who craved her parents' affection. The little girl believed their deception that this kind of activity was "normal" for liberally minded families.

Edward and Jane were careful, however, to tell Jennifer that society had strict rules, "just like Grandma and Grandpa" on both sides of the family. They would put Mom and Dad in prison and make a poor orphan out of her if she ever told anyone their secret. Jennifer had to swear she would tell *absolutely no one,* not even her best friend.

As Jennifer got older, she became increasingly uncomfortable with the sexual abuse. She tried to get out of the bondage, but her parents used threats, manipulation, and bribery with increased allowances as they demanded the continued incest. On several occasions she threatened to tell and was brutally beaten each time. After all, Daddy was an elected politician now. His career would be ruined if anyone found out.

Gymnastics Shored Up Jennifer's Sagging Self-esteem

As Jennifer's self-concept dipped lower and lower, she became more obsessed with gymnastics, something she had started at the age of six. She was soon spending four hours a day training as a gymnast, and she began winning meets in several different categories.

Gymnastics served several purposes for Jennifer: (1) It kept her away from her mother and father; (2) it gave her a sense of control in a world where she had no control over her own body sexually; and (3) it gave her a sense of self-worth in a world where she saw herself as a mere object to be used and abused, a piece of trash.

When Jennifer reached twelfth grade, one of her gymnastic friends invited her to attend Young Life meetings after school. Jennifer's parents tried to discourage it, and that only gave her more reason to go, because it was a way to rebel against their control. Jennifer enjoyed the Young Life meetings where kids got together, laughed, sang, and played games. They also shared gut-level feelings for each other, and they even—she could hardly believe it—*prayed* for one another. The Young Life kids were different from the "jerks" Jennifer knew at high school. Some of the Young Life guys were actually interested in who she really was rather than her body!

After a couple of months of fun, sharing, and Bible study, Jennifer decided to give her life to Jesus and ask Him to forgive her for all her sins, especially her family secret. She still couldn't tell anyone except God about that terrible secret, but she made up her mind she would never give her body sexually to her mother or father again.

"I Won't Tell If You Leave Me Alone"

Now Jennifer was scared because she knew how angry her parents could get and what they could do to hurt her. But her body belonged to God now, so she prayed for His protection. Jennifer decided to put off confronting her parents for a day or two because she had a big gymnastics meet coming up. She would tell them immediately after the meet, and she could only hope they would honor her decision, now that she was almost eighteen years old.

But then the thing she feared the most happened. Her parents came to her bedroom the night before her gymnastics meet. She tried to explain to them about her new faith in God and her decision to abstain from sex until marriage. She gave them her proposal, saying, "I will agree to keep the family secret if you agree to leave me alone."

Jennifer's hopes for a peaceful truce were dashed when Edward and Jane became filled with rage and began beating her. Jennifer had enough self-worth by now to defend herself, and she tried to escape. Her parents grabbed her, held her down, and slapped her and slugged her, ordering her to take off her clothes. When Jennifer continued to refuse, her mom held her while her dad bent her wrist behind her back farther and farther to get her to give in. Finally, the wrist snapped and blood squirted profusely out of a compound fracture!

Edward and Jane realized they had gone too far. His legal career was really in jeopardy now! What would they do?

They told Jennifer she had to go to the emergency room, but that they would literally murder her if she told the truth. Jennifer could tell her parents weren't bluffing, and she knew they were smart enough to cover their tracks.

Edward and Jane did all the talking at the emergency room, and Jennifer didn't say a word. She just wept with pain.

She had emergency surgery with the best orthopedic surgeons money could buy, but the results were still tragic. There was permanent nerve damage, and Jennifer lost forever her favorite pastime and escape mechanism, gymnastics. Doctors told her she would never regain full use of her right arm, hand, and fingers.

Edward and Jane told the doctors Jennifer had taken a fall off the balance beam during a late practice before the big gymnastics meet. Jennifer had kept her mouth shut, but now she knew she had to tell the truth, no matter what the cost might be. She prayed that God would protect her, and at the same time, wondered, *How could God let this happen when I promised to use all my gymnastics ability to honor Him in the future?*

Jennifer's Parents Plotted to Kill Her

The next time Ron and Sharon, Young Life leaders who had taken Jennifer under their wing, came to the hospital to visit her, she blurted out the whole sordid story. Ron and Sharon were dismayed, but they knew Jennifer wouldn't lie. They discussed the situation for over an hour before agreeing together to go through proper channels.

Ron and Sharon accompanied Jennifer as she reported her parents to the local child abuse agency, as well as the sheriff's office. When Edward was informed of his daughter's accusation, he made a quick call to a political friend who had the right contacts. Pressure was applied in certain places, and the social worker assigned to the case and the sheriff both kept their mouths shut and met with Edward privately. Edward explained that Jennifer had been under a lot of pressure lately and that she obviously must be cracking up; otherwise, why would she make such absurd accusations? Edward and his wife agreed to get a lie detector test to clear their names, and then get proper psychiatric help for their daughter. The sheriff and social case worker agreed to keep things quiet in return.

Edward and Jane knew just where to go for their lie detector test, and it came out fine, of course. They decided, however, that Jennifer had become a liability and they could no longer let her live. They would take Jennifer home, shoot her in the head, and fake Jennifer's signature on a false suicide note that would tell how she couldn't face life without gymnastics. Edward's political career would be damaged, but he would survive. They would adopt a new daughter and keep her away from religious fanatics as she grew up.

To help cover his tracks, Edward got his old friend, Dr. Jaxford, a psychiatrist, to do a quick consult on Jennifer. Edward had bailed Dr. Jaxford out of trouble on more than one occasion for sexual misconduct with patients, so "Dr. Jax" owed him one and was happy to cooperate.

"Incest? It Never Happened!"

Within hours, a meeting was arranged among the social worker, the sheriff, Dr. Jaxford, Ron, Sharon, and Jennifer's parents. Edward and Jane thanked Ron and Sharon warmly for all the help they had been to Jennifer. Then Edward praised them for the way they had handled the crisis. He told them they had done exactly the right thing in reporting the accused incest to the authorities.

Then the sheriff stepped in and told Ron and Sharon that the incest never took place. The lie detector test proved that. The social worker nodded in agreement. Dr. Jaxford told Ron and Sharon that he was treating Jennifer for depression and that she was temporarily having a delusion as a result of all the stress.

As a clincher, the sheriff, whom Edward had helped get elected, turned to Ron and Sharon, arched his bushy eyebrows, and warned: "If you act at all as if you believe Jennifer's delusions, not only will you be causing her harm, but you'll be guilty of slander toward this innocent public servant and his wife!"

Ron and Sharon thanked everyone and left the room, glancing at each other with a confused expression on their faces. Were they going a little crazy themselves? Could it really be a delusion?

Jennifer Had to Choose: Flee or Die

The young couple went back to the hospital to visit Jennifer just as the surgeon was leaving her room. Jennifer explained that the doctor had said he would send her home the next day and recommended frequent therapy sessions with Dr. Jaxford.

Then Jennifer grasped the hands of Ron and Sharon and gasped, "But I don't dare go home to my parents. When my mother came to see me today, she left the room for a few minutes, and I looked in her purse and found a suicide note with my name on it. So now I know they plan to kill me. I put it back just as I found it, and she doesn't know that I know what they're planning to do."

Ron and Sharon told Jennifer they had just been to a meeting where she had been accused of delusions, and Jennifer really looked frightened as she mumbled, "I should have known they would cover all the bases! It's all set up. But you do believe me, don't you?"

With tears in her eyes, Sharon gave Jennifer a warm hug. Ron was also near tears, but they both knew that they were all in a precarious predicament. If they helped Jennifer run away, they would break the law. If they encouraged her to go home, she would be killed.

Ron handed Jennifer $300 from his own wallet and a small white card. Then he wisely told her, "The money is a gift, whether you go home or not. Running away has to be your own decision. You're almost eighteen years old now, so I don't know if the police will come after you or not. If you do run away, I wish you would call Reverend Tom Davis at this number and address. He and his wife, Elaine, are close personal friends of ours, and they'll let us know how you are doing."

Jennifer set her travel alarm and slipped out of the hospital before daybreak the next morning. By the time the nurses made their rounds and found her missing, she was long gone. Three days later she turned up at the home of Reverend and Mrs. Tom Davis, hundreds of miles away. Ron had called them and told them the whole scenario, so Tom and Elaine welcomed Jennifer with open arms.

Jennifer Was Safe, But Suicidally Depressed

Jennifer lived with the Davis family for months. They fed her, clothed her, found her a job, showered her with genuine love, discipled her, and literally risked their lives for her. She took a GED test, went to a junior college, dated fine Christian boys, and had nice girlfriends, but was still suicidally depressed. She was so filled with self-hatred she would sometimes use a safety pin to cut slices on her wrist. The pain helped her feel relieved. It proved she really existed, and it appeased her false guilt at the same time. Tom and Elaine did their best to counsel her, but felt powerless to pull her out of her suicidal depression.

Finally they referred Jennifer to a Minirth-Meier Clinic. Because Jennifer was eighteen by now, we promptly admitted her to the adult behavioral medicine unit. A skilled therapist counselled her an hour a day, four days a week. One of our psychologists saw her in group therapy two and a half hours per day, seven days a week, and Dr. Frank Minirth and I took turns seeing her daily, seven days a week, to supervise her case. Together, our entire team treated her pain and false guilt and eventually got her to see herself as God saw her.

Jennifer also had to work through her rage toward God. How could a God of love allow her to go through all that suffering? We assured her that none of us knows the answer to that, or why God's plan for His own Son included so much suffering. We won't know those answers until we enroll some day in the University of Heaven.

After encouraging her to ventilate her emotions, I told her, "I really don't think it matters very much to God how well you perform at gymnastics or anything else. God cares a lot more about who you are becoming on the inside. Your real beauty and depth are becoming more apparent as you heal a little more each day."

And Jennifer had a lot of healing to do. Her many wounds caused by the abuse from two sadistic, Nth-Degree Jerks throughout her formative years were full of emotional pus. Along with her suicidal depression, she had a deep fear of intimacy with both males and females, and an even deeper distrust for any kind of authority figures, including God. And, oh, yes, there was the permanently damaged wrist and the ruined career in gymnastics, which had eroded great chunks of her self-worth.

When Jennifer came into our hospital, her excessive perfectionism caused her to fear loss of control. So deep was her fear of not being in control that she had serious side effects when given any antidepressant medicine, because her body rejected these medications due to actual anxiety symptoms. Her anxiety, including severe panic attacks, stemmed from a fear of getting in touch with how much rage she had stuffed inside herself during her formative years.

Jennifer Thought God Couldn't Love Her

Jennifer also struggled with a fear that God couldn't really love and accept her since she saw God intellectually through glasses that were colored by her parents' personalities as she grew up. After all, a six-year-old Jennifer praying "Dear heavenly Father" was really thinking, "Dear heavenly version of my earthly father," a phenomenon psychiatrists call projection.

During Jennifer's time in the hospital, we showed her that, ironically enough, although she had been horribly mistreated by her jerky parents, she was actually addicted to their twisted personalities.

"If you don't make some new decisions about how to get your needs met in healthy ways, you'll continue to be drawn toward this kind of person," I explained. "The reason you keep hurting yourself in various ways is because you are used to suffering. Because of a phenomenon we call transference, your natural inclination is to have romantic crushes on sociopaths like your father. You transfer your longing for the love you wished your father would have given you to irresponsible characters, and it's my guess you find responsible young men boring."

Jennifer looked at me in surprise and admitted that was precisely the case.

I cautioned Jennifer that at first she might feel guilty about learning to feel happy and lovable and be tempted to look for subtle, subconscious ways to regress into the misery of her past. I also warned her that some day down the road, if she eventually had several children, she might be tempted to sexually abuse them or possibly overly control them. This would be especially true of an oldest daughter she might have, because an oldest daughter would be most likely to remind her of her own unconscious faults and stand a good chance of becoming the scapegoat for Jennifer's future projections.

Why Jennifer Had to Learn to Forgive

When I told Jennifer that possibly her biggest task was forgiving her parents, she balked at first. The pain from all the years of abuse was simply too great. I told her I understood why she would find forgiving her parents difficult, but if she would do so it would clear up her suicidal depression.

"How can forgiving my parents do that?" she wanted to know.

"Your depression includes symptoms of insomnia, decreased energy, irritability, poor concentration, headaches, and decreased appetite," I explained. "All of these are a result of serotonin depletion in your brain. This serotonin depletion is caused by your anger, holding this huge grudge against your parents. Unless you get past this desire for personal vengeance and forgive them, you'll never get over your depression."

"But they were my *parents*," Jennifer said almost fiercely. "How could they possibly do such things to their daughter?"

"Look, Jennifer, there are nearly six billion out there on planet earth, some of whom are sick Nth-Degree Jerks and some of whom are nice people who are really worth loving. Your parents are only two of those six billion people, and they aren't any more important than two flies on a cow's horn. Why devote the rest of your life to getting vengeance on two flies on a cow's horn? Base your self-worth on what God thinks of you, not on what two people think of you. Sillier yet, why torture yourself with fantasies that they will ever change and love you? It's natural to think that you need them, but you don't. Grieve their loss and give up on them. Pray for them, but let God worry about them, and get on with your life and what you feel God wants you to do."

Vengeance Is God's—He Keeps Perfect Books

It took a while, but Jennifer was finally able to let go of her strong anger toward her parents and work toward forgiveness. She realized that she had reported them to the proper authorities, who, by the way, never did anything about it because of her father's political connections (welcome to the real world!). But she was finally able to turn the responsibility for vengeance over to God, who promised in the book of Romans to do a very good job of it,[2] even though we don't always understand how and when God evens up the ledger.

To help Jennifer with her anxiety and panic attacks, we got her in touch with her intense rage by encouraging her to use Gestalt techniques to release her anger. For example, I would place two empty chairs in front of Jennifer during a therapy session and have her pretend that her mom and dad were sitting in them. Then she had to verbalize her rage and sorrow directly at them, calling them by name. Another technique involved having her write a long letter to her parents, telling them goodbye forever. Then together we burned the letter.

Alexander Pope, a famous poet, once wisely said, "To err is human, to forgive divine." He was absolutely right.[3]

I still burn with rage myself when I think about Jennifer's parents still exerting their influence in powerful circles as I write this chapter, but holding grudges only hurts the bearer of the grudge, not the abuser. Jennifer prayed for divine help to forgive her Nth-Degree Jerk abusers—for her own sake and for God's.

And as Jennifer forgave her parents, the temptation to do more self-mutilation dissipated. Her self-mutilation was actually redirected rage. Her brain considered that much rage toward her parents unacceptable or "taboo," and so in her mind Jennifer found it more acceptable to be angry at herself—a form of false guilt.

Abused children blame themselves and feel like trash—as if they must have somehow deserved the abuse. Honestly feeling her rage, but then forgiving her undeserving sociopathic parents, was the best thing Jennifer could do.

After six weeks of intense, insight-oriented therapy in one of our hospital psychiatric units, Jennifer recovered from nearly all of her symptoms. To do the same amount of work on an outpatient basis would have probably taken one to two years of weekly, forty-five-minute sessions. It is true that Jennifer will never forget the abuse she received while growing up, but through proper therapy she became emotionally stronger than most people her age who had a "non-traumatic" childhood and a "functional" family.

Nth-Degree Jerks Come in Different Packages

So far we have looked at excessively sick, socially psychopathic Nth-Degree Jerks, such as Saddam Hussein, Adolf Hitler, and Jennifer's parents. But Nth-Degree Jerks can come in other packages that aren't so easy to spot. The difference between a Second-Degree Jerk and an Nth-Degree Jerk is that the Second-Degree Jerk will be controlling, dominating, and abusive, *but feel some guilt afterward.* The Nth-Degree Jerk, however, manipulates, controls, dominates, abuses, and even kills *with no feelings of guilt.*

Using some of the examples we applied to Second-Degree Jerks in Chapter 3, we see that it's quite possible to run across Nth-Degree Jerk bosses, drivers, teachers, and even Nth-Degree Jerk pastors.

The Nth-Degree Jerk driver, for example, would be competitive, controlling, and totally anti-authority. He would not care if others were harmed or killed as long as he suffered no consequences. I have sometimes been asked if a large percentage of people who are arrested for drunk driving are Nth-Degree Jerks. We cannot make a generalization about all drunk drivers, but it is quite likely that many of them are Nth-Degree Jerks who operate without guilt. They don't start out that way, but chronic alcohol abuse destroys the inhibitory areas of their brains, resulting in a literal deadening of the conscience. Many Nth-Degree Jerk abusers of alcohol also become manipulative storytellers (grandiose liars) who use and abuse others with no guilt whatsoever.

The Nth-Degree Jerk boss could operate much like the Second-Degree Jerk boss but, again, the one basic difference is that the Nth-Degree Jerk feels no guilt for intimidating employees or forcing them to work long hours for little or no extra pay. In fact, a major characteristic of the Nth-Degree Jerk boss is the tremendous high he or she might feel from having so much power and control over others.

Nth-Degree Jerk teachers also enjoy having power and control, but they are usually a little more subtle about it. I know of one Nth-Degree Jerk who, along with teaching social studies, also coached the girls' basketball team. After gaining the confidence, and even the admiration and affection of his players, he would pick out girls who were passive and vulnerable and start to be "extra friendly" with pats and hugs. If a girl did not act offended, he would move on to fondling her in discreet ways, and eventually he would invite her to have sex with him.

The coach was very successful and brought several state championships to the school, but eventually some of the girls blew the whistle on him. Ironically, the school principal and other school leaders knew about his sexual behavior from prior complaints, but they did not want to fire him. They wanted to sweep it under the rug because he was bringing state championships to the school, but the students and their parents would not back off. They threatened to turn him in for child abuse and other charges, and when he knew he had no choice, he resigned and left the area.

And just as you can find Second-Degree Jerks in the pastorate, you can find Nth-Degree Jerks as well. I have known many—yes, *many*—pastors who had affairs with parishioners and who engaged in other sexual immorality and perversion *without any guilt whatsoever*. This kind of pastor often feels entitled to do what he likes because he believes God's hand is upon him. This is particularly true if he is a good preacher and has excellent "results" in soul-winning and guiding people into a deeper Christian walk.

I know of one pastor, a superb speaker, who would preach on Sunday nights and then go out jogging. He would tell his wife he was driving to his jogging track, but, in truth, he would go to another part of the city where he would expose himself, particularly to young girls he might find coming out of a movie. Then, he would get up on Monday morning, go down to the church, and teach a Bible study.

Eventually he was caught, but he expressed no guilt or remorse at all. He was given jail time and later received therapy, which helped him realize what he was doing. At that point he did feel true guilt, dealt with it, and was able to recover completely from his sociopathic illness. He did not go back into the pastorate, however, but instead obtained a job in the corporate business world.

In another case, a pastor of a church of thousands of people, again, an excellent pulpiteer, rented a personal apartment that no one knew about, not even his wife. He would meet women from the church there and have affairs with them. When he was eventually caught and kicked out of his pulpit, he simply started up a new church in a different area, and many of the church members followed him. The opinion of those who were willing to put up with his behavior was, "Yes, we know he does it, but he preaches great sermons, and we don't care." You may find it hard to believe that pastors could do these kinds of things and not feel guilt, but I assure you that many of them could if their sense of entitlement were incredibly strong. It would be as if they started out wanting to be an example, but ended up telling God that they were an exception to His rules.

How to Spot an Nth-Degree Jerk

It is quite possible that many readers of this book are suffering abuse at the hands of an Nth-Degree Jerk. You might want to go through the following list of attitudes and practices of Nth-Degree Jerks to assess significant others in your home, work, neighborhood, even in your church. It is immoral to subject yourself to Nth-Degree Jerk abuse. To protect yourself, you must learn emotional self-defense, and the first line of that defense is to know some of the signs of an Nth-Degree Jerk.

In going through the following list of Nth-Degree Jerk characteristics, you will note that many of them are very similar to those of the Second-Degree Jerk. Indeed, in some cases it might be impossible to tell the Second-Degree Jerk from the Nth-Degree Jerk except for the fact that the Nth-Degree Jerk feels no guilt. The problem is that most Nth-Degree Jerks don't usually admit their guilt. Or, when confronted, some Nth-Degree Jerks may claim they feel guilty, but simply be lying to cover up. In many cases Nth-Degree Jerks can only be identified by the severe degree of how they act or what they say, which betrays their lack of guilt or remorse.

As with Second-Degree Jerks, there is no particular number of characteristics or attitudes that would qualify a person to be an Nth-Degree Jerk. Any combination of several of the above characteristics could mean Nth-Degree Jerk behavior and thinking and would make this person sociopathic and extremely dangerous to those around him.

Attitudes and Practices
of the Nth-Degree Jerk
(Male and Female Pronouns
Can Be Used Interchangeably)

_____ 1. Controls the conversation and focuses attention on herself with blatant disregard for what others think or feel.

_____ 2. Freely lets others know how good, fast, or successful he is, not only to make a good impression, but to control or intimidate.

_____ 3. Remembers nearly every offense against her and gains vengeance in one way or another—usually in a vicious and sometimes even fatal way.

_____ 4. Gets angry and retaliates in vicious and violent ways against anyone who shows anger toward him.

_____ 5. Spreads gossip freely with no concern for the harm she is causing to another's reputation. Enjoys ruining the reputation of others.

_____ 6. Never says "I was wrong" or "I'm sorry." Always has an explanation that puts the blame on someone else.

_____ 7. Has open dislike and disrespect for authority figures because they threaten his own ability to control and dominate others. Must be in a position of highest authority, if at all possible.

_____ 8. Has little or no interest in helping the poor, homeless, or hungry, unless there is a payoff of some kind.

_____ 9. Enjoys helping and protecting powerful, popular, or sexy people, but demands repayment of the favor and collects it one way or another.

_____ 10. Enjoys practicing chauvinism or bigotry and is openly proud of his "superiority" to the opposite sex, other races, and social groups.

_____ 11. Breaks traffic laws freely and when caught shows no remorse or concern. Often has dozens of warrants for his arrest or many unpaid tickets.

_____ 12. Is totally dishonest. Tells boldface lies with absolutely no guilt. May often lie when it would be more convenient or practical to tell the truth.

_____ 13. Engages in workaholism with no regard whatsoever for other family members. Often uses work to escape having to deal with family responsibilities.

_____ 14. Keeps all thoughts private and prides self in being strong and invulnerable. Would never admit any personal shortcoming.

_____ 15. In athletic events, winning is all that counts. Will cheat or hurt others in order to win.

_____ 16. Never gives in at any point during an argument. Is always right, period.

_____ 17. Sees self as irresistible to the opposite sex and enjoys gaining their attention, usually with the intent of having sex with them, if at all possible.

_____ 18. Particularly enjoys flirting with those who are married, with the full intention of trying to lure them into an affair.

_____ 19. Has no commitment or even intention to stay married for life. Will have repeated affairs and will even "date rape" someone if it strikes his fancy.

_____ 20. Sex with mate is entirely for personal gratification.

_____ 21. Openly admires members of the opposite sex, and often blatantly makes a play for their sexual favors.

_____ 22. Enjoys all kinds of soft and hard pornography.

_____ 23. Is a big spender, particularly when in control of other people's money.

_____ 24. Looks for ways to cheat store owners (for example, claiming that he handed them a $20 bill when it was really $10). Will steal without hesitation if given any opportunity.

_____ 25. Borrows from friends or anyone he can cajole into lending him money with no intention of ever paying it back.

_____ 26. Gives no money to other family members for any reason, and will often steal from other family members (to buy booze, for example).

_____ 27. Never forgives.

_____ 28. Has a short temper and will vent anger violently, verbally, and/or physically.

_____ 29. If not a workaholic, may go to the other end of the scale and be disdainful of anyone who works hard, thinking this is for suckers or fools.

_____ 30. Feels no guilt about any of his behaviors or attitudes and wouldn't dream of trying to change.

_____ 31. Refuses any kind of counseling or therapy.

_____ 32. Always tries to beat the system whether it be traffic laws, the IRS, or company rules. Acts and feels above the law, and, while afraid of punishments, will take great risks to prove his "superiority."

_____ 33. Will use his personal interpretation of the Bible to justify almost any kind of act. Feels that he has special permission from God to do the very things he preaches against, such as adultery.

If you have gone through this list and checked off several items with a certain person in mind, you may be wondering if that person really does these things without any guilt at all, or whether he or she might have occasional guilt feelings. There is no hard and fast line you can draw. Sometimes we have great difficulty in our clinics deciding if a patient is Nth-Degree or high-level Second-Degree.

As far as your own daily welfare and protection are concerned, use this list as a guideline to identify possible Nth-Degree Jerks and decide how to deal with them. Your best approach to Nth-Degree Jerks is sometimes to *confront* and, if you get no favorable response, to *flee*.

Note that I said "sometimes" it is safer to confront, but not always. To confront some Nth-Degree Jerks could be downright dangerous; therefore, sometimes it is much safer to flee an Nth-Degree Jerk and avoid getting badly hurt.

Suppose, for example, you have a spouse who exhibits several of the above characteristics. Perhaps you have put up with this behavior for years, but have had no idea of how to deal with it. If you made any complaint at all, you got a tongue-lashing or perhaps a beating for your trouble. You can go on being a punching bag for an Nth-Degree Jerk, or you can stop the abuse now. Confront your spouse and tell him or her that, unless he or she immediately seeks conjoint counseling and therapy, you will have to separate from him or her for your own protection and possibly for the protection of children who may be involved.

Obviously, this is no small step. You may need to seek the advice of your pastor, counselor, or a therapist for making this confrontation, but the important point is not to go on living with Nth-Degree Jerk abuse any longer.

If your spouse absolutely refuses to get any kind of therapy or counseling help, then you have no choice but to separate yourself from your spouse. This kind of action takes great courage and great sacrifice, but it is worth it.

If you find yourself in other Nth-Degree Jerk situations (working for an Nth-Degree Jerk boss, for example), you can use the same approach of confrontation and, if necessary, flight (seeking a different job). Again, this is never done easily and usually involves great difficulty and sacrifice. But the question is whether you want to continue with this abuse or whether you think enough of yourself to put an end to it.

This question is a very real one for many people because they have certain tendencies toward masochism, a term I will explain fully in the next chapter. A great number of us who are trying to live decent, kindly lives have masochistic tendencies due to abuse we suffered in the past, usually while growing up. These masochistic tendencies make us extremely vulnerable to jerk abuse.

You can learn various techniques to deal with jerks—how to say no, how to express your feelings, and how to stand up for your rights and state what you want. These techniques are all good and often very useful, but they only scratch the surface of the real problem, which revolves around recognizing how and why you are being masochistic. In the next chapter, we will look at how this is done.

CHAPTER
5

But Why Are We Such Pushovers for the Predatory Jerks?

All right, we've looked at the Nth-Degree Jerks, the really sociopathic sickos who lie, cheat, abuse, and even kill, all without guilt or remorse. Thankfully, their numbers are small—about 10 percent of society—but they are a very dangerous bunch who cause a lot of pain and discomfort for many people.

We've also analyzed Second-Degree Jerks, a much larger group, who willfully take advantage, control, lie, and cheat if they can get away with it. They feel guilt sometimes, but not enough to change their ways. From work with thousands of different cases, it's our guess at Minirth-Meier Clinics nationally that at least 40 percent of society could fall into the Second-Degree Jerk category in this age of "I gotta be me."

Nth-Degree Jerks and Second-Degree Jerks are what we call the "predators" of society, who prey on the rest of us who are First-Degree Jerks (or possibly mature adults). We First-Degree Jerks and Jerkettes mean no harm, but tend to make mistakes and be somewhat manipulative or careless at times. We definitely feel guilty about our jerkiness and are trying to be less jerky, but we wonder why life can be so unfair. Why do the Nth-Degree and Second-Degree Jerks seem to be able to manipulate, control, cheat, and abuse us so readily? Do we have some kind of built-in weakness that makes us easy prey for these predators?

As a matter of fact, many of us *do* have a built-in weakness, which I call masochism or masochistic tendencies. I mentioned masochism briefly in Chapter 1, and, as I said there, it usually has nothing to do with sexual aberrations. It is, instead, the tendency to put yourself in a position where you can get hurt, victimized, or taken advantage of. People who can't say no, no matter how busy or overscheduled they are, usually have masochistic tendencies. The kind of masochism I'm talking about is self-defeating behavior, which allows us to be used or abused by jerky people.

Notice that I used the pronoun *us.* The next few pages will be autobiographical as I use myself as an example to show you how a masochist is made, usually through the influence of his parents and family. I will share a few insights into why I started married life as a rather high-level First-Degree Jerk who could even do nasty Second-Degree things like throw soda on another driver. The roots of masochism always run deep, and they can usually be traced right back to the homes in which we grew up.

My Masochism Started Early

I've always had a strong personal tendency to be somewhat masochistic. I have a history of having a hard time saying no to people, and then being taken advantage of, especially in a financial way.

Through college, medical school, and the early part of my career, I was so weak in this regard that I usually wound up going out to eat with jerky friends who tended to be attracted to me because I would always treat them to meals. I no longer do this; in fact, now when I go out to eat with friends, we go Dutch treat, unless there are special circumstances.

For a long time, however, I was literally addicted to Second-Degree Jerks. The severe and sick Nth-Degree

Jerks never appealed to me, but Second-Degree Jerks, who had charisma and charm, did. In a sense, I unconsciously needed them in order to vicariously act out some of my own rebellious motives and emotions that I didn't even know were there until I got some personal therapy.

Interestingly enough, I did not grow up in a physically abusive or neglectful family. My German parents were good people who came out of a loving but extremely strict, conservative religious background. For example, we had family devotions *every day,* something I still greatly appreciate. However, we also attended a legalistic church, which meant complying with all kinds of rules that the church had concerning what was right and wrong. Many of these rules, by the way, had nothing to do with what the Bible actually says.

In addition to being legalistic and very strict, my dad was a workaholic, and had little time to spend with me. He never attended any of my basketball, football, or baseball games, which made me feel as if I were unworthy of his love. Until well into adulthood, I always struggled to get his attention and approval. A carpenter by trade, my father always worked very hard. In fact, in his mind, working twelve hours a day was how to show me and the rest of the family his love.

Today my parents are both in their eighties, and they are a lot more "hang loose" than they were when I was a small boy. Now we do things together that would have been considered a sin by that legalistic church we all attended many years ago.

For example, it was against the rule for me to use the scissors on Sunday (the Sabbath). I couldn't go to movies—not even G-rated Disney movies. I couldn't play with playing cards because they were considered evil, gambling tools. It was all right to play Rook, and other card games, but the regular playing cards were off limits.

Oh, yes, I also couldn't square dance in elementary school. I can distinctly remember being in third grade and watching all the other kids learning to square dance while I had to sit on the side, feeling angry and abandoned because my pastor had written a note to my teacher saying that God had killed fourteen thousand Jews for dancing. (My pastor didn't mention in his note that the fourteen thousand Jews had died for dancing as part of their worship of the false god Baal, something God had expressly forbidden them to do.)

I Learned Early, "Never Say No!"

In a very real sense, I suffered a type of religious abuse as I grew up, and that caused me to feel very insecure. I had a hard time saying no to anyone, because I thought I should do whatever anybody asked. In our church, the attitudes of Jesus were taken out of context and taught with a "letter of the Law" approach. For example, we were told that if somebody attacked us, we were to turn the other cheek, no matter what the situation might be. Likewise, we were taught that if someone wanted us to "walk an extra mile" for any reason whatsoever, we were to do it without questioning the other person's motive.

It wasn't until years later, however, that I learned a Christian should turn the other cheek or walk the extra mile if he is being slapped or hassled *for being a Christian*. The biblical text does not teach that we are to become masochists who allow people to abuse us whenever a whim suits them. But as a young boy, that's exactly what I thought—turn the other cheek and walk the extra mile, *no matter what*. It was no wonder, then, that I became a prime target for jerks who liked to take advantage of me.

During elementary school, for example, I helped my father build a garage, a task I thoroughly enjoyed. I did sixty hours of work, and he paid me fifty cents an hour. All of a sudden I was rich—thirty whole dollars! In my elementary school days, that was a great deal of money, and I made the mistake of taking it with me to school and showing it to my friends. All of a sudden I had a lot *more* friends, who all wanted to go to the candy store after school. My new friends lasted approximately two days, exactly as long as my thirty dollars lasted. When my money was gone, so were my new buddies. I had blown my entire thirty dollars trying to buy friendship and approval.

When I got into high school and then college, I had some

good friends along the way who didn't take advantage of me at all, but there were also plenty of those who latched on to me like sharks to their prey. When we would go out to eat, they would expect me to pay, and so, foolishly, I would do so. It wasn't as if I were loaded with money. Our family was never well off, and I worked my way through college, graduate school, medical school, psychiatry residency, and seminary. But even though I always paid my own way, I often ended up treating other students—the Second-Degree Jerks who knew I was an easy mark.

I Couldn't Resist Those "Dumb Doctor Deals"

When I finally finished all my schooling, I started becoming financially successful when the first few books I wrote or helped write sold very well. My masochistic tendencies continued to plague me, and I tended to be a real sucker for people who wanted me to invest in all of their "sure thing" propositions. You may have heard of "dumb doctor deals," which are tailor-made for physicians who have extra money, big hearts, and naive trust in their fellowman. Once I invested in a windmill that didn't exist. I also invested in an oil well that pumped barrels of salt water, but no oil.

In truth, I wasn't as much a "dumb doctor" as I was a "driven doctor" who wanted to please his investor friends. I couldn't—that is, I wouldn't—say no because I wanted their approval and friendship.

I made numerous investments over the years, and wound up losing a considerable amount of money. In fact, I wound up owing penalty payments to the IRS, whose agents really didn't believe anybody could be stupid enough to invest in a windmill that wasn't there. They actually thought I was deceiving the government when I was the one who had been deceived!

At one point, I cosigned on several big real estate deals as a favor for several friends who were in the same investment group. Normally, this kind of transaction calls for a cosigner's receiving a large amount of money for risking his money. I chose not to ask for any money for cosigning, however, because (a) I sincerely wanted to use my borrowing power to enable my friends who were in the investment group to share in my success; (b) I enjoyed the appreciation and admiration I received for being such a generous person.

Unfortunately, this investment group soon went out of business, and I got stuck with several large pieces of real estate worth less than one-third of what I (the cosigner) still owed on them.

In the wake of this disaster, I figuratively sat like a puppy whining in the corner, with my tail between my legs and my long ears covering my eyes. Winding up holding the cosigner's bag was only part of it. One of my investor friends used my name to make some other deals that I knew nothing about. As a young boy, I tried to buy friends with $30 I had earned by helping my father build a garage. Now, nearly thirty years later, I tried to buy the approval of my investor friends for the same basic masochistic reasons.

Jan, however, decided to go down and talk to the Federal agents who were trying to sort all this out at the bank to see if anything could be done. (At least she could let them know that I was not a crook.)

As Jan talked to the Feds, she asked, "What can I do to help Paul?"

The Feds answered quickly, "Put his hands in cement blocks so he can't sign any more 'dumb doctor deals'!"

As I look back over my life, I see that I had many friends who "took me to school," and I paid very high tuition. But along the way, however, I did learn some valuable lessons. I consulted with colleagues who were psychologists and psychiatrists, and shared what some of my struggles had been, which gave me insight into my masochism and self-defeating behaviors.

Eventually, I was able to make some important decisions that resulted in making new friends, the kind who wouldn't take me for a ride. My experiences are a key motivation for writing this book. I want to help other people who may be doing the very same thing I did for so long. Or perhaps I can prevent you from falling trustingly into financial bondage or other types of abuse.

Our "Shame Base" Makes Us Feel Unworthy

At several points in previous chapters, I have referred to patients as having "holes in their souls." These "holes in the soul" have usually been caused by abuse of one kind or another, and they are fertile ground for the planting of what we call a "shame base." In your personal shame base lie deeply buried pockets of false guilt that make you feel unworthy, of little value, and not entitled to have equal rights to the fundamental good things of life: your right to be angry within reason; your right to enjoy a healthy marriage; your right to feel happy and satisfied; your right to feel good about a good day's work; and your right to say yes or no, especially no.

When we talk with patients who have masochistic tendencies, these basic rights sound foreign to them. They say things like, "Some people may have the right to these good things, but I don't—I don't deserve them."[1]

This book is intended to help you avoid getting hurt by predatory jerks. It is not intended to be a book on child rearing, but it is crucial to understand that the roots of our masochistic tendencies usually go back to various kinds of abuse that we suffered during childhood. If you are making masochistic decisions today, it may be due at least in part to how you were brought up.

Parental Mistakes May Cause Masochism

While masochism is often caused by poor parenting, I by no means want to indict all parents as inept or abusive. Many parents do an excellent job of rearing their children, but their children make poor choices or sometimes suffer tragedies in their own lives that produce the very same kinds of results that come out of being abused. My own parents were wonderful people overall, but I still suffered from religious abuse (legalism) and made some poor choices of my own along the way as I became an easy target for predatory jerks who sensed they could take advantage of me.

Volumes have been written on the several hundred or more forms of child abuse, both major and minor, the effects of which we have treated in our clinics nationwide. But for our purposes in this chapter, I will list only some of the basic major, moderate, and minor forms of abuse that often produce certain levels of masochism and/or jerkiness in children by the time they become adults.

At the extreme end of the abuse spectrum, we have seen patients who are victims of horrible crimes, such as molestation, incest, rape, or date rape. We continually see the long-term effects of sexual abuse among patients in our Minirth-Meier Clinics. I've also studied many surveys of incidents of sexual abuse, and a very conservative estimate is that one out of twenty-five females in America is a victim of incest involving intercourse while growing up. Another 25 percent of all women in America have suffered some other form of sexual abuse. Also, about one out of fifty males in America has had intercourse with his mother or stepmother while growing up, and many young boys have been abused by homosexual men.

Any traumatic experience can and usually does cause a tremendous sense of shame in an individual, which leads to feelings of false guilt. In fact, all people who have been abused by jerks tend, to some extent or another, to blame themselves for getting abused. They actually feel that they deserved the abuse.

This kind of thinking is at its height in the eight- to ten-year-old child. For example, a ten-year-old's father dies in a car wreck or an airplane crash, and the child blames herself. The child believes that it's her fault that her father dies. She thinks God is punishing her for something she did wrong, and He took her dad away. Or she may think, *My dad died on purpose to punish me for not being good.*

Masochistic tendencies often develop out of the false guilt, shame, and rage that follow physical abuse, verbal abuse, lack of love, and too much or too little control of children as they grow up. We can even go back to things more basic than that. If children suffer deprivation of such basic needs as proper nutrition, hugs, warmth, friendliness, and affection, especially as infants, they can grow up with the misbelief that they do not, as adults, deserve these basic things.

A lot of what passes as good discipline is really abuse of children. Parents need to seek a balance between authoritarian heavy-handedness and permissive neglect. Lack of discipline actually lowers the child's self-esteem. Proper discipline and limit-setting tells the child he is worth all that effort, but too much discipline destroys much of a person's God-given curiosity and creativity.

Too much discipline often results in black and white, rigid, legalistic thinking. Many parents, for example, would do better to make the house *child-proof* rather than make the child *house-proof*. Instead of slapping your infant's hand for trying to satisfy natural curiosity, it would be better to remove precious knickknacks and other objects and put them in a safe place.

Overly strict and unloving discipline can also be abusive because it discourages children from sharing their honest, gut-level feelings, including their anger. Most three-year-olds are more in touch with their true feelings than most adults. When three-year-olds love you, they run up and smile and hug your leg until you pick them up to return their affection. When they are sad, they cry. When they are angry, they don't hesitate at all to let you know.

When parents teach their children in various ways to deny or stuff their true emotions, these parents are actually being abusive, whether they realize it or not. When children grow up hearing commands such as: "Stop being so angry—it's wrong to be angry," or "Quit your crying—big boys (or girls) don't cry!" they can wind up as adults who need therapy in order to be reunited with their true inner emotions. I have treated many intelligent, perfectionistic patients who didn't know their own anger from a hole in the ground! Because dealing with anger is so critical, we'll spend all of Chapter 9 learning how to handle it better.

Permissiveness Is Also Abuse

While it is abusive to be too authoritarian and harsh with
your children, it is equally abusive to be too permissive, because then they can grow up suffering from what we call
"expectation abuse." I'm talking about the *child's* expectations, not the *parents'*.

My Son, the Kindly Masochist

It's a bit early to tell completely how our mistakes may
have caused our children to have masochistic tendencies.
Each child has his or her own unique personality, but we
can see that all of them have a bit of masochism, which we
either unconsciously taught or which they unconsciously
caught from living with us.

The very week I was finishing up this chapter, one of our
sons was coming out of a supermarket when he heard a
woman scream from across the parking lot. A man had
snatched her purse and sped away in a pickup truck, leaving
her weeping hysterically.

My son went over to comfort her, and she told him that
she had just cashed her monthly welfare check and the man
had taken all her money. Now she would not be able to buy
food or pay the rent. Because my son's bank was only a
block or so away, he told the lady to wait, went down to his
bank, drew out all of the money in his account (several hundred dollars), returned to the parking lot, and gave it to the
grateful woman.

While we appreciated the fact that our son had such tremendous compassion for another human being in distress,
we were also concerned about his lack of foresight concerning his own financial situation. In being generous with the
woman who had been robbed, he left himself in a position to
be unable to pay his bills during the coming month. Also, he
could have been the victim of a scam by Nth-Degree Jerks.
But, as we tried to express our ambivalence about his gener-

ous act, he just shrugged. After all, it was "only money" and the lady needed help.

How the "Isms" Create Masochists

One of the most common forms of abuse that makes masochists out of many people is the "ism" abuse—the addictions of their parents. All addictions are shame-driven, and the addiction cycle (discussed in Chapter 8) moves from one generation to another. When moms or dads suffer trauma or abuse during childhood, they usually develop shame and low self-esteem. The pain of low self-esteem, even though unconscious, hurts very badly. In fact, the three greatest fears Americans have are (1) fear of failure, because it lowers self-esteem; (2) fear of abandonment, because it lowers self-esteem; and (3) fear of death—the ultimate threat to self-esteem, particularly for those who lack a deep faith in God.

The pain from low self-esteem may drive one or both parents toward a sedating, pain-relieving, addicting agent. The addictive agent winds up as an "ism," for example, alcoholism, sexaholism, sportaholism, spendaholism, or even churchaholism, to name a few of countless examples. I define a churchaholic as one who attends church so many hours each week that he risks incurring God's displeasure for ignoring the clear biblical teaching that those who fail to meet the needs of their own household are worse in the Lord's eyes than infidels.

Obviously, it would be better for Mom and Dad to get therapy, resolve their root problems, get rid of the pain those root problems are causing, and enjoy life without indulging in this "ism" behavior. But if they keep their "ism" during their children's growing up years, the children learn nonverbally that they are not of much value to their busy parents.

Parents become so involved and enmeshed in their "ism" that the child is left feeling neglected. Eventually, the child becomes so embarrassed and full of shame that he feels like trash. The child decides that he deserves to be rejected because he is of much less value than the parents' "ism." A child tells himself, "You deserve to suffer."

Eventually, the child believes all the lies that he hears in his own self-talk, which sets him up unconsciously for many unnecessary hurts as an adult. He may adopt his parents' "ism" or develop a new "ism" all his own (or both).

The Shame-filled Power of the Unconscious

All of the abuses described above—mild to severe—contribute to one's individual shame base, much of which lies deep in the unconscious. It is important to understand that the false guilt of our shame base permeates *all* levels of our consciousness.

The *conscious mind* deals with things you are thinking about right now that may or may not make you feel guilty. The *subconscious mind* touches on any thought, feeling, motive, or past event that you can call to memory. The *unconscious mind,* however—which probably is a reservoir for 80 percent of your thoughts, feelings, and motives—includes everything recorded in your brain that you *can't* call back to memory at the present moment.

In fact, we note in working with patients in our clinics that the more abusive or negative a person's childhood was, the less he will remember of his or her childhood. Nonetheless, all that stuff is down there affecting you in ways you don't even understand. Most of the hundreds of decisions we make each day are 80 percent unconsciously motivated, and only 20 percent consciously controlled or decided. It's a wonder we don't make more mistakes than we do!

One way to illustrate the conscious, subconscious, and unconscious mind is to roughly compare all three to an iceberg. One-eighth of an iceberg can be seen above the water, and this represents the conscious mind. The subconscious mind represents the next one-fourth or more of the iceberg, just below the surface. The rest of the iceberg, which is deep under water, represents the unconscious mind. In therapy we try to help patients bring things from the unconscious to the subconscious, and eventually to the conscious.

My own therapist has shown me many of my repressed

thoughts that become absolutely obvious once she brings them to my attention. Strangely enough, some of these interesting revelations are things my wife, Jan, has been telling me for years, but I never believed her!

Your shame base, especially the false guilt buried in your unconscious mind, is what can drive you into masochism and your own kind of "ism" (i.e., addiction). For example, it is quite possible to become addicted to jerks who will treat you badly—*jerkaholism,* if you please. I was a jerkaholic of sorts myself until I wised up and realized I was trying to buy the love and approval of people by being an easy mark and a soft touch.

In counseling thousands of patients in our Minirth-Meier Clinics nationwide, we have identified a common thread that runs through the lives of many, perhaps most, people. This thread pulls and tugs at their unconscious, affecting their judgment and actually robbing them of the ability to make a totally clear choice, even though they think they are making perfectly good choices. Our therapists and counselors, as well as many others in the field, have labeled this powerful force co-dependency, which in its broadest sense can be defined as "an addiction to people, behaviors, or things."[2]

In reality, jerkaholism is as valid a state of co-dependency as alcoholism, foodaholism, or any other addiction. Jerkaholism is a masochist's co-dependent addiction to jerks who, of course, are also co-dependent on the masochists they abuse. In other words, in my own case, jerks were co-dependent on taking advantage of me, and I was co-dependent on the jerks to fill my need to be accepted, approved of, and liked.

Masochists Are Often Rescuers

Regarding my own masochistic tendencies to allow people to abuse me financially, I had the benefit of being married to an extremely capable family therapist, who had particularly good insights into how I ticked. In addition, I worked every day with some of the best psychiatrists in the world, including my medical partner, Dr. Frank Minirth. They engaged me in some honest confrontations that helped me break free from my own mild to moderate jerk addictions, especially the drive to be a compulsive "rescuer" of acquaintances who then took advantage of my generosity to manipulate me and rip me off. Personal therapy was a luxury I am thankful I indulged in.

Rescuers are almost always masochists because they can't say no to anyone who asks them for help, even when helping that person might be harmful to him or her or to the rescuer's own family. Rescuing done to satisfy masochistic tendencies just doesn't make much sense, but it's exactly what I was guilty of. At times I even hired people we didn't need because I felt sorry for them and vainly thought I was the only one who could help them.

Those of us in the rescuing professions—psychiatrists, psychologists, pastors, missionaries, for example—would do well to identify our own masochistic tendencies. I feel that my own recovery from allowing others to abuse me financially has helped me become a better role model for clients who come to our clinic seeking to overcome their own masochism. I know from personal experience how it feels to move through the addiction cycle, and, more important, how to break that cycle and become free.

As you have been reading about my masochistic misadventures, you may have been trying to identify, but weren't able to do so completely. Perhaps you haven't been ripped off by making jerky investments as I did. Nonetheless, you have to admit that it seems that there are a lot of people who take advantage of you in one way or another. You may be wondering: *Am I really a masochist? Do I have masochistic tendencies that make me co-dependent on jerks whom I think I have to please or impress? How can I tell?*

At the risk of sounding a little overenthusiastic, I'd like to say, "I have just the thing that can help you!" I put the following fifty questions together after contacting many of our 300-plus Minirth-Meier therapists across the country to ask them what they have observed in the childhood backgrounds and current behavior of clients they are treating to overcome various masochistic tendencies. Out of their observations has come the "Minirth-Meier Masochistic Tendencies Test," which could also be labeled, "How prone are you to jerk abuse?"

Before you use this test, please realize that some people can suffer mild to severe abuse during childhood and beyond, and still manage to make the emotional and mental choices necessary to avoid any significant masochism and jerk addiction. You may score very low on the following test, but it will still be a valuable experience. In general, the higher one scores on the Masochistic Tendencies Test, the more likely it is statistically that you have a number of conscious or unconscious (deeply buried) masochistic tendencies.

Test yourself first, then, if you wish, go back and apply the questions to a significant other—your spouse, perhaps. Rate each statement from zero to three, with zero equaling "never," one equaling "rarely," two equaling "sometimes," and three equaling "often."

Minirth-Meier Masochistic Tendencies Test

	Self	Others
1. I tend to see myself as having been a victim in repeated situations in my past.	____	____
2. Sometimes I ask my friends for advice, then when they imply I should or could do something to protect myself from an abusive situation I use the words, "Yes, but . . ." to excuse myself from following their advice.	____	____
3. I tend to be late to meetings and appointments.	____	____
4. When my feelings are hurt, I have a tendency to pout.	____	____
5. I have a tendency to put things off (procrastinate).	____	____
6. When people ask me to do things I don't really want to do, I'll purposefully do an imperfect job so		

	Self	Others
they won't ask me to do that again the next time.	___	___
7. I tend to stay so busy that I never get caught up.	___	___
8. I have trouble saying no to people who ask favors of me.	___	___
9. I feel that if people could read my private thoughts they would reject me.	___	___
10. I have tension headaches or migraine headaches.	___	___
11. I tend to get physical illnesses more readily than the average person.	___	___
12. I tend to volunteer for too many activities (such as car pools, church jobs, committees, organizations).	___	___
13. I seem to have lingering feelings of guilt or shame.	___	___
14. When we go to eat, I wait for others to choose which restaurant to go to, even if I don't prefer that kind of food.	___	___
15. When we go to restaurants, I tend to pay for more than my fair share or even pick up the entire tab.	___	___
16. I have some compulsive tendencies, such as overeating, spending too much, workaholism, excessive volunteerism, excessive handwashing, excessive exercise, excessive television watching, excessive prescription drug use, churchaholism, hoarding things, or any sexual compulsion.	___	___
17. I have suffered physical abuse of some sort in the past ninety days without reporting it to the police.	___	___
18. I have been a victim of some form or forms of sexual harassment or abuse in the past ninety days and the perpetrator has suffered no consequences for doing this to me.	___	___
19. I have been a victim of some form of verbal abuse in the past seven days		

Self   **Others**

without telling the abuser how angry I truly feel about it. _____ _____

20. I feel sorry for myself for the suffering I experience now or have experienced in the past. _____ _____

21. When I was growing up, my parent of the opposite sex tended to be prejudiced against (or condescending toward) members of my sex. _____ _____

22. One or both of my parents tended to give me food or money as a love substitute. _____ _____

23. I seem to crave attention. _____ _____

24. I have either a father-vacuum (craving male attention), a mother-vacuum (craving female attention), or both. _____ _____

25. I felt as if I had to perform to get one or both of my parents to accept me. _____ _____

26. I spent an average of thirty or more hours per week in day-care centers during my preschool years. _____ _____

27. One or both parents tended to break promises to me. _____ _____

28. My parents relied on me to help settle *their disputes.* _____ _____

29. I feel lonely or abandoned. _____ _____

30. I was compared unfavorably to one of my siblings or friends. _____ _____

31. My parents gave me too many chores and responsibilities growing up—I was almost an extra parent. _____ _____

32. One or both parents imposed legalistic or rigid rules on me. _____ _____

33. My parents criticized each other in front of me. _____ _____

34. While I was growing up, one or both of my parents made decisions for me that I should have been allowed to make for myself. _____ _____

35. One (or both) of my parents verbally abused me by attacking my character. _____ _____

Self   Others

36. One (or both) of my parents slapped
    me in the face or slugged me during
    my growing up years.   _____   _____
37. One (or both) of my parents sexually
    harassed and/or abused me in any of
    the following ways: overt sexual acts,
    sexual innuendos, treating me as a
    substitute mate in subtle ways, sexual
    teasing.   _____   _____
38. One (or both) of my parents was
    unable or unwilling to attend my
    special activities as I was growing up
    (e.g., sports performances, musical
    recitals, birthday parties, PTA,
    graduations).   _____   _____
39. My parents seemed to be unable or
    unwilling to seek ways to develop
    genuine warmth and love for each
    other.   _____   _____
40. My parents seemed unwilling or unable
    to communicate their true emotions
    to each other in an assertive but loving
    and tactful way.   _____   _____
41. One (or both) of my parents was
    unhappy.   _____   _____
42. One of my parents was a masochist,
    and I seem to act more like that parent
    than the other one.   _____   _____
43. One (or both) of my parents expected
    me to excel in a certain area (such as
    academics, sports, popularity, music)
    that he or she felt inferior in when he
    or she was growing up.   _____   _____
44. One (or both) of my parents told me in
    verbal or nonverbal ways that I would
    not succeed in life.   _____   _____
45. My parents were unwilling or unable to
    take the time and effort to have
    regular, meaningful religious
    discussions or devotions with me when
    I was growing up.   _____   _____

Self   Others

46. I find it difficult to feel intimate with
   God the Father.   _____   _____
47. I felt like a scapegoat in my family—as
   if one (or both) of my parents was
   taking his or her anger out on me for
   some reason.   _____   _____
48. One (or both) of my parents implied
   nonverbally or even verbally that I was
   an "accident," or implied other "don't
   exist" messages.   _____   _____
49. I have difficulty remembering much of
   my childhood, particularly below the
   age of ten.   _____   _____
50. I have been verbally, physically,
   financially, or sexually abused by one
   or more nonparents, such as a sibling,
   friend, coach, teacher, pastor,
   neighbor, stranger, counselor,
   baby-sitter, or relative.   _____   _____
                                  TOTALS: _____   _____

Now add up your score to see in which category of masochistic tendencies you fall:

   0–30—few, if any, masochistic tendencies
   31–70—mild masochistic tendencies
   71–100—moderate masochistic tendencies
   101 or above—severe masochistic tendencies

Now repeat the test and score any significant others you wish to evaluate. Keep in mind that many adults have come from severely abusive childhoods, but have still learned to avoid being masochists. But if you have grown up to be a masochist of at least some degree, don't despair. My wife, Jan, and I are living proof that masochists *can* change.

In Part II of this book, I will take you through a Six-Step Plan to help you move from masochism (self-destructive behaviors and attitudes) to maturity. I hope that all you will need to do to conquer your own masochistic tendencies is simply read this book and complete the recommended exercises. It is possible, however, that going through the Six-Step Plan may convince you that you need the help of a counselor or therapist.

On a periodic basis, Jan and I have been seeing a woman therapist who has tremendous insights and has helped us stay on our road to recovery from masochism as we pursue the elusive holy grail of maturity. Jan, in particular, likes to tell people that early in our marriage her philosophy was, "Great men have great faults, and great women learn to live with them." Now she has changed her philosophy to: "Great men have great faults, and great women point them out—in a tactful, non-jerky way, of course!"

Nonmasochistic Approach to Money Management

Making a number of jerky investments that practically wiped me out financially taught me to take to heart some basic money management practices. Today I manage my money as nonmasochistically as possible, which automatically prevents me from being abused by predatory jerks who would otherwise take advantage of me.

The following are some commonsense financial practices that can protect you from unexpected financial stress and financial abuse. Check how many of these decisions you can claim as your own:

_____ 1. I will give approximately 10 percent or more of my income to any local church and/or responsible, accountable charities because it is really true that it is better to give than to receive. I will feel better about myself if I am making some sacrifices for the betterment of humankind, but on a controlled, stewardship basis.

_____ 2. I will put 10 percent of all my take-home pay into safe savings accounts, money market accounts, or short-term CDs. I will let this build until I eventually have one year's salary in my account, which I will use as "liquid assets" for any emergencies that might occur.

_____ 3. I will expect financial emergencies. For example, I will expect my car to break down. I will expect medical or even psychiatric emergencies. I will expect to lose my job at some time. Most people do. These are all realistic expectations. I will be prepared. I will protect myself financially.

_____ 4. If I follow the above suggestions, I must get used to the idea of living on 80 percent of my take-home pay. This may mean a smaller home, a less expensive car, fewer quality clothes, and less expensive entertainment and vacation habits, but I will get used to it. Materialism offers me a false sense of self-worth, but it never delivers. I won't be fooled by the consumer songs I hear all the time because I know I can be happier with less.

_____ 5. I will not cosign any loan for any friend, because in the end it hurts me and the person whom I helped make dependent by giving the loan. If I'm rejected for politely refusing, I have delivered myself from a potential abuser, and I will thank God for this.

_____ 6. If I use a credit card, I will charge only what I can pay off totally each month, thereby avoiding exorbitant interest rates. If I borrow money on a car, I will borrow no more than the resale value of that car. Then if I have an emergency and need to sell the car, I should be able to sell it quickly for at least what I owe on it.

_____ 7. I will not make investments of any kind until I have one year's worth of income saved in liquid funds and no debts at all, except for reasonable loans on my home and cars. When I do make an investment, it will be an amount that I can afford to lose if the investment goes sour.

_____ 8. There are two kinds of investment counselors. One kind charges by commissions or other kickbacks. The other charges by the hour and gives advice but gets no commissions or kickbacks. I will give preference to the latter kind of counselor. I will remain well aware that human nature finds it easy to rationalize, and I will never let another human being control my finances, no matter how well-meaning or how "brilliant" he or she might be.

_____ 9. I won't ever try to get rich quick. Ninety-nine percent of get-rich-quick "windows of opportunity" are phony, and the other 1 percent aren't worth looking at. If all these schemes work, why aren't all the investors wealthy and not in need of your money? I will just say no to get-rich-quick schemes.

_____ 10. I will be sure I have enough term insurance to protect my family. I can buy a half million dollars worth of term insurance from a reputable company for about $1,000 per year. When I can afford it, I will purchase whole life rather than term, because term policies get outrageously expensive as old age approaches.

_____ 11. I will be sure my mate and children are protected from unnecessary taxation and emotional or financial abuse by having a Last Will and Testament drawn up according to the laws of the state in which I live. If I move to a different state, I will have my will changed immediately in order to avoid probate court. Because rules vary from state to state, your safest approach is to always engage a lawyer to draw up your Last Will and Testament to help you get all details of your estate in order.

The above suggestions are just a few basic ideas to help you focus on being less masochistic with your money.

PART II

SIX STEPS OUT OF MASOCHISM TO MATURITY

CHAPTER
6

Meet the Enemy—He Is Definitely Us

STEP ONE: Take a Good Look at the Jerk Within

If you have any masochistic (self-destructive) tendencies at all, the Second- and Nth-Degree Jerks of this world are probably abusing you in numerous ways. If you ever hope to learn the art of psychological and spiritual self-defense against this host of predators—jerks from your past, jerks from your present, and future jerks you haven't even met yet—take Step One on your journey to maturity:

Examine the roots of your jerkism/masochism by going down deep to take a good look at where you came from and who you are today.

The Most Dangerous Jerk Lurks Within

When Pogo uttered his famous line, "We have met the enemy and he is us," he didn't know how right he was. He was referring to the one who has the most potential to cause us pain—and that is definitely the jerk within, to whom I have alluded to several times in earlier chapters.

The jerk within has two components or sides. On one side is the self-destructive masochist that is self-defeating and self-punishing due to your shame base. The other side of the jerk within is that sense of selfish entitlement that whispers, "You deserve to act, be, or have what you want." The jerk within is the self-centered narcissism that you didn't quite outgrow. Remnants of that sense of entitlement are still there, locked in your unconscious, but now and then they raise their ugly heads and climb into the subconscious mind and then finally poke through to our conscious awareness.

All of us have moments when we feel anxious but don't quite know why. At times like these, we are experiencing true anxiety, which occurs when our repressed thoughts, feelings, and motives are threatening to emerge, but we are afraid to look at them. I believe the process Christians call sanctification is the Holy Spirit pushing up these repressed thoughts and emotions from below while our brain keeps pushing them back down into the unconscious in order to avoid facing the painful truth. The tension between these two forces is what causes true anxiety.

As the prophet Jeremiah put it:

> "The heart is deceitful above all things,
> And desperately wicked;
> Who can know it?
> I, the LORD, search the heart,
> I test the mind."[1]

As the Lord searches our hearts, He pushes up only a little bit of our repressed thoughts, feelings, and motives at a time; if He pushed them *all* up, we couldn't stand it.

Because the brain is automatically self-protective against pain, it keeps pushing these repressed thoughts, feelings, and motives back down as the Holy Spirit pushes them up from below. But rather than facing the truth about ourselves, we prefer to use what psychiatrists call defense mechanisms to find ways to make the jerk within seem like a pretty good guy after all.

To understand why the jerk within is so comfortable to us, sort of like an old shoe, it helps to look at the various defense mechanisms that we all use almost every day. In earning our degrees, we psychiatrists spend many years studying forty or more defense mechanisms—the ways the brain deceives itself daily from the pain of seeing the truth. A standard definition of defense mechanisms is: "The ways people react to frustration and conflict by deceiving themselves about their real desires and goals in an effort to maintain their self-esteem and avoid anxiety."[2] It is no exaggeration to say that understanding how to deal with defense mechanisms is what psychology and psychiatry are basically all about.

Repression Is the Granddaddy of Them All

Repression means that unacceptable ideas, feelings, impulses, or motives are banished from conscious awareness; or unconscious ideas, feelings, impulses, or motives are prevented from coming into conscious awareness.

For example, someone brought up in the church is dying of cancer and feels great anger because God has allowed the cancer to develop. Because the patient is a devout believer, being angry at God feels unacceptable, so the patient represses his true feelings. At the same time, however, he stops going to church and having personal devotions, although he tries to tell family and friends he is "trusting God for healing."

If a close friend sees through the cancer victim's facade and asks him if he is angry toward God, the victim will profess shock and be insulted that the friend would even think such a thing.

Repression is the primary defense mechanism on which all other defense mechanisms are based. It is a "patriarch" with at least thirty-nine more offspring, although some psychotherapists would add more to the list. Let's look at some of the more common defense mechanisms and see how they illustrate jerkism and/or masochism.

Denial Just Can't See the Problem

A close cousin of repression is *denial*; thoughts, feelings, wishes, or motives are denied access to consciousness. When you use denial, your thoughts, feelings, wishes, or motives can be obviously wrong to those around you, but you can't see it. At least half of the alcoholics in this country use denial to fool themselves into thinking they could easily quit drinking "any time they felt like it."

Recently Jan and I went out to dinner with friends who were both therapists. During our dinner conversation, Jan mentioned an employee in one of our clinics who was taking advantage of me. I just smiled and said, "Well, it's at a tolerable level, and I don't think it's worth trying to change anything right now."

One of our therapist friends—the wife—observed, "Isn't denial wonderful?"

I laughed because I knew she had me cold. "Yeah, it really saves me a lot of hassle sometimes," I joked.

In reality, however, I realized I had been masochistically allowing myself to be taken advantage of by a jerky employee. I had avoided doing what I knew had to be done—that is, confront the employee and correct the situation. On the way home that evening, I told Jan I appreciated being confronted with my denial and that I would correct the problem as soon as a good opportunity came up. And I did follow through by speaking to the offending employee the following Monday morning.

Almost everyone uses denial. Take a moment right now and think of situations where you may be denying the truth because you don't want to face up to it. After making some notes, talk it over with your spouse or a good friend to see if they concur that you may well be using denial as a defense mechanism.

• I may be acting in a jerky way toward _____ because I don't want to admit _____
_____.

• I may be putting my masochistic head in the sand in regard to _____ because I don't want to admit _____

_____.

Projection Sees Faults in the Other Person

A defense mechanism almost all of us use at one time or another is *projection*: criticizing a fault, habit, or attitude in someone else when it's really *our* attitude, fault, or habit. Are there certain people who really bug you? When you're around them, do they have certain habits or mannerisms that make you anxious, frustrated, or even angry? Chances are, what you're seeing is an action or attitude that you are guilty of, but instead of wanting to admit it, you "project" this attitude or action onto them.

When I was in medical school, I would frequently become nauseated when a certain fellow student came to join the rest of us during lunch in the student cafeteria. I just didn't like being around him and felt anxious almost every time we had any interaction at all.

Then I took a basic psychiatry course and learned about projection. One day while studying in my room, I made a list of the things I didn't like about my classmate. My lengthy observations included:

> He eats too much.
> He talks too much.
> He's arrogant.
> He thinks he knows the answers to everybody's problems.

When I got through making my list, I looked at it for a few minutes and then realized: "Meier, you idiot, you're looking right into a mirror!"

I went to my fellow student, told him how nauseated he made me feel, and shared my list with him. He looked it over and said, "This is interesting. I have felt nauseated around you, too, for pretty much the same reasons!"

Instead of becoming sworn enemies, we both acknowledged the truth that neither of us had recognized to that point. We became good friends and for one three-month period shared a small office where we got along just fine, because we accepted the truth in ourselves without projecting it onto each other.

As we work with patients in our clinics, we find that the more paranoid a person is, the more he or she is likely to use projection. Just about everyone, however, will project their feelings, motives, or thoughts onto others at certain times.

For example, many perfectionists tend to be controllers who simply cannot delegate any task to anyone else. In fact, deep down, they aren't even satisfied with how they would handle that task; nonetheless, they project their own insecurities on the other person and assume that no one could do it right. The controlling perfectionist is caught between a rock and a hard place, telling himself, "I probably won't be satisfied with what I do, but if I ask someone else to do it, it will surely be done wrong. At least I'll do it 'less wrong' than he would."

When I covered projection in my seminary classes, I would ask my students to get out a sheet of paper and imagine they were going to a party. I asked them to imagine people walking into the party and think of three types of people who would really nauseate them or make them feel anxious or uncomfortable. Then I would ask them to list what it is about these people that "gets you."

I'd let them write for a while and even have some students share their papers with the rest of the class. Then I would make my point: "What you've listed—that's your problem—what you are fighting deep inside. It may not be the exact, same behavior, but the attitude is there. Whatever you see in others that bugs you and makes you anxious is very likely to be your kind of problem, deep down."

After completing this exercise, some of my students would challenge me, saying that there was no way they were like the persons they had listed. I replied that I understood their doubts, but to think about this: "We can be around certain people who have certain quirks or abrasive habits, but they never bother us. We don't become nauseated, anxious, or extremely uncomfortable. Why not? Because *that's* not our problem. But when we're around people who make us aware of something in our unconscious that we haven't been aware of to that point, *that's* when we get anxious and even sick to our stomach."

Projection is exactly what Jesus was talking about in Matthew 7:1-5 when He warned us not to judge others. Instead of worrying about the toothpick in someone else's eye, we should notice the log in our own, which I was finally able to do after our daughter ran away and we all wound up in the counselor's office. Just as I had done with my fellow student in medical school, I had been projecting my own faults onto my daughter, and she had been doing the same with me. (See Chapter 2.)

What about possible "logs" (or even toothpicks) in your own eye? Use the following questions to see if you've been using projection on anyone, for example, in your family, at work, at school, or in your church, perhaps.

• People who nauseate, irritate, or frustrate me *most of the time* include:

Name: _____

Fault: _____

Name: _____

Fault: _____

Now for the hard part. Do any of these "faults" remind you of yourself? Like any defense mechanism, projection is an act of your unconscious mind, and you may not be willing to admit that you have any of these faults. Talk it over with your spouse, a good friend, or possibly a counselor who can help you see the truth.

Rationalizing Excuses Our Jerky Behavior

Another familiar defense mechanism is *rationalization*: justifying unacceptable attitudes, beliefs, or behavior by inventing false reasons or excuses for that behavior. We use rationalization constantly. For example: "I had to drive 85 m.p.h. to get to work because I couldn't be late again"; or "I should have spent last night paying the bills, but I was tired and there was such a good program on television."

The jerky boss might rationalize: "I chewed her out for her own good—she's just not producing," when in truth he chewed this employee out because he wants her to make him look better in front of his superiors.

The jerky driver might rationalize: "I had to cut that pickup truck off because I couldn't go past my off ramp," when in truth she just didn't want to take the time to drive down to the next off ramp and then double back to her destination.

The jerky parent might give his child a severe thrashing and simply say, "I did it for his own good," when in fact he did it to relieve his frustration, anger, and hostility.

It is safe to say that rationalizing is one of the most popular defense mechanisms among Second-Degree Jerks in particular, although we all do it. The Second-Degree Jerk, however, *willfully* controls, manipulates, cheats, bullies, or abuses and then needs something to assuage his guilt. Rationalization is a perfect tool.

At the same time, masochists use rationalization to justify allowing jerks to abuse them. In my own case, I rationalized paying for the meals of jerks who took advantage of me by telling myself I wanted to be a good guy and, besides, "*real* Christians are always willing to go the extra mile." I assured myself that God wanted me to pay for freeloaders because it was a good way to "witness to them" and show them how a good Christian acts.

What about any rationalization you see in your own attitudes and behavior? Go through the following list of phrases and see if any sound like things you say to rationalize your own jerky/masochistic behavior at times:

_____ "I did it for his own good."

_____ "There just wasn't any alternative."

_____ "It was the only way I could see my way clear."

_____ "Everybody else was doing it."

_____ "My mate did it to me so . . ."

_____ "I needed the rest (or the break) or a good time for a change . . ."

_____ "I should have . . ."

_____ "I could have . . ."

_____ "I will if . . ."

_____ "Why not?"

_____ "She needs my help . . ."

_____ "He needs someone to talk to . . ."

We all use these rationalizations and many more. What to look for, however, is any pattern where you are continually excusing (rationalizing) certain behavior that is either jerky (you are abusing someone else) or masochistic (you are allowing someone to abuse you).

If you can identify any such "trigger phrases," they can serve as a red flag to tell you when you are rationalizing, and you can catch yourself in the act and quite possibly correct the situation.

Passive-Aggressiveness Rebels Against Authority

A defense mechanism we see more often in high-level masochists who tend to be abused by their more jerky counterparts is *passive-aggressive, unconscious behavior.* Passive-aggressive individuals have repressed hostility toward a certain individual (or organization) on which they are, or have been, overly dependent. Because they depend on this person (or organization), they dare not be openly confrontive or angry, so they learn to get unconscious revenge in nonverbal ways.

The passive-aggressive will pout, procrastinate, forget to call back, or stubbornly "tune out" the person (or organization) he is trying to rebel against. One example of passive-aggressive behavior would be the alcoholic husband whose domineering, mothering wife is trying to get him to quit drinking. The wife drives the alcoholic husband a little nuts with her nagging, but he is so dependent on her he doesn't dare express his anger. (In fact, he has repressed his anger and is not even aware of it.) But that anger comes out just the same as he gets even with her by coming home late from work or putting off doing simple chores around the house. Eventually, the passive-aggressive alcoholic husband gets ultimate revenge on his wife by dying of liver disease.

Three common ways to display passive-aggressive behavior are:

Pouting
Procrastinating
Performing poorly

Suppose a husband and wife disagree but he refuses to try to resolve it and just goes off to *pout*. He is being jerky toward his wife, as well as masochistic toward himself because he has to go through the pain of being estranged from her. Nonetheless, he pouts anyway to fulfill the masochistic "script" he has written for himself. Besides, it is a comfortable role, and he can wallow in self-pity as he consciously rebels against his wife (or perhaps against a parent whom he didn't want to rebel against openly in the past).

Procrastinating can be just plain jerky selfishness or laziness, but it is more likely to be used by the passive-aggressive masochist who *wants to fail* for whatever reason. This person puts off what needs to be done, finding excuse after excuse (rationalizing) to explain his behavior.

A friend of mine completed almost all of his work on an M.B.A. and had only one brief term paper left to do as a requirement. It was a rather easy assignment—only a few pages long—and should have taken only a few hours of work at the outside, but he drifted along *for five years,* never quite getting to it. Finally, the deadline for completing the program passed. He could no longer make up this last bit of required work, failed the course, and did not get his M.B.A. degree.

Why did my friend allow himself to fail? The degree would have given him a big boost in his career, and it also would have pleased his father to know his son had earned it. And there was the clue. His father had been severely critical of him all of his life, actually mean at times, and, in my opinion, my friend *unconsciously failed to get the degree to spite his father.*

In fact, he never did go back and complete the degree, which he could have done by repeating the course he had failed. Whom did he hurt? His father just shrugged and said, "I might have known he wouldn't do it." My friend hurt only himself, which is typical of the masochist.

Performing poorly is closely associated with procrastinating. Poor performance can be an act of out-and-out jerkiness, or it can be done "by accident" as a passive-aggressive way of rebelling against an overbearing spouse, a demanding boss, or, as in the case of my procrastinating friend, a parent.

Like procrastinating, performing poorly is something a masochist does without realizing it. He will insist that he tried as hard as he could, that he "gave it his best shot," but the truth is he set himself up for failure as a way of rebelling against some authority figure he didn't want to confront openly. So he took the passive-aggressive route and performed poorly as a way of getting back at this authority figure. An unemployed masochist, for example, will go to a job interview with the attitude "You don't want to hire me, do you?"

If you have masochistic tendencies, check yourself for passive-aggressive behavior. Any time you find yourself pouting, procrastinating, or performing poorly or inefficiently, ask yourself:

• Am I being (or was in the past) overly dependent on someone or some organization? Yes ___ No ___ Comments:

_____

_____

• Am I angry at this person (or organization)? Yes _____
No _____ Comments: _____

_____

• Could I possibly be expressing my anger in passive-
aggressive ways? Yes _____ No _____ Comments: _____

_____

• Do I pout, procrastinate, or perform poorly at home, in
my marriage and family? Sometimes _____ Often _____ Not
sure _____ Comments:

_____

_____

• The family member I may be rebelling against is:

_____

• Do I pout, procrastinate, or perform poorly at work?
Sometimes _____ Often _____ Not sure _____ Comments: __

_____

• The person at work I may be rebelling against is: _____

_____

As you look for passive-aggressiveness in your behavior,
keep in mind that denial and rationalization are tools often
used by the passive-aggressive person. It takes much more
than one defense mechanism to be a jerk or a masochist!

Displacement Takes Out Anger on a Safer Object

Still another very familiar defense mechanism is *displacement,* which means displacing or transferring your emotions (often anger) from the original object of that anger to a more acceptable and safer substitute.

The classic illustration of displacement is the man who is bawled out by his boss at work, but he is afraid to say anything because he wants to keep his job. So the man comes home that evening and takes it out on everybody in the family. He tells his wife that he is sick and tired of whatever she's made for dinner. He spanks his child for some nominal offense that he normally would have completely ignored. And somewhere along the line, he may even kick his dog!

(For a while I was thinking of including a chapter in this book on jerk abuse of pets, but because pets are so hard to interview I decided to leave it out. Suffice it to say, however, that abuse of pets by jerky people is done constantly. When the abuse is at Second-Degree Jerk level, it can be serious, and when the Nth-Degree Jerk abuses his dog or his horse, it can be fatal.)

Like all defense mechanisms, displacement can be used by jerks or masochists. In my work with patients in our clinics, I see masochists who are very angry at those who abused them, and they take out that anger on themselves in various ways. For example, women who were abused as children may sit and cut themselves, beat their heads on the wall, or inflict pain on themselves in any number of other ways, because they are angry at the person who has abused them and they are displacing that anger toward their own bodies.

A prime example of this kind of displacement would be Jennifer, the victim of incredible Nth-Degree Jerk abuse, described in Chapter 4, who was cutting herself with safety pins when she was admitted to our clinic. She was angry with her sadistic, incestuous parents, but she was taking it out on herself.

Another favorite displacement technique by a masochist

is to go through life continuing to be abused because he was abused when he was younger. Vivacious Vivian, the movie star who had five husbands, is a prime example. In order to continue ventilating her anger toward her abusive father, she kept marrying Nth-Degree Jerks who abused her. She felt she deserved their treatment, thinking, "I must be trash or I wouldn't have been abused by my father in the first place."

Displacement is also a favorite way to display jerky behavior. Suppose, for example, you get mad at yourself because you don't get the grade, don't make the sale, or aren't awarded the promotion. Deep down you know it is your own fault. You didn't study hard enough, you didn't hustle enough, you didn't produce, but instead of admitting your faults, you displace all your anger and point it toward authority figures who have caused all your grief: the teacher who gave you the *C*, the customer who turned down the sale, the boss who wouldn't promote you.

If you are a truly aggressive type, you will be confrontive—with the boss, for example, and possibly get fired or quit. Then you go on to another job where the same thing eventually happens. I have had many patients who had a record of going from job to job and unemployment line to unemployment line because they kept failing to see their own faults and displaced their anger toward their employer.

Another familiar approach finds a person who gets angry at work, for example, but doesn't confront his boss because he wants to keep his job. Instead, he will butter his boss up and praise him to his face, being very manipulative and phony. He may be very angry at his boss, but he would never say so. Instead, he displaces his anger by taking it out on fellow employees, his friends, or his family—those he can trust to continue to accept him in spite of his verbal outbursts. The most loyal and unconditionally loving friends are often the most victimized by displacement, an unfair fact of life.

Displacement isn't an easy defense mechanism to own up to because it suggests a certain amount of sneakiness or cowardice on our part. That's all the more reason to take a good look inside to see if you have any regular patterns that involve displacing anger toward innocent parties. If you discover such a pattern, you need to take two important steps: (1) Do not follow through with displacing your anger on the usual "safer target," such as your wife, your child, or your friend. (2) Muster the courage to confront the real target of your anger by letting that person know how you feel and trying to resolve the situation in some way.

Phariseeism Is "Holier Than Everyone Else"

A defense mechanism we often see in both Christian and non-Christian patients is Phariseeism. The person using Phariseeism is guilty of the same things Christ condemned in the Pharisees He encountered in the Gospels. Individuals think themselves better than others because of what they do or don't do. They become increasingly self-righteous, and they scrupulously adhere to a list of philosophical or religious rules or some other set of standards, all with the goal of avoiding becoming aware of their own faults, failures, and depravities.

Phariseeism is a defense mechanism often used by legalistic pastors. Young men grow up with unconscious inferiority feelings because of their repressed selfishness, hostility, and anger. These young men become Christians somewhere along the way and then feel "called" to preach. They go through seminary, eventually get a church of their own, and then feed their flocks a constant diet of legalism as they preach consistently against their own "dirty-dozen" list of sins and shortcomings.

As I mentioned, people usually engage in more than one defense mechanism, and Pharisaical pastors often use "reaction formation" by focusing on the sins they themselves struggle with at a conscious or unconscious level. For example, alcoholic pastors preach against drinking; sexaholics focus on fornication and adultery (for more on reaction formation, see the Appendix p. 243).

They actually think themselves to be more righteous and holy than others, particularly the less legalistic Christians whom they may condemn as "instruments of the devil" or as "demon possessed." Just as the Pharisees in Christ's day did, they love to be called on to pray (doing so with eloquent verbosity), and to preach long-winded sermons that are heavy on what not to do. They also like to set up certain cultural standards and make them spiritual qualifications—for example, length of hair or length of skirts.

Due to my strict and often legalistic German upbringing, I was something of a Pharisee myself as a young man. I went off to college with several lists of what I felt was right and wrong. One list I had contained twenty things I expected in a wife. After watching my father's chauvinistic approach to being a husband, I knew exactly what I wanted.

For openers, any girl I would consider marrying would have to be German, a Christian, beautiful, and smart. She would also have to be a hard worker, compliant, obedient, a good cook, and all those other things that my mother had been. Most important, however, she would have to be a committed, deeply spiritual believer, meaning that she had to be as super-spiritual as I thought I was.

I Thought I Had Found My Future Wife, But . . .

During my first week at school, which, by the way, was a very legalistic Christian university that had even more rules than my church back home, I found my future wife. Her name was Jan Verkler. On our first two or three dates, I wanted to make a good impression on Jan to assure her she was dating a very spiritual fellow, and I quoted Bible verses at every opportunity (and sometimes when there was no opportunity).

In the course of one of our conversations, I learned that Jan did not attend the Missionary Prayer Band, a special meeting held weekly on campus to pray for missionaries.

This was a serious black mark against Jan, and I had to prayerfully reconsider her as wife material. Should I even date her any longer? While I was struggling with my dilemma, Jan solved it for me. A genuinely spiritual girl, she had seen through my immaturity and decided that she would wait for me to grow up a little before thinking about dating me again.

While Jan's rebuffs hurt my feelings, I continued with my Pharisaical ways, spouting Bible verses at everyone for any reason. One day I confronted a fellow student I knew was spreading a "heretical" theological view around campus. We got in a heated argument, and I was so incensed by his "lack of spiritual insight," I turned him in to faculty authorities.

In reality, this student was not a heretic at all. He differed with me on one of Calvin's Five Points, but I "knew" he was wrong because he not only disagreed with me, the school taught the same position I believed in! When school authorities learned about this student's "heretical views," they asked him not to return to school the next semester.

Jan and I eventually did resume dating a year after she decided I had wised up, at least a little bit. I still had a lot to learn, however, and one of the first mistakes I made was to foolishly show her my list of twenty qualities that I wanted in a wife. Talk about high-level, First-Degree Jerkism! Jan read the list but was not impressed. "I'm all those things and more," she told me, "and I have my own list of what I want in a husband. You've got a little work to do!"

Undismayed, I indefatigably stuck with my original choice for a wife. I chased Jan for three years and she finally did marry me during our last year of college.

Pharisees Think They Are the Only "True Believers"

Keep in mind that Phariseeism is a defense mechanism people use to avoid becoming aware of their own faults, failures, and depravity. They unconsciously fear looking inside themselves to see what needs to be changed. They try to maintain that nothing needs to be changed and that only *they* are the true believers. It took me several years to rid myself of Phariseeism as a frequent defense mechanism. Jan was my finest ally, poking pins in my super-spiritual balloons whenever it was necessary. Even today, when I even hint at sliding back into Pharisaical thinking, Jan brings me up short in a hurry!

While I was teaching seminary for twelve years, every now and then I'd run across a student who would inform me quite confidentially that he was "sure only 10 to 20 percent of the entire student body were true believers." All the rest were carnal Christians at best, and a lot of them "weren't even saved." These Pharisaical students always had their own list of what it took to be a "real" Christian. If anyone failed to meet any criteria on that list, he was automatically excluded from God's Kingdom.

You can find Phariseeism in all kinds of settings, and not necessarily in the church. The only requirement to be a Pharisee is to have your list of requirements and then exclude or look down on others who don't match your requirements. There are, for example, political Pharisees. Every four years Democrats and Republicans don their Pharisaical robes and pepper each other with charges and counter-charges, gravely warning the voters that *their way* is the only possible solution to the country's ills. And then there are philosophical Pharisees, educational Pharisees, yes, even psychological Pharisees who are quite sure their narrow approach to the counseling profession is the only correct one.

When I get a couple in my office for marriage counseling, Phariseeism is often quickly detectable on the part of one or both mates. You may be wondering who is the most Pharisaical, the masochistic mate or the one who is more aggressively jerky. The answer is that the aggressive persecutor type of personality is usually the one who uses Phariseeism.

There is, however, no predominance of Phariseeism in men or women. Husband or wife may turn out to be the Pharisee as they reveal their paranoid perfectionism. The Pharisaical perfectionist mate is the one with grandiose ideas of his or her own wisdom and goodness. He or she is usually very controlling and very critical of the other spouse, who doesn't live up to his or her standards.

It's my hunch that there is a little Pharisee in all of us.

Sexualization Focuses on Sexual Prowess

Sexualization seeks to dominate the opposite sex. These persons typically boast of their "sexual athleticism" and they prove their prowess to themselves in one of two ways: through actual sexual encounter with other persons, or through sexual fantasies. In either case, the goal is the same—to "conquer" the opposite sex and enable themselves, temporarily at least, to feel less inferior sexually. In addition, they temporarily are able to ventilate their hostility toward the opposite sex.

Another form of sexualization can be seen in the sexual harassment of women by men, cases of which have made the news frequently in recent years. As women have attempted to enter professions or jobs formerly held only by men, they have had to endure all kinds of abuse, which, in many cases, is the defense mechanism of sexualization, used by certain males who feel inferior or hostile toward women.

I read recently about a woman who decided she could earn more money repairing and maintaining appliances, like dishwashers. She entered the field and was paired with a male coworker, who repeatedly told her, "I don't want you here."

The man harassed her and even threatened to sexually attack her. Whenever the woman reported him to her supervisors, they ignored her complaints. She eventually began carrying a piece of lead pipe to use on her nemesis, if he ever did decide to actually attack her when they were alone.

On one occasion he tried to set her up for serious injury, even death, by telling her to remove the knobs on a malfunctioning dishwasher after assuring her that he had already disconnected the power. The woman was smart enough to check the power herself and discovered that it had not been shut off. The appliance was still "live," and, in addition, there was a puddle of water directly in front of the dishwasher, where she would have been standing when she started to work on the machine. As the woman put it, "I would have been fried!"[3]

Recently my wife, Jan, was subjected to a "mild" form of harassment when a man we knew many years ago, while I was attending medical school, telephoned. When Jan answered, he immediately referred to her as "girl," as in, "Hey, girl, how are you folks doing up there anyway?"

Jan wasted no time in correcting him, "Please don't call me 'girl,'" she said.

"Why?" the man wanted to know. "That's what I call all the women I work with."

"Well, don't call me that," Jan insisted politely, but firmly. "I'm not your 'girl.'"

This is a typical example of the type of harassment that goes on daily in business and in many other settings. Women are referred to as "girl," "baby," and "honey," and while some men claim they are "just trying to be friendly," or even admiring, the underlying reason for these labels is to "put the woman in her place"—a sex object who is not quite equal to the person who is addressing her with that term.

The Goal Is Always the Same

Whether sexualization is played out in its most violent form—rape—or in its mildest form—verbal harassment—the goal is the same: *to conquer,* because the person using sexualization wants power. The goal of sexualization is to put down someone of the opposite sex.

Women, by the way, can be just as guilty of sexualization as men. For example, ultra feminism is every bit as chauvinistic as the behavior shown by "male chauvinist pigs," as the leaders of the liberation movement have labeled males in general. Sexualization is hardly an exclusively male defense mechanism.

A typical example of sexualization that I've seen many times is a female in her twenties who was sexually abused by her father as a child and/or a teenager. Her father ignored her most of her life and paid attention to her only when he wanted sex.

This young woman has a deep-seated and intense hostility toward her father, even though she claims she has forgiven him. Now in her twenties, she has a record of extremely pro-miscuous behavior, seducing men whenever possible to feed her ego. In fact, these men are married, and when she ruins their marriages it is even more unconsciously satisfying to her.

When confronted with her behavior, she claims that she is unaware of her hostility toward men. In fact, she insists that she "loves" men. The truth, of course, is that she hates men because she still has hatred for her father whom she cannot forgive. Once she truly forgives her father, she will be able to stop her promiscuous behavior toward men with the goal of seducing them. Wise King Solomon described in Proverbs the seductive woman as having sweet words but being "bit-ter as wormwood" (Prov. 5:1-4).

Like Phariseeism, sexualization is based on "feeling above" someone else, wanting to put someone else down and have power over them in some way.

We All Use Defense Mechanisms to Cop Out

I've given you this brief introductory course in defense mechanisms for at least two reasons:

1. To show you just a few of the ways our jerkiness comes out in our daily behavior.
2. To underline the fact that we all use defense mecha-nisms unconsciously as a way of protecting our false pride.

Defense mechanisms are unconscious, automatic reac-tions to frustrations and conflict that we all use to protect ourselves when we run into problems, trouble, arguments, or minor to major disputes. We use defense mechanisms to put the blame for the problem or conflict on someone else and never admit it to ourselves. (If you didn't happen to find yourself among the eight defense mechanisms just dis-cussed, see the Appendix, p. 239, for thirty-two other exam-ples of how we defend the jerk within.)

Although we use defense mechanisms unconsciously, I have tried to show in this chapter that it is entirely possible to bring the truth up from our unconscious, through the subconscious, and into our conscious mind where we can deal with the problem. Centuries ago, King Solomon wrote: "The wisdom of the prudent is to understand his way,/ But the folly of fools is deceit."[4] The wise, mature person will take time to analyze his or her behavior and admit fault when the fault is plainly to be seen. The immature person, however, seldom takes time to analyze his or her own behavior and attitudes, and keeps making the same mistakes.

The immature person fails to see his blind spots. Indeed, he uses defense mechanisms to blind himself. For example, a classic sign of a Second-Degree or Nth-Degree Jerk is the inability to ever admit that another point of view might have some merit (a sign of denial, rationalization, or Pharisee-ism). Second-Degree or Nth-Degree Jerks often lose friends, but they seldom lose arguments. Their defenses are just too strong.

Defense Mechanisms Shore Up Our Self-esteem

Defense mechanisms can be traced right back to the shame base we mentioned in Chapter 5. When we feel guilt (true or false guilt, it doesn't matter), we look for a way to shore up our self-esteem, and we often use a defense mechanism that suits our purposes. What we are really trying to do is deal with our anxiety, which is basically a fear of the unknown. That's why repression is foundational to every other defense mechanism. We fear that we might become aware of something, some thought, desire, or motive deep within that is unacceptable, even horrible or perverted. This would only increase our guilt and decrease our self-esteem still more, so we use a defense mechanism to block that possibility.

Another related reason we all use defense mechanisms is that everyone has inferiority feelings to at least some degree.

We unconsciously keep trying to prove that we have significance—that we are "somebody."

The workaholic, for example, is sure that he's putting in eighty hours a week for his wife and family, when, in fact, he is unconsciously trying to prove his significance and worth, while staying too busy to get in touch with his true inner pain.

The churchaholic spends so much time at church that he neglects his family, but he keeps telling himself he's doing it "for the Lord." Actually, he is doing it for himself and using obvious defense mechanisms, such as rationalization ("I'm only trying to serve God"). If confronted, he uses the mechanism of denial and will not even entertain the possibility that he is neglecting his family with too much church activity.

One of the major dangers in defense mechanisms is that they "seem to work" for the individual. In fact, many psychologists and psychiatrists encourage people to use defense mechanisms as a way of coping with life's frustrations and problems. Extensive research data on defense mechanisms shows that all human beings are basically self-deceiving; nonetheless, many therapists encourage their use to prevent insanity.

At the Minirth-Meier Clinics, however, we believe that the best way to cope with life's frustrations and problems is not to deny our depraved desires and motives but to turn them over to God through faith in Jesus. While facing up to our jerk within can be painful, in the long run it is the far better approach because the truth, indeed, will set us free. We believe, by the way, that the only Person who never used defense mechanisms was Jesus, the God-Man, whose self-esteem was so secure that He had no sinful motives or desires of any kind.

The unpleasant truth is that we lie to ourselves daily. We may not realize we're lying, but we're lying, nonetheless. What does logic tell you, then, about what must exist inside of each one of us? Yes, it's the jerk within, who is fighting for control over the other part of us—the part that wants to do good and be good.

Who Discovered the Jerk Within?

Around one hundred years ago, Sigmund Freud became "the father of modern psychiatry," describing the human personality in three parts: the ego (the will), the id (basic human drives), and the superego (the conscience). In truth, Freud was merely repeating the discoveries of Johann Christian Heinroth, a psychiatrist who published books and scholarly papers in Germany in the early 1800s. Heinroth divided human personality into: (1) the *überuns* (conscience), (2) the ego (mind, emotions, and will), and (3) the *Fleisch* (basic drives, including what Heinroth believed was man's sinful nature).

Obviously, Freud only repeated what Heinroth put down but with a totally different interpretation. Freud, a Jew, grew up in an area where Jews were despised and persecuted by self-righteous types who called themselves Christians. It's no wonder that Freud overracted, becoming an atheist and calling all religion "the universal neurosis of mankind."

Freud taught that the ego is an unconscious slave to the id (man's basic drives). For Freud, the only practical approach was to simply deaden the superego (the conscience) and thereby avoid the guilt that might cause mental illness. Heinroth, on the other hand, was a Bible-believing Christian who believed the ego is a slave to the Fleisch—the "flesh" the apostle Paul referred to in Romans 7. For Heinroth, however, victory didn't come by living a pragmatic life and deadening the conscience. Instead, victory came through the power of the Holy Spirit working in the life of the born-again believer.

Because most modern psychiatrists are secular in their outlook, they lean toward Freud's point of view because they simply can't accept the possibility of dealing with man's basic drives through putting faith in Jesus and depending on the Holy Spirit for a "Higher Power" source of victory over our addictive tendencies.

We Travel Different Roads to Self-discovery

As a physician/psychiatrist, I wish a machine existed that could X-ray our souls. I could X-ray myself and my patients, flash the results on a screen, and say, "Here's what you need to do to fix it!" But that's only fantasy. Psychological testing helps, but it's not gospel either.

Each of us has to travel his own road of self-discovery, and the best place to start is to look at your relationships. At its very base, this book is about your relationships to "jerks without"—the people with whom you deal in your life, on a long-term or short-term basis. How you deal with these people is directly connected to your relationship to the jerk within.

Where did the jerk within learn certain defense mechanisms and how to use them? To answer that question, the best place to go is back to your family of origin. There you will gain insights from those who knew you best and who imprinted you with positive and negative messages that you still carry with you to this day.

Sooner or later, all psychotherapy, whether done in the psychiatrist's office or in the comfort of your easy chair as you read this book, has to go back to your parents. Your parents may have been wonderful, so-so, or abusive monsters, but one thing is unquestionable. The impact on your life was *tremendous*. For good or for ill, their stamp on you, although correctable, is forever. The road from jerkism/masochism to mature adulthood must go through taking a good look at your family system, the role you played in that system, and the "injunctions" your parents hammered into your brain as you were growing up. We will do that in the next chapter.

CHAPTER
7

Are Mom and Dad Still Parenting You?

STEP TWO: Finish Leaving Home Psychologically

W hen I was about to graduate from high school, my father called me aside one evening and showed me a beautifully bound book printed in German.

"Paul, this is the Meier family history," he said proudly. "This story of our family goes back one hundred and fifty years. Your ancestors were German, but they lived in Russia. How our family gained its wealth and lost it all to the Communists—it's all here in this book."

At the time I was only mildly interested and just glanced at the book. Years later, however, after I began studying and practicing psychiatry, I realized this carefully bound record of our family history was a gold mine of psychological information. I eagerly devoured the book, cover to cover, and, as I examined our family's history back at least four generations, I learned a great deal about Meier strengths and Meier weaknesses and why I am who I am today. I saw how my parents had influenced my life and how their parents had molded theirs. I came to better understand the biblical passages that dramatize the influence fathers have on their children to the "third and fourth generation."[1]

Hard Work Paid Off for My Ancestors

My ancestors settled in Franzosan, a German city within Russian borders along the Volga River in the 1770s, around the time of the Revolutionary War, which led to the founding of the United States of America. The Meier clan was moral, hard-working (workaholic, in fact), and wealthy. Besides large tracts of land, they built and owned a large machinery factory in Franzosan, lots of horses, and a large home with servants' quarters in the back.

One day about 150 years ago, something happened in the city of Franzosan that had a profound impact on my life today. Two shoe repairmen came to town. That doesn't sound too life-shaking until you realize that these two shoe repairmen fixed the holes in the soles of people's shoes only to earn a livelihood. Their real goal was repairing the holes in people's souls—the aches and longings in their hearts.

They went door-to-door throughout the entire city, telling everyone that God loved them. They encouraged people to acknowledge Jesus as the Christ, the promised Messiah of the Old Testament, who died to take the punishment for all their sins. Not only that, but they could obtain forgiveness of their sins by depending on what Jesus did on the Cross to give them eternal life.

One-third of the citizens of Franzosan became Christians. Two-thirds only got the holes in the soles of their shoes fixed. Among that one-third that found help for the holes in their souls was the Meier clan, all of whom trusted Christ as Savior and Lord. My great-great-grandfather Meier was elected to be pastor of a new church that was organized.

The two shoe repairmen stuck around just long enough to train my great-great-grandfather in the Bible and to start additional Bible studies in the city. Six months after these two strangers entered the city, they vanished and were never heard from again!

When my great-great-grandfather died of old age, his son became the pastor, and then his son, my grandfather, became pastor after him. Grandfather Meier loved God and was an ardent student of the Bible, but he was also a workaholic with several jobs—pastor, factory owner, and land baron. My grandfather had inherited the family's machinery factory, as well as vast holdings of land and livestock.

My dad was born in Franzosan in 1910, as was my mother, who was the daughter of a loving middle-class family, who also had the name Meier but were not related to my father's family.

Dad literally grew up a millionaire. His family was waited on by thirty servants living in the quarters behind the main house. At the same time, however, my father was expected to be up at 4:30 A.M. every morning in order to do many chores before going to school.

The Communist Revolution Changed Everything

In 1917 when my dad was about seven years old, another life-changing event happened, which made a profound effect on what and who I am today: the Communist Revolution. If you have ever seen the film *Dr. Zhivago*, you have an idea of what life was like in Russia during those times. My parents tell me that the film is quite accurate.

First, all of my grandfather's money, which was in cash, became worthless due to decrees by the Communists. Next, the Red Army came marching into Franzosan, took away all the family possessions, gave my grandfather's favorite horses to their soldiers to ride, and used the family home for their headquarters.

Then they proceeded to "draft" all able-bodied men in the town into the Communist Army. Two of my parents' uncles refused to join and were promptly shot and killed before the eyes of their families, a terrible scene also witnessed by my father and my mother, who were only seven or eight years old at the time. Other members of the Meier clan "enlisted" to save their lives, managing to escape just a few nights later, while their commanding officers were asleep.

My father's family was left practically destitute, but miraculously a wealthy family friend and member of my grandfather's church who had most of his wealth in the form of gold came to their rescue. After being stranded for a year in Saint Petersburg, he financed their escape to East Germany, where they settled in Prussia and lived for several years. My mother's family, helped by the same generous benefactor, also managed to get away to Germany. You could say that my mom and dad grew up together, but they had no idea they would someday marry.

Both of their families lived in Prussia for several years. My father still had to follow the strict policies of his father—up early in the morning, plenty of hard work, and, oh, yes, getting straight A's in school. My father entered college at age sixteen and got a one-year degree in bookkeeping. His real trade, however, would be carpentry, which he would learn as a young man after arriving in America.

On to America and the Great Depression

In 1929, the kind family friend, who still had some gold hidden away, financed both my father's and my mother's families in making the journey to America and a new life. My father and mother arrived in the U.S.A. as teenagers, just in time for the Great Depression of 1930. Their families settled in different cities in Kansas and eked out a poverty-stricken living for several years.

Then, Mom and Dad accidentally ran into each other in the little town of Peabody, Kansas, in 1936. They were each delighted to discover that the other was still single. They dated a short time and then got married. They have been lovers ever since. Now in their eighties, they still go on long walks holding hands and thanking God for bringing them to America because they truly appreciate what it means to be able to live in "the land of the free."

As newlyweds, my mother and father honeymooned in Michigan and, because the climate and scenery reminded them so much of their own roots back in Russia, they decided to settle there. My father often worked two jobs as a carpenter. He was also a churchaholic (Sunday school superintendent and deacon) and an ardent student of the Bible.

In his love of Scripture, my father was like his father, his grandfather, and his great-grandfather, the original pastor of the Christian church founded in Franzosan, after the two shoe repairmen evangelized the town. I recall many times that we children would read a random verse out of the Bible, and my father could usually tell us what chapter and book of the Bible we were reading from.

My mother was a homemaker, but she worked so hard that she filled a role that was more like a family servant than wife. My parents had grown up in a very chauvinistic culture where the men were expected to be scholars, tradesmen, and providers of the family income. The women were taken out of school after the third grade and then became servants in their own family or a neighbor's family where they were taught to sew, cook, and wash clothes. Marriages were often pre-arranged, although in my parents' case, they chose each other, and then got married—with their families' blessing, of course.

Spoiled by Mom, Ignored by Dad

My parents had a son, Richard, then a daughter, Bettye. Then I came along and my baby sister, Nancy, was born four years after I was. I was a compliant child, close friends with my mother who spoiled me because I was the youngest boy.

My father was gone most of the time, either at work or at church. He did eat dinner with us every night and read a chapter out of the Bible after supper. Then we would sing a hymn, hold hands, and pray briefly for each other. (I've often thought of how those two shoe repairmen had an impact, not only on the people they talked to, but on generations to come, even 150 years later.)

On Saturdays, my father would give me a long list of chores to do, and I was also required to practice the piano. Failure to do the chores or learn my piano lesson meant facing my father's paddle, and, not being fond of pain, I usually did as I was instructed.

While my father had little time to spend with me personally, I was fortunate enough to have my big brother, Richard, who played the role of father in many ways. He took me everywhere he went and bought me gifts from his own hard-earned money, which he made working in a drug store.

Eight years older than I, Richard taught me self-defense and how to play sports, such as football, basketball, and baseball. At times, he was more of a father to me than my own dad.

My Best Was Never Good Enough

I grew up filled with what could be called "spiritual ambivalence." I loved God, His Bible, Christian music, and Christian friends, but I really resented "religion" and church, because it seemed to me that these things were keeping my dad away from me. I never doubted that my dad loved me, but his workaholism and churchaholism gave him little time to spend with me, and when he did take time, he often criticized me for not doing better, or at least not doing as well as he thought I could.

As I look back, I recall never being spanked by my mother, but I was spanked too often by my dad. In Mom's eyes, I could do no wrong. In Dad's eyes, there were many times when it seemed I could do no right. He loved me, but he was hampered by his own strict German upbringing, the traditions of his father, and the generations before him.

Besides having to walk a rigid line at home, my dad attended schools that had an atmosphere similar to a Marine boot camp. On one occasion, as my father sat in his high school class, he whispered to someone across the aisle. The professor saw him, strode directly to his seat, and slapped him hard across the face. This kind of corporal punishment was commonplace in German schools, which demanded perfection in every way.

It's not too hard to understand, then, that my father always wanted me to do my best—actually, be perfect—and when I didn't measure up, he disciplined me "for my own good." I wound up feeling that, no matter what I did or how hard I tried, it was never quite good enough. But the older he became, the kinder he became, and he and I are close friends today.

In high school I took classes in architecture and I still treasure the memories of how my dad let me play amateur architect and design a house that he and I built together. Later, our family moved into it and lived there for a year or two before my father sold the home at a nice profit. The entire experience gave me a tremendous amount of confidence and self-respect. Not only did I spend a lot more time than usual with my father, but I also gained his approval for the most part.

As I look back now, I can see that my mom's permissiveness is what encouraged my high level of First-Degree jerkism. On the positive side, her confidence in me gave me courage to take risks in life to create and succeed. On the other hand, my dad's strict ways and lack of time for me gave me masochistic tendencies, which led me to allow people to take financial advantage of me in the hope that I would be accepted and loved by these so-called friends. On the positive side, my father's strict expectations gave me the self-discipline to survive the unbelievably demanding rigors of medical school.

Every Family Has a System

In recent years, counselors, psychologists, and psychotherapists have been using a "systems" approach to the family. One of the more popular approaches to family systems has been the work of John Bradshaw, whose TV series on "The Family," was seen on PBS channels throughout the country by millions of people. In addition, his book by the same title became a national best-seller. According to Bradshaw:

> The family as a system is a new reality. Only thirty-five years old, the concept of families as systems helps explain a bewildering array of behaviors. . . . The fam-

ily systems model shows how each person in a family plays *a part in the whole system.*[2]

In our Minirth-Meier Clinics we have also taken a systems approach to the family. One of the questions we frequently ask patients is: "What roles did (or do) you play in your family of origin?"

There are many different roles people can play in a family, but the most common triad of human behaviors includes *persecutors, victims,* and *rescuers.* As the following diagram illustrates, persecutors display jerky behavior. Abuse victims, for the most part, display masochistic behavior. Rescuers come to the aid of victims and may display masochistic and/ or jerky behavior, depending on the situation.

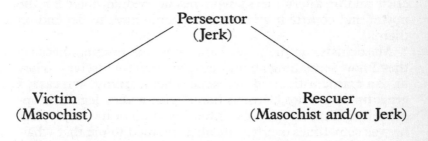

Persecutors will abuse others in the family (as well as outside the family, for that matter) verbally, physically, sexually, mentally, or emotionally. It is possible for a high-level First-Degree Jerk to be a persecutor, but the more hard core kind of persecutor would be your Second-Degree or Nth-Degree Jerk. The word *persecutor* suggests someone who willfully tries to control, dominate, or abuse for one reason or another. It is possible, however, that a person can be a First-Degree Jerk but simply be unaware of how blustering, intimidating, and abusive he or she is at certain times.

Victims are the passive, frustrated, somewhat frightened members of the family who see themselves as helpless to fight back or stand up for their rights in any way. Favorite phrases that victims like to use include: "I should have . . . "; "I could have . . . "; "I might have . . . "; and the ever popular, "If only. . . . "

As we have seen in many of the illustrations in this book, victims may have terrible things happen to them. But what makes you a "victim" is not what happens to you but how you respond to what happens. Victims almost always have masochistic tendencies and many are high-level masochists who continue to put themselves in a position to be abused because it's "easier" to be a victim than to take initiative and fight back.

Rescuers are the ones who obviously try to come to the aid of the victims. They ride in on their white horses to do battle with the persecutors or to help the victim with whatever situation he or she is in.

As the diagram above suggests, a rescuer can be a masochist and/or a jerk. Jerks who rescue people do it for the power and control it gives them. People have to depend on them.

Masochists, on the other hand, become rescuers because they know something about being victims themselves. They have a masochistic need to rescue others. In my own case, I grew up in a strict German home with a very legalistic approach to Christianity. My father loved all of us deeply, but he was sometimes overly critical. It seemed to me that whatever I did always fell a little bit short.

That feeling of falling short or not quite being good enough carried over into all my relationships. As a young boy, I started trying to be a rescuer, trying to help people where I could, particularly if they wanted me to spend money on them. That's why my thirty dollars lasted only two days when my friends learned that I had all that money and was just itching to spend it on them at the candy store (see Chapter 5).

When I was sixteen, I became good friends with a young surgeon who was a member of our church. "Dr. Bob," as I liked to call him, invited me over to his home one night, where he showed me books on medicine and told me how hard medical school was. As I showed interest, he suggested that I memorize Proverbs 3:5-6:

Trust in the LORD with all your heart,
And lean not on your own
   understanding;
In all your ways acknowledge Him,
And He shall direct your paths.

We went over those verses several times, and I committed them to memory that very evening. Later, when I got home, I got down on my knees beside my bed and rededicated my life to God. For reasons that I thought only God knew, I felt certain that He wanted me to serve Him someday, helping people as some sort of medical doctor.

I'm not questioning at all whether God called me that night or not. I believe He used the unconscious need in my soul to be a rescuer and directed me toward a positive goal. As I have met hundreds of people in rescuing professions, I have learned that most of them are masochists of some kind. They all have the hole in their soul that they fill by helping others.

There are a few persecutor jerks who are rescuers—arrogant and domineering surgeons and specialists, for example—but I believe that, for the most part, people in healing and helping professions are there to rescue others out of a sincere desire to benefit mankind.

I know of many wonderful physicians who have become disillusioned by having to suffer through frivolous and unfair lawsuits. In one case, a female "psychic" went to a neurologist because she had been having continuing migraine headaches. The neurologist did an MRI brain scan to check for a brain tumor but found nothing wrong.

Later, the woman claimed that the brain scan had robbed her of her psychic powers—and her ability to make a living. She filed a lawsuit, claiming that the neurologist had not warned her that the MRI might cause her to lose her powers. The jury awarded the woman one million dollars. The neurologist appealed to a higher court and was finally able to get the ruling overturned, but not before spending several hundred thousand dollars in legal fees.

Everyone Plays Out His Role

The family system is where the different members play out their roles, and family dynamics is how they go about it. Who, for example, were the persecutors in your family? Your father? Your mother? How did you interact with those persecutors? Perhaps, for example, you recall an older brother who beat you up all the time and threatened to beat you up again if you ever told. On the other hand, perhaps *you* were the persecutor who worked over your little brother.

Who were the rescuers in your family? Who always felt sorry for the victims and tried to help and aid them? In our family, my mother was the rescuer and my dad was a mild persecutor of sorts, not because he was an unfeeling, Second-Degree Jerk, but because he was a strict German who was trying to be sure all his kids toed the mark.

Dad was really a nice man, and he would have never knowingly persecuted me with intent to really harm me. He was, nevertheless, a stern disciplinarian, and, when things got a little too hot for me, I would run for cover and hide behind my mom, who would protect me, saying, "Now, Alex, he didn't mean any harm. He makes mistakes . . . he's only a boy."

And who were the victims in your family—the scapegoats who were often the targets of displaced anger? In other words, who got persecuted the most or victimized the most? In my own case, I was partly victim (of my dad's strictness) and partly a persecutor (i.e., jerk) who took advantage of my mother's tendency to spoil me. In fact, while I was a scapegoat of sorts, I was also a rather high-level First-Degree Jerk who had a strong sense of entitlement.

For example, I can remember being in third or fourth grade and coming home from school. I'd throw my coat on the floor and kick off my shoes, letting them fall near my coat. My mother would hang up my coat, shine my shoes, and put them away, and then offer me a sandwich and a glass of milk. As I ate, she would often massage my back. My jerk within never had it so good!

My older and younger sisters didn't have it so easy. When

they got home from school, they had to wash the dishes, clean house, and iron—all the chores expected of the women in the family. In a sense, my sisters were victims—at least victims of chauvinism.

Try Analyzing Your Own Family System

Stop right now and look at your own family's "system." Identify who played what role, and particularly look at the role you played (and probably still play to a lesser or greater degree) in that system.

• What role did you play in your family of origin's system? Keep in mind that many people play more than one role. Were you the persecutor? The victim? The rescuer? _____

Comments: _____

_____

• Analyze the other members of your family. The persecutors were: _____

_____

The victims were: _____

_____

The rescuers were: _____

_____

• Think about the dynamics of how your family system played out its own "drama of life." Did one particular family member have a serious addiction, such as alcoholism? Did anyone use a certain defense mechanism in a jerky or masochistic way? (Review Chapter 6 and the Appendix.)

As you analyzed your family's system and the role you played in it, it will be of use to think about who you identified with the most as you grew up. Your father? Your mother? Or someone else in the family? Whose personality traits did you adapt or copy to the letter?

In most families, it is easiest to identify with the more aggressive members and become more the persecutor than the rescuer or the victim. There is no hard and fast rule, however, and people can go in any number of directions. For example, a girl growing up in a home where the father persecutes the mother is likely to become a victim, too, because she identifies more with her mother on a sexual basis.

There is no way to accurately predict who a child will identify with because choices are always involved. In our clinics, patients want to believe that their problems are all inherited (in the genes), or they will want to blame it all on their environment (how their parents brought them up). Genetics and environment are two powerful forces, to be sure, but in the final analysis *we all make our own choices* concerning who we will become.

One of the major premises at Minirth-Meier Clinics is that people can change. They are not doomed to live out their lives playing a certain role or being hobbled by crippling personality disorders using the same old defense mechanisms over and over. *You can choose to change, if you want to.*

Looking at your family's system and the role you played in it is useful, but there is possibly an even more important area to examine—parental injunctions, the messages your parents used to program you, literally for life.

Everyone Inherits Parental Injunctions

The primary thing we inherit from our parents is not their money, or even the color of their eyes, but their *parental injunctions*. When parents die, the usual procedure is to leave a Last Will and Testament, which explains which of their assets and funds they wish to pass on to us. But, while they are alive, they also pass on a "Psychological Will" to use in the form of subtle and sometimes not so subtle injunctions or life messages, if you please, that give us their directions about how they really want us to live and what they want us to accomplish.

Following are some common examples of parental injunctions that my psychiatric patients have shared with me during therapy. In many different ways, their parents told them to:

1. Be perfect.
2. Be rich.
3. Always impress your parents' friends and neighbors with what good parents you have.
4. Be the substitute mate for a parent emotionally and sometimes even sexually.
5. Succeed in life at any cost.
6. Fail in life so a parent can feel he or she is better than you.
7. Fail in life because a parent doesn't really like you and you deserve to fail.
8. Fail in life to punish yourself for not living up to parental expectations.
9. Succeed in life at any cost to the highest level of fame and fortune you possibly can to make your parents proud.
10. Rescue everyone you possibly can. Never say no to anyone, particularly those who ask favors of you.

The above list is only a brief sampling of hundreds of parental injunctions that I've heard patients mention over the years. Most of the above list have negative connotations, but there are positive parental injunctions, too, such as:

1. Love God and others.
2. Always tell the truth.
3. Work hard—always pull your own weight.
4. Be fair to everyone.
5. Be honest—never cheat.
6. Go to church and worship God regularly for your spiritual benefit, not as a duty.
7. Read your Bible every day and seek to become like Jesus.
8. Forgive others when they trespass against you.
9. Do unto others as you would have them do unto you.

The list of "good" parental injunctions could go on and on. As we grow up, we hear hundreds of messages, some good, some not so good, and some that can form the basis for our jerky or masochistic tendencies. For example, parents subtly or not so subtly tell their kids:

- "I'd be better off if you didn't exist."
- "Don't get emotionally connected to your dad because I want all his attention myself."
- "Succeed at some major area I failed at, whether you like that area or not!"

My Parents Wanted Me to "Replace" Billy Graham

As I grew up I received many injunction messages from both of my parents. My dad never made more than $8,000 a year as a carpenter, and in order to supplement our income, my mother did catering and housecleaning for the families of medical doctors. In a way she idolized doctors because they seemed to be so successful. She would say, "Dr. So-and-So said this . . ." or "Dr. So-and-So's wife gave me this . . ."

In one case, Dr. So-and-So's wife gave my mom a mink coat that she didn't want anymore, and Mom put it on the line to air out the mothball odors. She left it out overnight, and before morning there was a real downpour. The coat was ruined and for my mother it was a real tragedy.

Mom hoped that I, too, would become a medical doctor, and both my parents also wanted me to "replace" Billy Graham in one way or another. In fact, they threw in replacing Dwight Eisenhower and Richard Nixon as well. With all those assignments and the role modeling by both my hardworking parents, there was no question I would become a workaholic.

The good side of my mother's permissiveness was that she was always interested in what I had to say, and as she shared her day's experiences with me, she taught me many positive injunctions as well. Early on she taught me to memorize

Bible verses, and I decided to trust Christ personally when I was only six.

When I was around ten years old, Mom had me memorize Psalm 1, which speaks of delighting in the law of the Lord and meditating in His law day and night. That psalm is burned into my memory bank, and Bible reading and meditation is a habit I continue until this day. Now, however, I am more apt to listen to Cliff Barrows reading the *New King James Version* on cassette tape while I'm stuck in freeway traffic. Or I might choose to memorize Bible verses as I roll along.

For a while as a teenager I fantasized developing a father-and-son, home-building business someday, which I was sure would have done quite well in America, the great land of opportunity. But my father kept urging me to get an education so I could "get a really good job" and restore the family wealth, which had been lost in the Communist Revolution.

Somehow my father didn't, or couldn't, realize that carpenters need trained minds as well as skilled hands in order to compute the materials they need and build to specifications. As we worked together on the house I designed, he would say, "Paul, you're a smart boy. I want you to work with your brains, not your hands. I don't want you to do what I've had to do all my life—slave away doing carpenter work, twelve hours a day. The Russians took away what our family had passed on from generation to generation. I don't have anything to pass on to you except this instruction: Use your mind, not your back, to make a living."

All of Us "Take Off the Parental Overcoat"

I fulfilled some of my parents' injunctions, but not all. I did become a medical doctor, but replacing Billy Graham or Dwight Eisenhower wasn't in the cards. And I did do my best to develop and use my mind, as my father had instructed.

When the very first copy of the first book I wrote—the

one on child-rearing—came off the press, I presented it as a
gift to my perfectionistic, German father. He looked at it,
and didn't mention how proud he was of me or how wonderful the book looked. Instead, he talked about a well-known,
contemporary Christian leader who had written at least three
hundred books. My dad's message was clear: "One book
isn't good enough. You need to write several hundred
more!"

One of my favorite role models has been Paul Tournier,
the wise and loving Swiss psychiatrist, author of many insightful books and articles. Tournier was a master in offering
hope to anyone who wanted to become a whole person, even
though he or she lived in a broken world. When he died a
few years ago, I joined thousands of others who grieved his
loss. Tournier wrote the forward to *Happiness Is a Choice*,
the first book that Dr. Frank Minirth and I wrote together as
medical and psychiatric partners. Tournier has taught me
much concerning parental injunctions and how to become
your own person.

In his writings, he speaks of "taking off" parental injunctions much as you take off an overcoat, a dress, or a shirt.
You begin doing this as a teenager when you start to question your parents in many areas. You may even go through a
stage where you become arrogant, defiant, and self-
righteous. The classic teenager, who knows everything
and whose parents know nothing, is well-known, and
we have seen thousands come through the Minirth-Meier
Clinics.

But the interesting thing about a teenager "taking off"
the overcoat of values and injunctions given him by his parents is that he will examine what he has been taught, and
usually keep much of it for himself. He will put the overcoat
back on, but now it is *his* overcoat instead of just being what
his parents have told him is "right."

This process of examining parental injunctions is called
"leaving home psychologically." I began doing it myself as a
graduate student at Michigan State University, and I have
found that I need to continue to do it as I have passed on
through my adult career. Becoming a mature, functioning
adult means that I should be ready to examine parental

injunctions—the prejudices, morals, and values that I have been taught since childhood—and reevaluate all of these in the light of the Bible and my current level of maturity. I am free to discard all of these injunctions, but I am also free to put any of them back into my own overcoat of spiritual values.

That day when I was thirty and came to my dad with the first book I had ever written, and he gave me his injunction to "go write three hundred more," I had to continue my process of leaving home psychologically. I had to sort out just what my dad's injunction meant to me. Would I rebel? Would I try to obey? Instead, I decided I would keep on writing books, not because I hoped to become "good enough," but because I love writing and I want to do the task that I believe God has given me.

No one has ever had perfect parents. I am no exception, and neither are my six young adult children who are currently ages sixteen through twenty-two. As I observe them taking off the parental overcoats Jan and I have given them, I keep reminding myself they are free to make their own choices, even when some of those choices are distasteful to me.

Leaving home psychologically is a painful process when you go through it yourself, and you experience the pain all over again as you watch your own beloved offspring doing the same thing. I now understand in a small way how a mother eagle feels when she lovingly pushes her young eaglets out of the nest, hoping they will learn to fly on the way down.

We gave our kids boundaries when they were young. Now we mainly attempt to offer them unconditional love and acceptance. We also offer them our emotional responses to their decisions, and we attempt to interpret to them why we are concerned about their choices. Unfortunately, at the present time, we seem to hold our many years of education and experience in much higher esteem than our children do! We are happy, nonetheless, to see our children take off their "parental overcoats" and try their own thinking on for size, because that is how all of us must make the passage from childlike dependency into adulthood.

Some Adults Remain Trapped by Parental Injunctions

Leaving home psychologically means different things to different people, but for everyone it means no longer viewing their parents as the dominating influence in their lives. Now they strike out on their own to build new relationships, the most important of which for many is learning to cleave to a mate in a healthy, interdependent marriage.

In a healthy marriage, the partners are not two totally independent people who happen to share the same dwelling place. Nor are they two overly dependent people, depending totally on each other for their happiness. Instead, they are two mature *interdependent* people who learn to trust and love each other, accepting each other as they are. All of Chapter 11 will be devoted to what it means to bond with your mate or some other highly significant person in your life.

Unfortunately, many children—including children who have reached adulthood—are extremely fearful of the conditional rejection of domineering or abusive parents. Crippled by an unhealthy self-concept, fear, and anxiety, they remain totally compliant to the psychological will (parental injunctions) handed down to them by Mom and Dad.

Michelle came to our clinic at age forty-five, single, lonely, and depressed because she had been erroneously taught that even adult children should obey their parents, and she had never learned to take off this unreasonable injunction and discard it. For one thing, the Bible doesn't talk about adult children obeying parents. In Ephesians 6:1, the original Greek word refers to *young* children, not those who are fully grown.

Michelle's domineering and selfish mother used her as a lifelong personal slave. Michelle happened to be the youngest child, so her mother laid a guilt trip on her whenever she dated men or even began forming close relationships with other females her own age. At age forty-five, Michelle needed to leave home physically as well as psychologically. She had to move away from her seventy-five-year-old mother and develop a life of her own. She did so, and, sure enough, her mother totally rejected and abandoned her. Nonetheless, Michelle was able to go on to live a significantly happier life with a much better sense of her own self-worth.

It's easy enough to look upon Michelle with a mixture of compassion and disapproval for wasting so many years in psychological bondage to her mother. None of us, however, can deny the existence of powerful, unconscious, emotional rivers that flow into the ocean of our own personal decision-making process. "Leaving home" means many different things to different people. It all depends on what your family of origin was like.

Suppose you are the daughter of a workaholic father who refuses to change. Leaving home will mean giving up the desire to have a healthy relationship with him. Instead, get on with your life. There are six billion people on Planet Earth, and Dad is just one of them. You can survive without him. I promise.

You may think your self-worth depends on Dad's approval and love, and that the pain of your lonely inferiority feelings will be unbearable if you give up the foolish fantasy he will come through for you—someday. But you are wrong—dead wrong! Stop wasting time with foolish fantasies and move on. Fill that "father-vacuum" by getting connected in a mature and moral way to your mate, or to some other significant person. But never depend on anyone, not even a mature mate, for your self-worth. Only you and God can team up to provide such a precious commodity! (For more on achieving a healthy sense of self-worth, see Chapter 10.)

Or suppose you have a domineering mother who calls you daily. Suppose she's telling you how to run your life as she depends on you to be her only close friend. Cold and cruel as it sounds, it's time to cut the umbilical cord!

Get advice from a professional counselor or perhaps your pastor as to what is a reasonable amount of contact to have with your mother. One or two ten-minute phone calls per week might be one place to start. The idea is to establish boundaries with your mom, letting her know that, even though you love her very much, you will not allow her to tell you how to run your life anymore. If she does not listen, you can politely hang up on her and call her back in a few days.

The whole point is that you choose not to let her manipulate and control you through false guilt. She may get upset when she is forced to respect your boundaries and honor your decisions, but if she rejects you, cuts you out of her will, or tries to get other family members to take vengeance on you, remain respectful but refuse to play her jerky games. Let her know that you will always love her and respect her, but at the same time I would encourage you to thank God that you are being delivered from her dominance.

The above examples are typical scenarios that we see in many of our patients' lives. Deciding to leave home psychologically is a crucial step, but it is not done in an instant. It usually takes years and, for some, a lifetime. You may or may not need professional counseling to determine what steps you need to take if you want to finish leaving home, but be aware that it may very well be a painful journey. The more abusive the family of origin, the more painful leaving home tends to be.

Take courage in remembering that God teaches baby birds to fly out of their nests. He teaches baby lions how to catch their own food. And He teaches young adult human beings how to examine the parental injunctions, sort out the ones they want to keep, and discard the rest. Please begin living your own free life today if you haven't already done so. The rewards will far outweigh the pain.

CHAPTER
8

Why Not Sing
Your Own Song?

STEP THREE: Break the Jerk Addiction Cycle

Patricia was a talented little girl with a beautiful voice, and a domineering, controlling "stage mother" who had her performing from the age of three. Patricia could sing just about any kind of music: western songs at rodeos, religious songs in churches, and patriotic songs at political campaigns. She even had different costumes to wear, depending on what kinds of songs she was singing and what the setting might be.

When Patricia turned eighteen, she learned that a highly regarded orchestra was coming to perform in her community. The orchestra leader had heard about Patricia's voice and had written to her, inviting her to sing a solo during their performance. Enclosed in the envelope was the music that Patricia would be using, and she practiced daily for hours to get the song just right.

On the day before the orchestra was to perform, Patricia got a phone call telling her the orchestra was going to be late getting into town, and they wouldn't have time to rehearse her solo with her. At first Patricia was quite upset, but then she thought, *I've practiced for hours—I know I can do it.*

On the night of the program, Patricia waited nervously

offstage until her solo was announced. She walked out on the stage and bowed to the welcoming applause of her many friends and neighbors who had known her practically all her life. The maestro raised his baton, and the orchestra began to play, but something was wrong. Patricia couldn't believe her ears. The orchestra was playing a different song from the one she had practiced!

Patricia's first reaction was panic, followed immediately by anger. Once again she felt like the little mannequin being controlled by others. Yes, she knew the song the orchestra was playing by mistake. And, true, she could follow the lead of others and probably do that song fairly well without even having rehearsed it once. But at that moment, up on that stage, something inside Patricia snapped, not her sanity, but the leash she had figuratively felt around her neck all her life.

I practiced on my own song too many hours to change now, Patricia told herself. *In my heart it's the one I really want to sing, and I'm going to sing it!*

For literally the first time in her life, Patricia followed her heart instead of the control and lead of others. Regaining her composure, she took a deep breath and began singing *her* song. The keen ears of the maestro instantly detected the difference. He smiled, waved his baton at his well-trained orchestra, and within a few notes the musicians were following Patricia as she sang her song, not the one they thought they were to play.

Patricia never sounded better. As the last notes of her solo died away, the hometown audience rose to their feet, cheering and clapping. Tears streaming down her face, Patricia bowed again and again as she acknowledged the standing ovation.

Patricia made two major choices that day. The first was the split-second decision she made to follow her heart and sing her own song, not somebody else's. The second was a long-range decision that led Patricia to take hesitant but firm steps toward being her own person. She didn't become rebellious or disrespectful to her mother, but she did start being more independent and assertive. Instinctively, Patricia realized she had been controlled all her life and it was time to take control of herself for a change.

Through the recommendation of the mother of one of her good friends, Patricia paid a visit to a Minirth-Meier Clinic, where she began a lifelong process of taking control of her own life. In therapy, she quickly saw that she had never been aware of how powerless she had always been until that day she sang her own song. Because she could sing so well, she thought she was the one in control, but she soon realized that others were controlling her, not only her domineering mother, but her steady boyfriend, who soon became an ex-boyfriend.

Is Your "Ism" Controlling You?

Thousands of our patients nationwide who have come to us for help because they were addicted to substances, behavior patterns, or even jerks (jerkaholism, if you please), all tell us the same thing: They think they are in control of certain areas in their lives, but the exact reverse is true.

If you are ever to gain real self-control, you must do what Patricia did, which is the essence of Step Three:

Determine in your heart to sing your own song. Make the decision that you will progressively resist being timid and allowing your life to be controlled by parental injunctions, jerk addictions, failure scripts, or the expectations of others. Choose to replace your timid passivity with God's gift of loving and powerful self-control.

Vivacious Vivian Was a Super Masochist

As I said in an earlier chapter, jerkaholism—masochistic addiction to the abuse of overpowering controlling jerks—is one of the key problems we treat in Minirth-Meier Clinics nationwide.

One of the passages of Scripture we often share with our patients contains the words of the apostle Paul, who would have made a good psychotherapist. On one occasion he wrote to his close friend Timothy, who was being criticized and controlled by the jerky members of his church: "God has not given us a spirit of fear, but of power and of love and of a sound mind."[1]

But breaking the grip of severe jerkaholism can be a real struggle, as it was in the case of a thirty-five-year-old movie actress I treated several years ago, whom we'll call Vivacious Vivian. She had checked into the hospital for "exhaustion," but after her internist ran all the tests and couldn't find anything wrong with her physically, he began thinking she was suffering from a psychological depression.

When he broached the subject she got angry with him. The truth was that she was so severely depressed she could no longer function. She didn't want to admit to herself that she was depressed. Instead, she desperately wanted to blame it on hypoglycemia, mitral valve prolapse, chronic fatigue syndrome, TMJ (temporomandibular joint) syndrome, or *anything* other than some kind of psychological depression.

This is not to say that some people don't have the physical ailments named above, as well as any number of other physical problems. That is why the first thing that doctors check is a depressed person's physical condition. In Vivian's case, however, there was nothing physically wrong, and so she finally reluctantly agreed to see a psychiatrist. I was called in because she had heard of me through some of my books.

Because I had been warned that she was quite beautiful and openly seductive, I protected myself legally by taking a nurse with me when I went to see her. All the warnings had been true. When we walked in, I noted that she was wearing a see-through negligee that left nothing to the imagination. It was obvious that Vivian knew that she was attractive and that she liked to display it, especially for anyone of the male gender. I'm sure that if she had put on one of the famous hospital gowns that never quite meet in the back, she would have preferred to wear it backwards!

After asking Vivian to put on a robe, I proceeded to ask her a number of questions and learned that she had insomnia, poor concentration, no energy, and crying spells—all the symptoms of a clinical depression. She had been having these symptoms for three straight months, and they had driven her to the brink of suicide. She also admitted that she had had these same symptoms at other periods in her life as well, along with chronic headaches and chronic trouble with real and imagined physical illnesses.

I asked Vivian, "Did anything happen around three months ago that may have triggered a lot of anger in you?"

"Just a little over three months ago I left my fifth husband and filed for divorce," she admitted.

I asked Vivian why she had divorced her fifth husband, and she told me that she had discovered he was running around on her. When she confronted him, he beat her up.

"So I got rid of the jerk," Vivian said vehemently. "I ditched him, just like all the others."

Vivian Thought All Men Were Nth-Degree Jerks

"All the others" interested me a great deal. When I asked her about her fourth husband, her third, her second, and first, I learned that all of them had run around on her, some with other women, others with other men. Overall, all five of Vivian's husbands had been physically, not to mention mentally and emotionally, abusive. All of them had been drug addicts or alcoholics as well.

Vivian had a simple explanation for all this. She was merely the victim of incredibly bad luck. She had also come to the conclusion that all men must be Nth-Degree Jerks, and all women were "innocent victims."

Vivian was locked into black-and-white thinking, and not very straight thinking at that. Gently I pointed out, "Obviously if *all* men are Nth-Degree Jerks, then you couldn't have been the victim of bad luck because luck wasn't really involved. It's time to realize that you have spent years of suffering with jerky husbands because you are addicted to jerks."

"Addicted to jerks? How can you be addicted to a jerk?" Vivian wanted to know.

To help Vivian understand her jerkaholism, I explained how clinical depression often occurs. Anger depletes levels of serotonin, an important chemical in the brain. The result is loss of sleep, loss of energy, loss of concentration, and even thoughts of suicide, which are all symptoms that Vivian had been exhibiting. Vivian's symptoms were "physical" in a sense, but all of her symptoms were actually a physiological response to her deep-seated anger. (How deep-seated anger can lower your serotonin level and cause clinical depression will be discussed in depth in Chapter 9.)

I further explained that unless she got extensive therapy to uncover the emotional wounds from her childhood, which were driving her to these self-destructive choices, she could never take conscious control of her life.

"Around 80 percent of our thoughts, feelings, and motives are unconscious—out of our conscious awareness," I told her. "We have no idea that these thoughts and feelings are driving our decisions. We think we are in control, but we're not."

"What's that got to do with striking out five straight times with five lousy husbands?" Vivian asked.

"We've treated thousands of patients who have had problems similar to yours. We can't completely explain it, but it's as if you have 'unconscious antennas' coming out of your brain, in a figurative sense. These antennas go ZAP whenever you meet a really jerky guy. It is my guess that your father must have been a real Nth-Degree Jerk. Am I right? How old were you the first time he sexually abused you?"

The shocked look on Vivian's face told me that my guesses were on target. Then she spilled out her story about how her father had sexually abused her at age thirteen. She thought I had the ability to read minds, but I assured her that I can only read age-old patterns that I see over and over in hundreds of patients.

"Let me do a little more guessing," I said. "You are a beautiful woman, and lots of really nice, moral, attractive guys have asked you out as well as the 'body only' jerks who just wanted to get you to bed. But you have probably found the moral, loving guys boring and the jerky types exciting."

"Right on the money, Doctor," Vivian responded. "I've always preferred men who were hard to get and a little mean and wild to boot."

After seven weeks of intense, insight-oriented therapy, several hours per day, seven days a week in our Minirth-Meier hospital unit, Vivian got over her suicidal depression. Eventually, she told me she felt like a lifelong slave who had just been set free. Then it took eighteen more months of outpatient therapy to finish cleaning the emotional pus out of all the wounds from her past, and to teach her how to take care of herself for the rest of her life without the need for psychotherapy (or for Nth-Degree Jerks to replace her father).

How the "Addiction Cycle" Causes Masochism

As we treated Vivian, an important part of helping her learn how to overcome her masochistic addiction to jerks, or any other kind of addiction for that matter, was introducing her to the "Addiction Cycle," which anyone goes through when addicted to people, behaviors, or things (see chart on p. 157).

To understand how the Addiction Cycle is part of one's masochistic tendencies, we will walk through the cycle together, using Vivian as an example.

Point One in the cycle is some form of emotional, physical, and/or sexual abuse. This abuse occurs because of how the person is reared in the family of origin, or because of some major life trauma. In Vivian's case, her Addiction Cycle began when her father ignored her needs, but sexually abused her while her mother failed to protect her. For Vivian, suffering became a habit.

Point Two in the cycle involves receiving negative messages, sent by your own self-talk. Vivian, the little girl, began telling herself that she had to be the cause of what her father was doing to her. Somehow she convinced herself that she deserved this kind of abuse. To Vivian, masochistic suffering became the logical thing to do.

Point Three is the development of false guilt (the shame base). As Vivian sent herself negative messages, she experienced overwhelming feelings of false guilt for taking her mother's sexual place in the marriage. A young child takes responsibility for what is done to her and feels guilty, rather than realizing the abusing adult is the guilty one. For Vivian, masochism became a way to get vengeance on herself to pay for her false guilt.

Point Four is the development of feelings of low self-esteem. Because Vivian blamed herself for her father's sexual abuse, she felt like trash. Somebody once said, "God don't make no junk!" but junk is exactly what Vivian felt like as she grew up. Junk deserves to be kicked around, and masochism is again a logical choice. As my wife, Jan, often says, "If you act like a doormat, people will step on you."

Point Five in the cycle involves emotional pain that is an inevitable part of feelings of false guilt and low self-esteem. This kind of pain can be more real and intense than the pain from a broken arm. Vivian had no idea of how to "grieve out" this pain. She could only feel it and, therefore, at best she went through a kind of boomerang syndrome, always having the pain come right back and burrow deeper into her soul and eventually become the chief cause of her suicidal depression. Many masochistic patients who recover from their pain actually miss their pain for a while until they get used to experiencing peace, joy, and love.

Point Six is finding an addictive agent to numb the pain that comes out of low self-esteem and false guilt. As the Addiction Cycle progresses, and a person suffers physical, sexual, emotional, or spiritual trauma, that person becomes more addiction-prone. Three major factors affect the kind of addictive agent a person will subconsciously choose: (1) genetic predispositions; (2) environmental factors; (3) personal preferences or attractions.

For example, some people choose food and become overweight or bulimic (involved in binge eating, followed by compulsive vomiting, which can lead to death from an electrolyte imbalance). Nearly all overweight people use food as a pleasurable, numbing addictive agent to kill the emotional pain that comes out of unresolved root problems. That's why crash dieting without resolving the root problems seldom works. Thirty-five out of thirty-six people who lose a great deal of weight gain most or all of it back within one year because they failed to resolve the shame issues (false guilt) that are driving their food addiction.[2]

Other typical addictive agents that we treat include workaholism, drugs, alcohol, various sexual addictions, power (control), and even churchaholism—going to so many church meetings each week that you ignore personal and family needs, and make God angry with you for doing so.

Vivian was surprised to learn that one of the most common addictions we treat at our Minirth-Meier Clinics is jerkaholism. She had always turned to high-level Second-Degree Jerks, or even Nth-Degree Jerks, as her addictive agent. In fact, the more they were like her Nth-Degree Jerk father the better. Nice guys were boring. The wild kind were exhilarating to her masochistic instincts, and this led to the next step in the cycle.

Point Seven is the anesthesia the addictive agent provides. The taker of drugs would call it "getting high." The workaholic experiences his anesthesia in the absorbing satisfaction he receives through working long hours and accomplishing more and more. The workaholic who tries to slow down without getting therapy feels tremendous pain and shame. He stays busy, to the point of exhaustion, and then wakes up the next morning and rushes back to work to avoid the pain of insight. Work acts as anesthesia from the pain. On the other hand, therapy would make the pain go away.

For Vivian, jerky husbands brought her a kind of "rush" that made her feel good—until they started beating her up and running around on her.

Point Eight is the "fallout" that occurs from any addiction. Fallout can be a very complex and variable thing, but it usually involves the bad things that can happen to you in several areas of your life due to your use of the addictive agent: physical illnesses and symptoms, financial losses, emotional losses, and spiritual losses.

In Vivian's case the fallout was obvious. She came to us exhausted, unable to sleep or concentrate, and subject to crying spells—all symptoms of suicidal depression. Jerks had taken such a toll on Vivian that she was ready to check out of life completely. She had also lowered her moral standards in various ways as part of the spiritual fallout from her addiction. Interestingly enough, as her therapy progressed to outpatient status, Vivian started dressing and acting much less seductively. She also became active in a church near her home.

Point Nine is a violation of values, which is the other major consequence of seeking anesthesia through the addictive agent. While fallout is usually quite visible and very measurable, violation of values is more profound and intensely private.[3]

To violate one's personal values almost always results in unbearable pain. Contradicting your personal code of ethics leads you to realize you are a hypocrite, saying one thing and doing another, and you hate yourself for it. Part of you understands what is right and what values you should embrace. But because of your shame base, insecurity, low self-esteem, and emotional pain, you are driven to act in ways that are contrary to what you know to be correct.[4] A bad conscience is very painful. A masochist may repent and "clean house," only to quickly return to violation of values in order to get vengeance on herself.

Vivian was a perfect example of violation of values. As a teenager she vowed to God and to herself that she would never marry *anyone* like her dad. Unfortunately, while the spirit is willing, the flesh of the masochist is weak. Driven by unconscious forces she didn't understand, Vivian chose to break her vow and marry five men just like dear old Dad before she was thirty-five years old. She also violated various other moral standards and values along the way, which added true guilt to the false guilt already in her shame base.

Point Ten in the Addiction Cycle is true guilt. When we violate our deep inner values, we are overwhelmed with true guilt, which gets piled onto the big heap of already existing false guilt that accumulated during our childhood. This awareness of true guilt leads to more shame, which leads to lower self-esteem, more emotional pain, stronger cravings for an addictive agent, anesthesia, fallout, further violation of values, and still more true guilt, which then revolves into still more shame—and the cycle becomes a bottomless pit.

When Vivian came to us, she was at the bottom of her

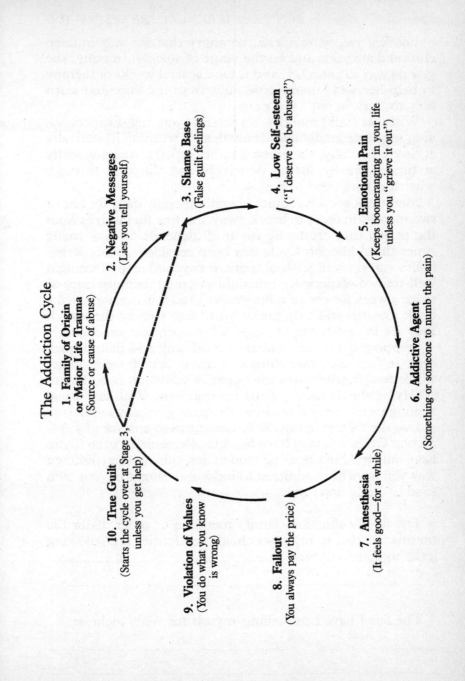

The Addiction Cycle

1. Family of Origin or Major Life Trauma (Source or cause of abuse)

2. Negative Messages (Lies you tell yourself)

3. Shame Base (False guilt feelings)

4. Low Self-esteem ("I deserve to be abused")

5. Emotional Pain (Keeps boomeranging in your life unless you "grieve it out")

6. Addictive Agent (Something or someone to numb the pain)

7. Anesthesia (It feels good—for a while)

8. Fallout (You always pay the price)

9. Violation of Values (You do what you know is wrong)

10. True Guilt (Starts the cycle over at Stage 3, unless you get help)

bottomless pit, so to speak, so angry that she was in deep clinical depression and on the verge of suicide. Initially, she saw no way to get relief, and it took several weeks of therapy to help her sort out the true guilt from the false and learn how to "grieve out" her pain.

With her background as an actress, you might expect Vivian to grieve loudly and dramatically, weeping hysterically at times. Actually, she grieved rather quietly, weeping softly at times, usually sitting pensively and thinking through what had happened to her.

Many jerk addicts require hospital therapy daily for one or two months in order to break away and free themselves from the prison they are living in. It all depends on how many times the Addiction Cycle has been recycled. Other jerkaholics can do well with outpatient psychotherapy (seeing a well-trained, experienced, insight-oriented therapist once or twice a week for one or more years). And it is my hope that a book like this will help many break free *without* therapy, if they are in early or mild stages of masochistic jerkaholism.

Stepping out of masochism is a difficult and painful process. In fact, the inner pains and drives actually tend to get worse temporarily when the negative addiction is no longer satisfying the demands of the unconscious. With emotional healing over a period of time, the pain goes away.

Use the following interactive exercises to analyze any Addiction Cycle you may have been in. Remember, even if you have only mild masochistic tendencies, this says in your own way you have been addicted to jerks and caught in your own kind of Addiction Cycle.

• The family situation, family member, or other major life trauma that led to my masochistic tendencies and allowing jerks to abuse me was: _____

_____

• The lies I have been telling myself for years include:

_____

_____

• The false guilt feelings that make up my personal shame base include: _____

_____

• I admit that I have low self-esteem because I often feel:

_____

_____

• I admit I have emotional pain that needs to be grieved out. This pain is centered around: _____

_____

• The addictive agent that I have used to numb my pain has been allowing jerks to abuse me in the following ways:

_____

_____

• The anesthesia I've felt as I've allowed people to abuse me can best be described this way: _____

_____

• The fallout—the price I've paid—for having masochistic tendencies is: _____

_____

• Personal values that I have violated in allowing jerks to take advantage of me are: _____

_____

• The true guilt that I feel, and which I want to sincerely confess to God, is: _____

_____

• Other addictive agents I have come to depend on from time to time include: _____

_____

No Grief, No Gain—and More Pain

Grieving through the "ouch" of emotional pain is a key step in breaking the Addiction Cycle. In fact, grieving through the pain is absolutely necessary before peace and joy can even become possible. I know it sounds odd, even weird, to talk about grieving the loss of being addicted to a jerk, or anything else, for that matter. Nonetheless, grief is absolutely necessary. Whatever our addictions are, they meet a need and to some extent fill the holes in our souls. Take away the addiction that plugged that hole, and the hole reappears, bigger than ever.

As you work on ridding yourself of masochistic tendencies—your jerkaholic addiction, if you please—it may hurt worse for a while than it did when you were resigned to being abused by the predatory jerks who seemed to always get the better of you.

For example, as you analyze the parental injunctions that you have heard all your life (see Chapter 7), you may have to grieve the loss of an idealized family image. It may mean taking Mom and Dad off their "pedestal of perfection" and bringing them down to real human being status.

You may have to grieve abuses you have suffered at the hands of people you trusted to love you and take care of you. You may have to grieve a lost childhood, as you realize you were deprived of the fun and freedom you should have experienced as a child.

Any time we work on leaving home psychologically (see Chapter 7), grieving may need to be done. You may have to grieve the lost fantasy that one or both parents will someday come through for you and be there to give you emotional and even physical support.

If you've been in any co-dependent relationships, you may have to grieve the loss of having someone make your decisions for you, someone to blame when you fail, someone to bail you out of trouble, and someone to punish you to ease your own guilt.

In more extreme cases, it may mean grieving the loss of a jerky mate who may decide to divorce you rather than get therapy because you've "gone healthy" on him or her and will no longer be abused or misused by your mate. And it may mean watching your beloved children go through this same process and that will mean grieving that kind of pain.

Getting Through the Five Stages of Grief

Any time you try to really make a change and break habits that have literally become addictive, you must be prepared for pain. But there is a way to decrease the pain and speed up your recovery from the grief process. It involves understanding, anticipating, and facilitating the five stages of grief. If you know what these five stages are, you will know what to expect. You will know that what you are going through is normal and you are not going crazy. You will be in control, even though it may not always seem that way. The five stages of grief include:

1. Denial—actually a form of the defense mechanism discussed in Chapter 6. The pain is so great you simply want to deny whatever happened to you.
2. Your anger turns outward—at those you think have caused your pain, other persons, and/or God.
3. Your anger turns inward—you experience true and/ or false guilt.
4. Intense grieving—which may or may not include a great deal of weeping and emotional upset.
5. Resolution—you make sense out of what happened, accept it, and move on.

Jack's Jerky Wife Caused Him Pain and Grief

To demonstrate all five stages of grief, I will use the story of a patient of mine we'll call Jack, who was married to a high-level Second-Degree Jerk we'll call Jezzy.

In fact, Jezzy seemed to cross the line into Nth-Degree behavior. She had numerous affairs and acted repentant only after Jack would catch her—usually in the act. Eventually, however, Jezzy ran off, moved in with another man, and finally divorced Jack for "incompatibility." Fortunately, they had no children, but Jezzy saw to it that her Great White Shark lawyer took Jack for everything he had.

Jack was in total clinical depression when he came to us. He was also wallowing in the first stage of grief—denial. When Jezzy had wandered into her other affairs, Jack had denied that truth and told himself that "Jezzy has changed this time" each time she came back to him. Now that she had actually run away with another man and divorced Jack, he was in the most serious kind of denial, telling himself that Jezzy would repent, divorce her new husband, and come back to him. Jack couldn't see that Jezzy had come back to him all the other times simply because he was a convenient meal ticket.

You might call Jack's denial naiveté, but he was doing what many people do when they suffer a significant loss or realize that they have been abused significantly during their adult lives or when they were children. Their first reaction is, "This didn't really happen. It's all going to change back, and everything's going to be okay."

People in the denial stage of grief desperately grapple with reality, telling themselves:

This hasn't really happened—it's just a bad dream.

Everything's going to be okay. Things will be just the way they were before.

Jack kept using the "things will be the same as before" line during our first three sessions together. He kept assuring me that Jezzy would divorce her new husband and come back to him, but I kept pounding on his denial until it cracked. When Jack finally realized that Jezzy wasn't coming back, he moved into the second stage of grief as his anger turned outward—toward Jezzy.

Jack raged on and on as he paced my office floor. But as he

verbalized his anger against his former wife, its intensity diminished with each session.

Using a familiar, but often effective, Gestalt technique, I suggested to Jack, "Pretend that Jezzy is sitting in an empty chair here in my office. Go ahead and tell her off and then forgive her for your own sake." Jack did as I asked and was amazed to find out how much better he felt by talking to an empty chair! But his grief cycle wasn't over.

The next time Jack was in my office, he appeared to be in the third stage of grief, with his anger turned inward. He paced the floor of my office, verbally abusing himself, saying, "If only I had earned more money for Jezzy . . . If only I had taken her on more vacations . . . If only I had helped her more around the house . . . ." Jack went on and on with his "if only's."

As any true masochist is prone to do, Jack was blaming himself for his wife's problems. Jack wasn't a perfect husband. Who is? But he was a pretty good one. Yes, he had faults and he had made mistakes with Jezzy, but as we talked it appeared that Jack had perhaps 10 percent true guilt, mixed with 90 percent false guilt, and he had come to a totally wrong conclusion. I finally was able to convince Jack that Jezzy had only been using him and would have left him for more dollars and cents even if he had been "perfect."

Jack was now ready to enter the fourth stage of the grief cycle—genuine grieving—although some people might wonder what he had to grieve about. It would be easy enough to tell Jack: "You really didn't lose very much. You should be giving thanks to God that Jezzy left you now, instead of hanging around a few more years and putting you through all the more pain and grief."

The way Jack saw it, however, he had lost a great deal and the pain was very real. He had enjoyed the social status of being married to a really great-looking woman, and he had kept idealizing Jezzy into something that she was not. In truth, she was a superficial friend, an occasional sex partner, a lousy cook, and a part-time housekeeper, at best. But in Jack's eyes, Jezzy had been "wonderful." He had to weep over all his "losses," even while seeing Jezzy realistically for the first time.

As the scales drop from our eyes and the truth is revealed, we can come to the fifth stage of grief, resolution.

For Jack, resolution didn't come automatically after he did some genuine weeping and grieving over losing his jerky wife, Jezzy. Nothing is automatic in the grief process. In fairy tales, the villain is defeated, the good guys ride off into the sunset, and everybody lives happily ever after. In real life, however, many villains continue to be successful, the good guys may have to ride off on a rainy day into an uncertain future, and "happily ever after" is a term better fitted to theological discussion of life after death than life on this fallen planet.

Grieving Takes More Than "Five Quick Steps"

Giving yourself permission to experience the stages of grief will lessen the intensity and duration of any pain you're feeling as you try to make changes, give up jerk addictions, and stop masochistic behavior. But as Jack and so many others have learned, the grief process isn't over in four or five quick steps. There can be painful moments for many years to come, even after you've done "proper" grieving.

Looking at the truth helped Jack get over Jezzy's running off with another man. Weeping over his losses also helped Jack lessen his pain and shorten his grief. But I recall Jack wept again when his wedding anniversary rolled around. He also went through a very blue time when he experienced the first Christmas without Jezzy. Even a year later, as he looked through a photo album and saw pictures of himself and Jezzy together, he still got tears in his eyes.

During these brief periods, Jack needed to experience "re-grieving," and he needed to rehash some of the facts of his story with me, ventilate some more anger, and do some "re-forgiving."

Jack came to resolution only as he grew more mature, less co-dependent, and less masochistic. He forgave her, deeply regretted the divorce, but realized he was better off without

Jezzy, who remained unrepentant and soon moved on to still another man with an even higher annual income.

We cannot avoid some of the normal crises of life and the natural grief reactions that follow, but we can learn to choose how to avoid harboring prolonged bitterness and vengeful motives toward the jerks who may have hurt us. If we don't learn to make these right choices, we may choose to deny our emotions and "stuff" our grief.

Resolution of grief requires that we be honest and willing to admit the gamut of emotions that are coursing through our pains: rage, guilt, doubt—and more rage. Once we face the truth about our anger, we must move on to true forgiveness of all who have contributed to our pain. In extreme cases, resolution may require hospitalization or outpatient therapy. In other cases, you can resolve the pain yourself, but you still have to go through this same grief process if you want to get rid of the masochistic tendencies that keep setting you up for abuse in a world full of jerks. Keep in mind, too, that painful emotions come and go in waves that can last a few hours or for days at a time. In other words, resolution takes time and plenty of patience.

God Is Often a Scapegoat for Our Anger

Whether you grieve the loss of a loved one who has been killed by a jerk in a drunken stupor, or whether you grieve over the loss of self-esteem because a jerky spouse or jerky fellow workers keep putting you down, there are two universal factors with which you must deal: anger and forgiveness.

When you face the truth, it's quite natural to feel angry. Don't try to shut this anger off. If you aren't really angry over the masochism that you've been engaged in, you'll never be able to move toward maturity.

In fact, you may even get enraged. Sometimes what really happens is that a person gets in touch emotionally with the rage that has been there all his or her life, but denial and repression have kept it stuffed deep inside, out of conscious awareness.

And it's quite normal to want to deflect and project some of your rage onto God. I've seen it happen hundreds of times in patients in our clinics. God doesn't force the jerks in your life to do the right thing, and so you become mad at God because you wish He would shape them up.

If you were God, you tell yourself, you would make all the jerks turn into good people (or maybe just blow all the jerks away). Fortunately, however, none of us can be God. And even more fortunately, God never forces anybody to do anything. He doesn't even force you to give up your own jerkiness and your own masochism. He only promises to help you do the work yourself while becoming interdependent on Him for guidance and strength.

Two passages from Paul's letter to the Philippian Christians apply perfectly to the idea of becoming interdependent with God:

> Work out your own salvation with fear and trembling; for it is God who works in you both to will and to do for His good pleasure. (Phil. 2:12-13)

> I can do all things through Christ who strengthens me. (Phil. 4:13)

When you are trying to change lifelong habits and attitudes in order to break the bonds of jerkiness or masochism, phrases such as "God is working in me" and "I can do all things through Christ" take on a new and powerful meaning.

When dealing with your anger, you need all the help you can get and, ironically, God is willing to help us, even when we get mad at Him! Fortunately, God is omniscient. While we are ignorant of so many things, He knows everything. Above all, He knows all about you and me—what we have been thinking, what we are thinking, and what we will be thinking in the future.

When I get angry with God (and this still seems to happen once or twice a week), I tell Him how I feel, even though He knows it already anyway. I tell Him that I realize my anger toward Him is a form of displacement and that I'm really angry with somebody else. He knows all that, too.

Then I ask Him to help me trust Him, even though I don't understand why He allows suffering in this world. I ask Him to help me work through my rage toward Him for not letting me have His job. Yes, every now and then my jerkiness becomes incredible arrogance, and I keep thinking about what I would do if I were in God's shoes. Have you ever thought that perhaps you're a little smarter than God— at least about some things where you are "better informed"? I have, and I still do on occasion, but I'm thankful that I'm becoming a tiny bit wiser with each passing day.

To paraphrase King Solomon, "The beginning of wisdom is realizing it is silly to think that you are smarter than God."[5] That's really what's going on, you know, when you hold a grudge against God or anyone else. Holding on to your anger and nursing it, perhaps behind a big smile and facade that assures everyone that "I have no problems," will keep you in a state of chronic grief and can lead you to bio-chemical depression (more on this in Chapter 9).

It isn't a question of "you ought to forgive," or even "you should forgive." You *must* forgive others who have done you wrong, and you must forgive God, although He hasn't done anything wrong. Bitterness and the vengeful motives in an unforgiving spirit will all do their hurtful work unless they are given up. We must peel them off like layers of an onion. In our clinics we have seen that it can take months, sometimes years, for someone's *gut* to forgive, after that person's brain has made the conscious decision to do so.

We all know that we should not let anger eat away at us, and we have all heard from childhood that we must forgive those who trespass against us. But how does forgiveness really work, and how is it done?

Because forgiveness is such a vital part of learning to become a mature adult and less of a masochist, we will devote Step Four to learning ways to forgive "seventy times seven"—in other words, forgive jerks indefinitely for the rest of our lives.

CHAPTER
9

You Can't Stuff Your Anger Forever

STEP FOUR: Bury the Hatchet, Handle, and All

Approximately fifteen thousand Americans will come to Minirth-Meier Clinics across the country this week for insight-oriented therapy. They are people of all ages, from infancy to senility, all races, all creeds, and all socioeconomic backgrounds. The diagnosis for 75 percent of these clients will be either clinical depression or some sort of anxiety disorder. The other 25 percent will be a scattering of about fifty different diagnoses.

The official psychiatric diagnostic manual does not have a diagnosis called "jerk abuse," but it should. In reality, 95 percent of all cases of depression are caused by repressed anger toward an abuser or toward oneself. A majority of anxiety disorders involve a fear of becoming aware of our unconscious repressed anger toward our abusers or toward ourselves.

Without any hesitation, then, I can say that a majority of the mental health problems we will potentially face in life can be avoided by becoming skilled in doing Step Four:

Learn how to use forgiveness and other tools to deal with the daily anger that we are bound to feel from the effects of jerk abuse.

That includes learning how to live successfully with "jerks without" who take advantage of us as well as the "jerk within," who can make us very angry, indeed, particularly if we are perfectionists and subject to strong feelings of false guilt.

We have dozens of case studies in our files that demonstrate the corrosive power of anger. Following are three prime examples.

Pete and Joe Both Ran Out of Serotonin

About a decade ago, two seminary students—we'll call them Pete and Joe—were referred to our Dallas hospital unit in the same month. Both had been verbally abused as children by perfectionistic parents who were never satisfied. Pete and Joe had become perfectionists, and as grown young men they now expected too much of themselves. They both erroneously thought God expected too much of them also, because they confused the true God of the Bible with their father-projections.

Pete and Joe took excessively heavy course loads in seminary. They made it through their freshman year without any problems, but by the middle of their sophomore year, both of them started showing symptoms of depression. What had happened was that both young men had become subconsciously angry and bitter at God because He was demanding too much of them. Actually, they were displacing their anger from their perfectionistic earthly fathers to their heavenly Father.

The seething anger that consumed Pete and Joe depleted the serotonin in each young man's brain. Serotonin is a natural chemical found in the synapses, or spaces, between all of our brain and nerve cells. When we think or move, serotonin moves from cell to cell, across the synapses, and transmits the proper messages.

Since our brains run on serotonin like a car runs on gasoline, both men "ran out of gas," mentally and emotionally. When we become bitter, our brain dumps serotonin into the blood stream, and it is broken down into by-products that are lost in the urine. When this occurs, we suffer from the classical symptoms of depression: insomnia, decreased energy, decreased concentration, despair, headaches, and thoughts of suicide.

Antidepressant medication will give temporary relief to the clinically depressed person by rebuilding the brain's serotonin level, but until the root cause of a patient's depression is dealt with, the depression returns within days after he is taken off the antidepressant drug. In most cases, repressed anger is the root cause of the patient's depression and, until the patient can truly forgive the person or persons who have caused this anger, his brain will continue to dump serotonin and he will continue to be depressed, possibly for life.

Helping a patient learn to forgive and rid himself of repressed anger is a process that usually takes several months. During that time we keep the patient on an antidepressant to be sure he has had enough time to resolve his anger through counseling and other therapeutic processes.

When the patient gets proper therapy and truly forgives, his brain is able to hold on to the serotonin that his body produces naturally from a chemical called tryptophan (found in foods like bananas, milk, fruit, and whole grains). A patient can be depressed for many years, then forgive the one who caused his repressed anger and totally recover from the depression, because his serotonin has been restored naturally and the brain is able to work correctly. However, this restoration takes months without the help of antidepressant medications, and only a couple of weeks with the medication.

Neither Pete nor Joe tried to get help for their depression, because they just thought it was part of "getting through seminary." Eventually, however, each man got more and more depressed and developed a dopamine imbalance in his brain. Dopamine is another natural chemical that moves between the synapses of the brain. During some severe depression, however, the dopamine is blocked and cannot get from cell to cell.

When a patient's dopamine gets blocked, he becomes psychotic, thinking he hears voices that aren't really there, and developing delusions of grandiosity, compensating for severe feelings of inferiority by believing grandiose things about himself. Or he may suffer paranoid delusions of persecution and project his repressed rage upon others. Thinking others are "out to get him" is safer than owning up to his own intense anger toward his past or present abusers.

Dopamine malfunctions are much more serious than serotonin depletions. Six months of a dopamine malfunction with its resultive psychosis (loss of touch with reality) nearly always results in a permanent, lifelong, psychotic disorder—usually incurable. But in the first six months, medication with major tranquilizers can usually cure or vastly improve the dopamine pathways and restore the person to sanity.

Why Pete Recovered and Joe Did Not

Pete and Joe both became psychotic due to a dopamine malfunction during the same month, and the seminary referred them both to our hospital for treatment. Pete came from a biblical church whose pastor supported the use of psychotherapy. We gave Pete a major tranquilizer to restore his dopamine function, then antidepressants to restore his serotonin. Later, when he could handle looking at the truth about his perfectionistic parents and how they had abused him when he was young, we gave Pete intensive, insight-oriented therapy. His recovery went beautifully, and he became a successful pastor and family man.

Joe also came from a biblical church, but one that was far more legalistic than Pete's. In fact, Joe's pastor was guilty of the same kind of thinking that was prevalent among pastors of legalistic churches of the 1780s. Back then, it wasn't unusual to hear ministers call Benjamin Franklin's invention of bifocals "devil's eyes," and to say things such as, "If God wanted you to see clearly, He would have given you better eyes, and if you had faith, He would heal your vision without bifocals!"

Over two hundred years later, this same kind of legalistic thinking is still with us. Today the legalists wear bifocals, but they are condemning psychotherapy by calling it "psychoheresy" and claiming that all psychology and psychiatry is pagan and secular, not to be used by any "Bible-believing Christian."

Despite Joe's obvious psychosis, his pastor persuaded him to check out of the hospital by quoting Bible verses that Joe could not really comprehend because his dopamine and serotonin were so out of balance. It proved to be a tragic decision for Joe.

As I stated earlier, if a person goes six months or longer without correcting a dopamine imbalance, the psychotic effects nearly always become permanent. Once past a certain point, there is no cure, and Joe went past that point. He was literally the victim of "pastor abuse" and to this day, a decade later, he still hears voices and lives in a world filled with delusions.

Joe's pastor blames it on Joe's "lack of faith," but in reality it was Joe's faith in his pastor's ignorant and self-righteous thinking that destroyed his life. Even if Joe got treatment now, he could improve only about 20 percent, because his dopamine pathways have become permanently damaged. I have high hopes, however, that psychiatric research will develop a medication to "cure the uncurables," perhaps in the next decade.

Why Masochists Get Depressed More Often Than Jerks

Insight-oriented therapy is designed to help the depression sufferer become aware of all repressed anger and vengeful motives toward self, others, and/or God. The real cure comes from forgiving the jerk who got you angry in the first place whether he or she deserves it or not. It's no wonder that nice, conscientious masochists get clinically depressed much more than Second- or Nth-Degree Jerks. The jerks get even with people and verbalize their anger too much. The masochist holds anger in, denies he is angry, holds unconscious grudges, and causes his own demise through serotonin depletion.

Interestingly enough, King David listed many of the symptoms of serotonin depletion when he wrote certain psalms nearly three thousand years ago. He held grudges toward some of his enemies, as well as toward his own "jerk within" because he had committed adultery with Bathsheba and then arranged for the murder of her husband. He complained of weight loss, aching bones, insomnia, decreased energy, and "drenching his couch with tears" (see, for example, Ps. 6).

The Scripture contains sound psychology concerning how to deal with anger. Paul referred to Psalm 4:4 when he told the Ephesians: " 'Be angry, and do not sin': do not let the sun go down on your wrath."[1] In other words, they had the right to be angry over injustice and other violations of their true rights, but they were not to harbor their anger and bear grudges day after day, which would have been sinful. All true sins hurt either yourself or someone else, and all sins are examples of jerkiness or masochism. Allowing anger to simmer deep in your soul is exactly what brings on the depletion of serotonin and clinical depression.

Whenever we are wronged and become angry about it, we have the strong temptation to get revenge. Paul warned the Roman Christians not to try to get even with anybody, no matter how big a jerk that person might be. They were to leave all vengeance to God, who has promised to get even eventually with all the jerks in the world who haven't sincerely asked Him for forgiveness.[2]

As somebody has said, carrying a grudge is a heavy burden indeed. When you realize that 90 to 95 percent of all clinical depressions are anger related, you have to ask, "Where does all this anger come from?" Our experience with thousands of patients shows that the anger accumulates from grudges toward jerks we knew in our childhood, grudges toward ourselves for jerky things we have done in the past or present, grudges toward God for allowing jerky events in our lives, or grudges about life in general because we are under too much stress or have unrealistic expectations that haven't been met.

Almost All Depression Is Avoidable If . . .

Getting angry is not, however, the only way to deplete your serotonin. Approximately 5 percent of clinical depressions are caused by one or more of the following, all of which lower the serotonin level:

1. Not getting seven or eight hours of sleep per night.
2. Regular use of alcohol or marijuana.
3. Most addicting prescription medications, including many minor tranquilizers prescribed by physicians.
4. Beta blockers used for blood pressure problems (deplete serotonin in about 20 percent of the people who use them).

Various illnesses and diseases can cause serotonin depletion, including hypothyroidism, brain tumors, many forms of cancer, anemias, and many viral infections, including mononucleosis and the flu.

Probably half of all Americans will suffer from clinical depression at one time or another in their lives. Some victims will stay depressed for their entire lives, but 100 percent of all victims can be helped if they get the right treatment.

A small number of depressions are caused by a condition called "genetic bipolar disorder," which occurs because the patient inherits a brain that dumps its serotonin, even though he may not be angry or holding grudges. At other times, however, the patient with bipolar disorder undergoes another chemical change in his brain that makes him hyperactive and hypertalkative to a psychotic level, with grandiose delusions.

Bipolar disorder was once referred to as "manic depressive illness," but because "manic" sounds too much like "maniac," the term for the condition was changed to bipolar disorder. The term *bipolar* does not refer to any actual location in the brain, but is a figurative way of describing high mood and low mood. When the patient is "high," he is at the "north pole"; when he is low and depressed, he is at the "south pole."

Bipolar disorder can be controlled by giving the patient antidepressants for his depressive dips and lithium for his manic highs, enabling the patient to live a relatively normal life.

Bipolar disorder occurs in approximately 1 percent of all human beings. The vast majority of depressed people are not bipolar and can best find help through therapy and antidepressant medications, combined with getting in touch with their anger and learning to forgive. Learning how to be aware of one's anger, verbalizing it, and forgiving the jerk who is making you angry are critical factors in overcoming clinical depression.

That's why learning about jerkism in ourselves and others, and how to avoid getting hurt by jerks, is so vitally important if we want to live happy lives. Clinical depression is totally avoidable for most of us, *if we are willing to get to the root of the problem and protect ourselves.*

If a person only takes an antidepressant, but fails to resolve the anger he is holding inside, he will seem to improve because his serotonin will replenish and he will feel less symptomatic. As soon as he quits taking the antidepressant, however, his serotonin will deplete again rapidly and he will be depressed once more. Until a person resolves his grudges, conscious or unconscious, he will suffer serotonin depletion and depression and have to rely on taking the antidepressant. In other words, he will be treating the symptom (the depression) but not the cause (his repressed anger).

If you or someone you love is showing signs of clinical depression (fatigue, little energy, pessimism, anxiety, sleeplessness, weepy spells, tension or migraine headaches, upset stomach, to name a few), I recommend that you do more reading on the subject[3] and also consider seeing a professional counselor.

A very serious sign of clinical depression is suicidal thoughts. If you or someone you love has continuing thoughts of suicide, I recommend hospitalization in a psychiatric unit or behavioral medicine unit. It is better to be safe than sorry. (Minirth-Meier Clinics are located throughout the United States. For information concerning the one nearest you, call toll free 1-800-545-1819.)

It is possible to suffer such severe serotonin depletion that otherwise normal persons can start seeing suicide as a very logical solution to their depression—like a mercy killing. After they are treated for their depression, however, they can't believe they almost killed themselves!

If you have a loved one who has committed suicide, you may have been erroneously blaming yourself for what happened (many people do). Or perhaps you have been blaming the one who died by his own hand. It may help to realize that it is quite possible this person had a serotonin depletion and made a very poor decision. Forgive him or her for making a terrible and irrational choice that probably was based in great part on faulty brain chemistry.

By now, I hope you are convinced of the dangers of carrying a grudge, which really involves repressing anger and stuffing it deep into the unconscious where it can fester, deplete your serotonin, and cause all kinds of other havoc. You may be tired of reading serotonin horror stories and want to know what you can do about dealing with your anger more effectively. The rest of this chapter will give you some practical ideas.

But Isn't It a Sin to Be Angry?

You would be amazed at how many people come to our clinics believing that all anger is sinful. They were told as children, "You are *not* angry! . . . *Stop* being angry! . . . Anger is a *sin!*"

But the Bible doesn't teach this at all. James, the half-brother of Jesus, wrote a letter to Christian believers and told them that they should be *slow* to become angry, but He did not say, "*Never* become angry." James did make it clear that anger "does not bring about the righteous life that God desires."[4] It is clear from the context of what James is saying that he is speaking about flaring, raging anger that goes uncontrolled.

For most people it is normal to get angry once or even several times a day, but just what is anger? It is common to associate anger with screaming, shouting, hitting, cursing, and being out of control, in general. Patients often tell us, "I didn't really get angry over what she did to me, but I was hurt"; or "I wasn't angry, but I was irritated"; or "Angry? Not really, but I was frustrated."

What they don't understand is that being hurt, irritated, or frustrated are all related to anger and are really forms of the same thing. Anger is not always an explosion; often anger is a sputtering fuse that burns on and on deep inside while on the surface you may be smiling and saying, "I'm not angry—I don't believe getting angry makes much sense."

The "sputtering fuse" is repressed anger. Actually, explosive anger that involves shouting, screaming, and even hitting is not as dangerous in the long run as repressed anger. The person who explodes gets over it and "cools off." But the person who stuffs his anger does not get over it. He thinks he's fine when in truth he's a walking time bomb.

What to Do When You Start Feeling Angry

The first step in dealing with anger is simple: *Admit that you are angry!* Yes, this includes small irritations as well as major ones. But feeling the emotion of anger is not a sin, per se. Jesus got angry but was "without sin" because He channeled His anger in ways that glorified God.[5] It is the attitudes that sometimes lead to our anger (selfishness, jealousy) and the ways we handle our anger as we are experiencing it that can become sinful.

There are many systems and techniques for handling anger. A simple plan that we recommend to patients or callers to our radio program is a three-step process that calls for:

1. Analyzing your anger rationally and calmly.
2. Verbalizing your anger as lovingly as possible.
3. Neutralizing your anger through forgiveness.

How to Analyze Your Anger

Analyzing your anger is a several-step process in itself. When you experience angry feelings (including frustration and irritation), ask yourself, "Which of my rights is being violated right now?" It's amazing how this simple question can tone down your anger and even defuse it.

You may recall that one of the chief characteristics of being a jerk is a sense of selfish entitlement, which simply means that you think you have a right to do as you please. Often when we are becoming angry, we are exercising a "false right," one of the many ways we choose to live selfishly. One of the best ways to detect whether or not you are exercising a false right is to ask yourself the next question: "Is this a God-given right—that is, if I think one of my rights is being violated, is it a God-given legitimate right or something else?"

For example, suppose I'm doing 70 in a 55-mile-an-hour zone and a policeman pulls me over and gives me a ticket. According to my own experience and the admissions of many people I've talked with, a typical reaction to a speeding ticket is to get angry—perhaps it would be better to say "irritated." If I'm angry over a speeding ticket, which of my rights is being violated? If I analyze it, I see that my right to drive as fast as I want is being violated, but there is no such right, is there? It is a false right, and that means that my anger is illegitimate.

My next step is obvious. I must give up my false right, and that means giving up my illegitimate anger instead of expressing it and usually abusing somebody in the bargain.

The three major causes of illegitimate anger are selfishness, perfectionism, and paranoia. If selfishness is controlling me, I will feel angry almost all the time because I expect too much. I expect people to get out of my way when I'm driving. I expect people to let me go first in line. I expect people to never challenge me, cross me, argue with me, or correct me. In a word, I expect far too much, and when my expectations aren't fulfilled (which they seldom will be), I am angry. Therefore, it follows that I will be angry most of the time, serotonin depleted, and unhappy.

Some of the angriest people I know are perfectionists. When you let perfectionism rule your life, the first person from whom you demand flawless behavior is yourself. That's enough to cause continual anger in itself, but then you also expect flawless behavior from your mate, your children, your pastor, your friends—in short, you expect perfection from everyone and when they don't deliver, or you don't deliver, you get angry.

The old cliche says "nobody's perfect," but like so many cliches, it contains a giant truth. Some Christians point to the words of Jesus in His Sermon on the Mount when He told His followers, "Be perfect, therefore, as your heavenly Father is perfect."[6] The Greek word translated in many versions of the Bible as "perfect" is *teleios*, but it does not mean flawlessness or "never making a mistake."

A better translation of *teleios* would be "mature" or "full grown." When Jesus asked His followers to be perfect as God is perfect, what He was saying might sound like this in contemporary terms: "Grow up and become what God has in mind for you to be. Shed yourself of jerkiness, masochism, repressed anger, and depression, and go on to fulfill the purpose for which you were created."

Paranoia—feeling that everyone is against you, doesn't like you, or is out to get you—is another classic example of illegitimate anger. Paranoia is characterized by a supercritical attitude. As you go through your day, you can find any number of reasons to get angry. You mumble a soft "hello," and the other person fails to answer back. Anger flares because you *know* the person snubbed you. In truth, the person was probably distracted and didn't even see you or hear you.

Paranoic anger is good at misinterpreting the actions, words, and even arched eyebrows of other people. Paranoia can actually become a personality disorder, and—if severe enough—can develop into a psychosis (loss of touch with reality due to a dopamine impairment in the brain).

What Are My "Legitimate" Rights?

When we speak of false rights, we are implying there are legitimate, God-given rights. I have treated some Christians who hold the legalistic idea that Christians have no rights at all, but this simply isn't true. The Golden Rule clearly teaches that we should treat others as we would want others to treat us. To violate the Golden Rule, then, violates the right of other persons to be treated with the human dignity that God accorded to us all. Whenever we treat people less than what the Golden Rule demands, we violate their God-given rights.

In many places the Bible speaks directly of our rights or at least strongly implies that we have certain rights, for example, the right to sexual relations with your spouse (1 Cor. 7:3-5).

Scripture makes it plain we have the right not to have people lie to us. Proverbs tells us "a false witness will not go unpunished,/ and he who pours out lies will not go free."[7]

The right not to have your face stepped on or beaten in is clearly taught in passages such as Exodus 21:18-27 where all kinds of rulings are made about punishment for striking people in various situations. Does Christ's teaching in Matthew 5:39 on "turning the other cheek" negate the laws in Exodus? Jesus said He came to "fulfill the Law," not negate it. In His Sermon on the Mount, Jesus is telling His followers that when they are *abused for being Christians*, then they are to turn the other cheek. He is not telling them to never defend themselves against violent attacks.

In Matthew 5:40, Jesus tells His followers that if someone wants to sue you and take away your tunic, you should let him have your cloak as well. But if someone comes up and demands your coat, your shirt, and possibly your wallet, you have a right to call a cop! Stealing and robbing are clearly condemned in Scripture (see, for example, Lev. 19:11).

The Bible also condemns gossip and slander (see Lev. 19:16), which implies that you have the right not to have your character attacked and disparaged.

Even with the Golden Rule principle as a measuring stick,

it is not always easy to be sure if your God-given rights are being violated. One practical approach, which my brother, Richard, often suggests in counseling situations, is to ask yourself, "Is this a five-cent issue or a five hundred-dollar issue?" If whatever was said or done appears to be a nickel issue, it probably didn't involve one of your legitimate rights. If it is more in the five hundred-dollar category, however, that is a good indicator that someone has broken the Golden Rule and your legitimate rights were violated.

How to Verbalize Your Anger

Unfortunately, human beings are very human. They violate each other's God-given rights in many ways. What do you do with your anger when one of your God-given rights is violated? That brings us to our second technique in the three-step approach to handling anger: verbalize your angry feelings, but be sure to "speak the truth in love."

In his letter to the Ephesian Christians, Paul urges believers toward unity and deeper knowledge of Christ in order that they might become perfect (mature) and achieve the stature and fullness of Christ Himself. Paul doesn't want Christians to be children tossed to and fro by every wind of doctrine or by the trickery of men (jerkiness, jerk abuse). Instead, he wants Christians to *speak the truth in love* so they can grow up and become like their Head, Jesus Christ Himself.[8]

While it's true that Paul has right doctrine primarily in mind in this passage, the phrase "speak the truth in love" is excellent advice when we seek the best way to deal with someone when we are angry. How then does one "speak the truth in love"?

For one thing, when you are angry, you can verbalize it gently, respectfully, and tactfully. To speak the truth in love means using the "I" message rather than the "you" message. Examples of "you" messages would include:

"You should have called."
"You shouldn't have said that!"
"You are such a slob!"

How can we turn these "you" messages into "I" messages? Let's try:

> "I was upset when I didn't hear from you. I got worried."
>
> "I don't think what you said was fair, and I didn't appreciate it."
>
> "I get very irritated when the kitchen (bedroom, bathroom) is left messy."

"I" messages are a simple device, but it's not easy to learn to use them consistently. The normal tendency is to use the same kind of "you" messages we have heard all our lives. Work on using "I" messages, particularly when you're feeling angry. When phrasing your "I" message, think through the situation carefully and don't exaggerate. The key to using "I" messages is to put the responsibility for your own feelings on yourself. Do not accuse, demean, or attack the other person.

Forgiving Is Love's Toughest Work

The final step in dealing with your anger is the hardest. You must learn ways to neutralize your anger by forgiving the one who has offended or abused you. Forgiving is 180 degrees from the thing that we naturally want to do, which is get revenge or at least settle the score.

I often talk to patients who believe that to forgive the spouse or parent or friend who has done them wrong "just doesn't seem fair." After all, this person just doesn't deserve their forgiveness.

I tell these patients that they're absolutely right. When we are treated unfairly, the jerks who abused us don't deserve our forgiveness, but *we* deserve to give it to them anyway because it's the only way to be fair to ourselves.

I like what Lewis Smedes, the award-winning author of *Free to Forgive*, says about getting even. He calls it a "loser's game," which leaves you frustrated and in more pain than you got from the original offense in the first place.[9]

During a Minirth-Meier broadcast, we were spending the entire week on the subject of forgiveness when we received a call from a pastor's wife who was obviously still very angry. With a trembling voice she told us how one of their parishioners had been cleaning out the church and somehow this person had thrown out large quantities of rare organ music that were irreplaceable. The pastor's wife, who was, of course, the church organist, was distraught. Even though the dumping of the organ music had not been done on purpose, she just didn't know how to get past her anger and grief.

My brother, Richard, often joins me on Minirth-Meier broadcasts, and he was with me in the studio that day. Together we gave the lady several ideas for dealing with her problem.

First of all, we suggested that she might want to forgive herself for any mistakes she may have made. Perhaps she was angry at herself for leaving the music out where it could be found and tossed like any other pile of trash. Then we urged her to go to the person who had tossed out the music and forgive that person in a face-to-face encounter. Finally, we suggested that she forgive God for letting this tragedy happen.

One of the most practical suggestions made to this pastor's wife came from my brother, Richard. He told her to set aside a half hour a day for the next seven days to feel that anger and grief. He suggested that she find a quiet spot where she could sit down and grieve, weep, scream— whatever it took to express her anger over losing the valuable manuscripts of organ music. After seven days she would be far more ready to give up her anger and go on with life.

And that, after all, is the bottom line: letting go of whatever has made you angry, forgiving whoever hurt you unfairly, *and getting on with life.* The apostle Paul knew that when anger is kept in the heart, it turns into animosity, hatred, and a grudge that you can bear for years, possibly until you die. Along with all that, anger and bitterness can set you up for demonic jerk abuse. That's why Paul wrote to the Christians at Ephesus and said: "If you are angry, don't sin by nursing your grudge. Don't let the sun go down with you still angry—get over it quickly; for when you are angry you give a mighty foothold to the devil."[10]

Lewis Smedes calls forgiveness "love's toughest work," and so it is. But forgiving is the best kind of work you will ever do for your own sake, for the sake of the one who has wronged you, and for God's sake.

To Avoid Jerk Abuse—Avoid the Jerks!

You've undoubtedly heard the old saying, "Forgive and forget." We never use it in Minirth-Meier Clinics. Forgive, yes, but forget, no. You see, we don't forget, and it's probably just as well because some things should not be forgotten. They should be coped with, worked through, and remembered as a warning not to get into the same situation again.

If you have been or are being victimized by jerks, take a tip from how the apostle Paul dealt with jerk abuse in writing to his pastor friend Timothy. As he wound up his second letter to Timothy, Paul mentioned several people, some of whom had forsaken him, and some of whom had stuck with him. And then he went on to say: "Alexander the coppersmith did me much harm. May the Lord repay him according to his works. You also must beware of him, for he has greatly resisted our words."[11]

Taking the very same advice that he gave to the Roman Christians, Paul had left vengeance on Alexander to God; the Lord could repay Alexander according to his works. Who knows? Alexander may have repented and asked forgiveness. On the other hand, if he went unrepentant and an enemy of Jesus and the gospel, he would eventually face the vengeance that belongs only to God, who deals with every one of us in perfect fairness.

I believe Paul forgave Alexander, but he also learned from his experience. He had set some boundaries about dealing with Alexander, and what he was simply telling Timothy was, "Watch out for this guy. You are to love him, but don't trust him." In other words, beware of jerks who can do you harm.

In Paul's comments we can see all three steps in dealing with anger. First, Paul analyzed his anger, and it's fairly obvious that one of his legitimate rights had been violated—he had the right to preach the gospel, and Alexander was opposing his work in very jerky ways.

Second, Paul verbalized his anger by telling Timothy that Alexander had done him harm and that Timothy would be wise to beware of any dealings with this man.

Third, Paul neutralized his anger by turning vengeance on Alexander over to God. Paul forgave, but he also faced facts. To that point, at least, Alexander was an unrepentant jerk and needed to be dealt with cautiously.

This is a key lesson for anybody with masochistic tendencies to learn. Forgiving a jerk who abuses you doesn't mean that you have to cozy up to that jerk and become fast friends. In fact, in most cases, you will need to keep away from jerks who abuse you. Avoid them, if possible. If necessary, change jobs, golf partners, or the route you drive to work.

If you're married to a jerk, get counseling. If the abuse by a jerky partner gets too severe, separate until your mate gets counseling and the situation is safe. Moving out of masochism into maturity does not mean becoming a doormat. In fact, that's what a masochist is—a doormat who has probably been stuffing his or her anger and trying to believe that this is the way to be "spiritual."

After working with tens of thousands of patients in our clinics through the years, we have developed many psychological and spiritual techniques to help them forgive their jerky abusers. One of the most helpful tools, perhaps, is a daily devotional book written by Frank Minirth and myself, which contains 365 brief pointers for learning how to deal with those tough-to-get-rid-of grudges that we may still be carrying inside. If you have grudges you can't seem to get rid of, you may find real help in *Free to Forgive: Daily Devotions for Adult Children of Abuse* (Nashville: Thomas Nelson, 1991).

The Best Way to Forgive

I believe that learning to forgive is an active process, not a passive one. In the final analysis, the best way to forgive is to turn to the Author of forgiveness Himself and ask Him for help. In one of many books Corrie ten Boom wrote about her experiences in a Nazi concentration camp, she tells of being assigned with her sister, Betsie, to load pieces of wrecked airplanes onto big trucks. The work was heavy, far too much for Betsie, who was very frail. When one of the guards saw Betsie picking up only the smaller pieces to load, she snapped out orders to pick up the heavy ones also. Betsie replied kindly, "Don't give me more to do than I am trying to do already, because I am not strong enough to lift these heavy parts."

"You don't decide what you do. *I* decide," the guard snarled, and she started to brutally beat Betsie. Corrie became enraged and would have attacked the guard had the other prisoners not held her back.

After the guard left, Corrie ran to her sister and tried to wipe away the blood that was streaming down her face. Betsie said, "No, don't hate, Corrie, you must love and forgive."

"I cannot!" Corrie exclaimed, still in a rage. "I am not able."

After the prisoners returned to their barracks that evening, Corrie climbed out of a window and went for a short walk to talk with the Lord. She prayed, "Lord, I cannot forgive that brutal woman. It is more difficult to forgive when people you love suffer than when you suffer yourself."

At that moment Corrie felt sure that the Lord was reminding her of a passage from Romans. She reached under her dress where she had a tiny Bible hidden, opened it and read: "The love of God has been poured out in our hearts by the Holy Spirit who was given to us."[12]

Corrie relates that as she read that verse she realized that the Lord, who lived in her heart, was able to do what she could not. She thanked God for this verse that had come to her mind, and for His love that she felt within her, which was stronger than her hatred for the guard. She writes:

> At that moment when I was able to forgive, my hatred disappeared. . . . Forgiveness is the key which unlocks the door of resentment and the handcuffs of

hatred. It is a power that breaks the chains of bitterness and the shackles of selfishness. What a liberation it is when you can forgive.[13]

What liberation indeed! There is an old joke about "burying the hatchet but leaving the handle sticking up," which is a good description of repressed anger. But when God empowers you to forgive, you can bury the hatchet, handle, and all!

CHAPTER

10

Why Keep Running the Rat Race?

<u>STEP FIVE:</u> Become Your Own Best Friend

Our regular radio listeners have probably heard me say this a thousand times, but I plan to keep on saying it wherever I can:

> *There are six billion of us on Planet Earth, and all six billion of us feel inferior to some degree.*

Why is that rather negative bit of news worthy of repeated mention? Because feeling inferior is the driving force that makes all of us want to go through life running a meaningless rat race to feel significant. Deep down we feel like nobodies and we spend most of our time, energy, and money trying to prove to the world that we're really "not nobodies."

Despite all the academic shingles hanging on my walls, I, too, have pain of inferiority feelings from time to time, even though I apply everything I know in an attempt to avoid or alleviate that pain. But some pain is still there, and always will be, until I breathe my last on this earth.

According to the extensive psychiatric research I've read over the years, only a small percentage of people claim they have *no* feelings of inferiority, but if these same people agree to psychological testing, the results show they feel so extremely inferior they can't even admit they have inferiority feelings!

Where do these inferiority feelings come from? Are we born with them or do we develop them? While you can never completely rule out genetics, it's clear that the greater part of our inferiority feelings are developed as we go through our first six years of life.

We form 85 percent of our personality by our sixth birthday, and if you think about it, during those first six years, we *are* inferior to most of those around us—in size, in strength, in knowledge, in coordination, and in ability to reason and comprehend. During the very years you are forming your basic personality, you truly are "less than" to the key people around you, particularly your parents. If your parents did a perfect job of bringing you up, most of these inferiority feelings would be sharply reduced, but, unfortunately, your parents were brought up by their parents, who made mistakes with them.

A common mistake that parents make with their children, without realizing it, is slipping into the use of defense mechanisms, such as projection and displacement, both of which were described in Chapter 6. Projection, as you may recall, is what we do when we "project" onto other people our unconscious faults, thoughts, feelings, and motives. Projection is what Jesus was describing when He cautioned against seeing the speck in your brother's eye instead of the plank in your own.[1]

"Displacement" happens when we displace or "switch" our anger or other emotions from one object to another object. Almost everyone has times when he will displace the anger he actually feels toward himself, his boss, or somebody else, and take it out on a convenient scapegoat.

Unfortunately, parents often use these defense mechanisms on their children. For example, all parents project to some extent onto their children. A father tends to project most on his oldest son, and a mother on her oldest daughter. That's one reason why it's tough to be a firstborn, or even to be the oldest child of your sex.

In addition, parents often displace the anger they might feel toward themselves, their employers, or their own parents onto convenient "scapegoat" objects. And what objects are most convenient? Very often it's the children.

Think about it. When you were growing up, your parents had those times when they were legitimately angry because you were disobedient or selfishly rebellious. But what about those times they scorned you or even punished you and you didn't quite understand why? Very likely, it was because you were innocently reminding them of their own unconscious faults, and they projected those faults onto you.

But this wasn't all. At other times you were probably the object of your parents' scorn or rage because they were displacing anger they truly felt toward themselves, other people, or their employers, and you happened to be the handy scapegoat. After all, was it safer for your dad to be angry at his boss, or even your mother, or at you?

So what does all this have to do with your sense of self-worth—your self-esteem? Just about everything. Most human beings tend to base their self-worth on their parents' opinions of them. Unfortunately, parental opinions are almost always colored by defense mechanisms such as projection and displacement. And if parents don't use these two common mechanisms, they may use any number of the other thirty-eight defense mechanisms that are commonly seen in psychiatric practice (see Chapter 6 and the Appendix, p. 239).

The bottom line is that we grow up developing a self-concept and sense of self-worth that had little to do with us and an awful lot to do with the hang-ups and problems our parents had. And, of course, our parents developed their self-concept and sense of self-worth from being reared by *their* parents, who used defense mechanisms on them!

Can you see, then, why all human beings have a certain amount of inferiority feelings? Can you see why so many people suffer severe pain from false opinions of themselves? The reason all six billion of us on this planet have inferiority feelings is that somewhere along the line our self-concept (sense of self-worth) got twisted or damaged, if not by our parents, then by significant others, such as teachers, coaches, and schoolmates, who were also using projection, displacement, and any number of other defense mechanisms. (See the Appendix, p. 239.)

Fortunately, no matter how badly damaged your self-concept may be, there is always help. No matter how old you are, you can always improve and increase your sense of self-worth. As the rest of this chapter will show, change is always possible in anyone who is willing to be changed.

How Much Are You Worth?

A damaged sense of self-worth is a primary, driving reason why many people become masochists—prone to jerk abuse. When we get addicted to jerks, we are co-dependent upon them. In a way, we are slaves, trying to satisfy our addictive compulsion. We run around seeking constant approval, attention, and influence. We are in a rat race, and the prize is significance; the only problem is that we never get to the finish line!

In the race for self-significance, nothing seems to work for very long. Getting an academic degree doesn't feel good forever. Winning a tennis or golf tournament doesn't last forever. Having an affair may afford an initial thrill, but it ends up destroying lives and lowering self-worth even more in the long run. Money is always fun, but how much is enough to keep feeling good? We always need a little bit more!

While all of us feel inferior to some degree, we all have a current up-to-date opinion of our value as a human being, relative to the other six billion human beings roaming around Planet Earth. Some of us feel more valuable than others. We call this feeling self-concept, self-worth, self-significance, or self-esteem, but all of these labels boil down to the same thing: How do I feel when I take an honest journey into me?

Imagine for a moment that you have a written document before you called a "Certificate of Worth." Take a moment to fill out this certificate and base your answers on how you have tended to think about yourself during most of your past:

CERTIFICATE OF WORTH

My Name: _____
On what do I tend to base my self-worth:

_____

In whose pocket do I tend to put this certificate of self-worth (in other words, whose opinion affects my feelings of self-worth the most)?

_____

My best human friend is: _____
On a scale of 1 to 10 (with 10 meaning "as high as possible"), my estimated net worth as a human being is: _____

How did you fill out your certificate? Did you base your worth on your sexual prowess? Your good looks? Influence, power, or control over other people? The neighborhood where you live? The kind of clothing you wear? Your religious dogma or level of superspirituality? Your abilities—to masochistically rescue others, for example? The "what" of one's sense of self-worth could be just about anything.

The "who" behind your self-worth is even more important than the "what." Who really carries your Certificate of Worth in his or her pocket, so to speak? Whose opinion makes your sense of self-worth go up and down like a yo-yo? Your mother? Your father? Your siblings? Your peers? Your teachers? Your pastor? Your relatives? Your coworkers? Your employers or employees? Your past schoolmates from junior high, high school, or college? Your past lovers? Your mate or ex-mate?

Stop and reflect carefully on each of the above possibilities. It may be no surprise that the ones who have your certificate of worth in their pocket are your past and/or present jerky abusers. Very few human beings have decided to place their "Certificate of Worth" in their own pockets. Most of us tend to place that certificate in *someone else's pocket*, whether we realize it or not.

And when we do, we become masochists, prone to jerk abuse and co-dependency. Basing your sense of self-worth on the opinions of others is a foolish and childish thing to do, but we all have a tendency to do it anyway. That's why Step Five is critical to moving toward mature adulthood:

> *Put your personal Certificate of Worth in your own pocket, and no one else's, by developing a healthy accurate self-concept.*

What Is a Self-concept Made Of?

One of the best books on self-concept that I have ever read is *The Sensation of Being Somebody,* by Dr. Maurice Wagner who holds degrees in theology and psychology. In describing a person's self-concept, Wagner speaks of three feelings that "work together like legs of a tripod . . . if any one of the three feelings is weak, the self-concept totters like a camera on a tripod when one leg is slipping."[2] The three feelings Wagner believes make up our self-concept are:

1. Belongingness
2. Worthiness
3. Competence

"To belong" means to feel wanted and accepted, cared for, and enjoyed as a person. In our Minirth-Meier Clinics nationwide, we deal with many people who don't feel they belong. In fact, they complain of "being on the outside looking in" all their lives. They didn't belong at home, they didn't belong at school, they don't feel as if they belong at work, they're just not in the in group. They have spent their lives on the outside, looking in.

"To feel worthy" means that you can tell yourself, "I am a good person" or "I am right." We get this feeling when others in our lives approve of us and affirm us. If we are criticized, put down, or gossiped about, we lose our sense of worthiness.

Wagner describes a man who had picked out a car he

wanted to buy but had made the mistake of describing the car to his domineering older brother, who immediately told him in no uncertain terms that such a car was a poor investment. Besides, he was sure his younger brother couldn't afford the payments. The younger brother had, in fact, carefully worked out a plan to pay for the car, and he had the money, but in order to keep his older brother's approval, he backed down and canceled his plans to buy the car. Not surprisingly, the younger brother wound up feeling depressed.

If this younger brother sounds like a masochist, you're right, because he is. It's more important for him to keep his brother's approval than it is to make a decision he feels good about and go ahead with it.[3]

Wagner points out that an offshoot of this younger brother's attitude is the kind of person who prefers not to even try to make a decision. This person continually asks for the opinions of others, no matter how simple the choice might be. As Wagner says, "These people never developed a good sense of worthiness through making good decisions for themselves, and they are very dependent upon others."[4] Again, we see another typical description of someone with masochistic tendencies.

The masochist's sense of self-worth is relatively weak, and that's why he believes everyone else's opinion tends to be worth more than his.

The person with a strong sense of worthiness (strong self-worth) makes his own decisions and, when criticized, he doesn't let it erode his self-concept. If the criticism is unfair, he might tell himself, *Well, they just don't understand . . . they've never been in my shoes . . . he's usually negative anyway.* If the criticism is fair, the person with strong feelings of worthiness may think, *He's right. I'll do better next time. . . . So I blew it, it isn't the end of the world.*

A strong sense of worthiness is one of the best defenses against the manipulations and abuses of the jerks of this world. Unfortunately, it is one of the hardest legs of self-concept to develop, particularly if you have masochistic tendencies and a strong need to please others.

Perhaps you grew up in a home that had a lot of rules and

regulations. You may have felt that you belonged, but you were always hearing, "No, you're wrong . . . don't do that . . . that's not right . . ." Because of all this negative input, you learned to send yourself negative messages through your self-talk. (We'll look at ways to change self-talk from negative to positive later in this chapter.)

"To feel competent," the third leg of the self-concept tripod, is what Wagner calls the "'I can' feeling of being able to face life and cope with its complexities."[5] This feeling of competence is tied to words like *adequate, courage, hopeful,* and *strength.* In short, competence says, "I can do it." The teenage years are crucial times for developing a feeling of competence. Obviously, successes make one's feelings of competence grow while failures make it diminish.

While the "tripod" metaphor is helpful in understanding self-concept, it should not be pushed too hard. Feelings of belongingness, worthiness, and competence aren't three separate entities. They flow back and forth into one another. Feeling worthy depends on feeling that you belong, and feeling competent comes out of belongingness and worthiness. A healthy self-concept includes all three basic feelings.

I Was a Workaholic and Then Some

I sometimes run across people who are trying to make up for a lack of belongingness or worthiness by being "competent." Who they are depends entirely on what they do, their skills, their abilities, their talents, or the amount of money they make. But without feeling that you belong or that you are worthy, skills and achievements turn to dust in your mouth. I understand how these people feel because the same thing happened to me.

Early in our marriage, I became a workaholic in order to pursue the "holy grail of significance." By the time I was thirty and was finishing my psychiatric training, I was spending almost no time with Jan and the children. Instead, I was trying to achieve significance by obeying the parental injunction of my German workaholic father, who often told me as I was growing up: *Arbeit macht das Leben süss* ("Work makes life sweet").

I was very much the religious workaholic who was following in the footsteps of his ancestors—and then some. But I had not yet learned that becoming a workaholic does not make life sweet at all. While teaching full-time at Trinity Seminary near Chicago, I practiced part-time psychiatry in Milwaukee, a sixty-mile drive one way. I also began working on a seminary degree by taking courses at Trinity. In addition, I fulfilled my masochistic tendencies by giving seminary students and their spouses free counseling almost every night in my home. I also did charity work in the ghetto on Saturdays and did seminars and other teaching in churches on Sundays.

And I began writing books. Ironically, my first book dealt with child-rearing and personality development. Totally addicted to my workaholic lifestyle, I happily wrote my book on how to be a wonderful Christian parent, unaware that while I was a very spiritual fellow, getting up at 5:30 every morning for devotions, I was mostly ignoring my wife and three small children, a pattern I had learned during my childhood.

As this routine went on for several years, I honestly thought that I was doing the best I could to serve God and my fellowman. At the ripe young age of thirty, however, I began feeling the effects of burnout.

One morning I awoke at my usual time, opened my Bible to Matthew 11, and read Jesus' words: "My yoke is easy and My burden is light."[6] I remember looking up toward heaven, shaking my fist, and saying to Jesus, "How can You say that? Your yoke and burden are *overwhelming!*"

I made a long distance call to my friend Frank Minirth, who was teaching at Dallas Seminary at the time. I shared my frustrations over Jesus' words about an easy yoke and a light burden, but Frank was unimpressed with my criticisms of the Almighty.

"If God says His yoke is easy, then His yoke is easy," Frank told me. "If you're overwhelmed with the yoke you think you're under, then you're getting that yoke from the way your parents modeled workaholism while you were growing up."

As Frank and I talked, he also reminded me not to confuse my heavenly Father with my earthly father. I was embarrassed that I hadn't seen these obvious truths for myself. I had yet to learn that it's easy to see certain dynamics in others, but personal insights can be painfully difficult because of our own blind spots. And even psychiatrists have these blind spots.

From Workaholism to Computer Bridge

I sat down with Jan, and we had a long talk. We discussed my workaholism and how I had been ignoring her and the children. Jan admitted she hadn't really minded that much because she, in true masochist style, sort of enjoyed having the weight of our entire family on her back. Those conversations between Jan and me resulted in some major decisions on my part.

I re-prioritized my life and changed my daily schedule to fit my new priority list. That new list included Jan's needs, spending more time with her, and spending at least eighteen hours a week in positive, noncritical time with my children. I also vowed to stay at home at least three weekends a month, instead of going out to do free counseling, charity work, or teaching in a nearby church.

But while my road to maturity was paved with good intentions, I got sidetracked. I thought I had handled my workaholic addiction quite nicely, but I was soon hooked on another addiction—of all things, computer bridge. During all that quality time I was spending with my kids, they introduced me to video games and eventually I wound up playing video bridge by the hour, rationalizing my actions by saying, "I'm doing it to relax." In truth, I was still trying to distance myself from my family, something I had learned from my father, who had distanced himself to some extent from his family through workaholism and churchaholism, both of which kept him away from home a great deal of the time.

I Decided to Restore the Family Wealth, But . . .

About this time I also succumbed to one of the major parental injunctions I had heard all my life from my dad: get a high-paying job and restore the family wealth that had been lost in the Communist Revolution. I decided to look for a full-time position in psychiatry that would pay far more than I was making at the seminary.

In a matter of weeks, I got an excellent offer from a psychiatric clinic in the Chicago area, well into the six figures, but before I could quit and take the new high-paying job, a good friend of mine on the Trinity Seminary faculty was killed in a car wreck. He was Paul Little, a godly man who may be best known for his book, *How to Give Away Your Faith* (Downers Grove, Ill.: InterVarsity Press, 1966). One of the speakers at Paul's funeral was Leighton Ford, a man I respected for his many years of evangelistic work with Billy Graham.

As Leighton spoke about Paul Little's pioneer spirit and his willingness to serve God and man, he asked some pointed questions that stabbed deep into my heart: "When you are old and look back on your life, what do you want to see? Will you have spent your life earning money and 'success' or will you have spent it as a pioneer, using the talents God gave you to benefit your fellowman as Paul Little did?"

I recalled a phone call from Frank Minirth just a couple of days before. Frank had invited me to join him in teaching full-time at Dallas Seminary, where we could pioneer a new counseling program. The full-time pay was $12,600 a year!

A tug-of-war went on in my brain as I tried to sort out the parental injunctions I had heard all my life. Should I try to "replenish the Meier family wealth" at over $100,000 a year? Or should I be a servant of God for $12,600 a year? As tempting as the six-figure salary sounded, I kept remembering all those Bible verses about serving God that my mother had taught me. Yes, it was true I could be a "servant of God" in a psychiatric practice, but I had a strong feeling that God would prefer that I serve Him at Dallas Seminary, and I sat down and talked with Jan to see how she felt. Jan agreed, so we took our "poverty vows" and moved our family of three small children to Dallas, Texas.

If you have been a follower of God for any time at all, you know that He has a way of changing our plans and predictions. Jan and I had planned on poverty, but we were soon busy counting our blessings. Once settled in my job at Dallas Seminary, I joined Frank Minirth in co-authoring several textbooks, all of which sold surprisingly well in the popular market. As some of our students graduated from seminary, they went into TV and radio work and began to get us involved. Soon Frank and I were appearing on single radio broadcasts here and there, which featured our answers to spiritual and emotional problems of listeners who would write or call in.

People who read our books and heard us on the radio wanted Frank and me to treat them, but we simply didn't have the time because we were too busy with our seminary teaching, as well as a part-time psychiatric practice that we had started together in Dallas in 1976. Soon the demand became so great we began hiring like-minded psychiatrists and psychologists to work for us, and our part-time venture evolved into the first full-fledged, Minirth-Meier Clinic.

In no time at all, we were so busy we both had to battle our tendencies to be workaholics. And, as human beings are prone to do, I began to feel a bit smug, all in a very spiritual way, of course! I felt I had my jerk within well under control and was well on my way to being a mature adult.

In truth, however, the masochist in me was running wild. It was during this time that I began making numerous poor financial decisions as different people came to me with sure-thing investments, the "dumb doctor deals" that I mentioned back in Chapter 5. But for a while I thought I was a smart doctor, indeed, and that whatever I did could only turn to gold. "Restoring the family wealth" seemed possible after all, as an unexpected gift from God.

In 1985 I got my comeuppance in two ways, first on a rocky mountainside in Turkey and, second, in a financial avalanche that wiped out most of Texas—and my bank account.

I Was Invited to Help Find Noah's Ark

Early in 1985, I was invited to be the team doctor on an expedition to discover Noah's Ark, which scholars have always thought landed on top of Mt. Ararat in Turkey. The group that invited me to join their expedition wasn't operating on a mere whim. They had gained access to secret aerial reconnaissance photos which showed exactly where the remains of the Ark were. Joining the expedition meant taking time out from my busy schedule at the seminary and clinic, but I jumped at the chance anyway.

Our expedition left for Turkey in August, where we planned to rendezvous with Jim Irwin, the American astronaut, who was leading his own team to the same area. I was filled with all kinds of noble feelings as I thought I was risking my life on Mt. Ararat totally for God and mankind. What I didn't quite realize, however, was that my jerk within was definitely still operating. Unconsciously, I wanted to go on this expedition because it would mean fame, glory, and the opportunity to have my name in history books.

Our expedition team arrived in Turkey and went through customs without incident, except for one snag. For reasons still unknown to me, a Turkish bureaucrat decided something was wrong with my papers and would not allow me to climb Mt. Ararat with my expedition team.

Two nights after the team started its climb, I lay sleepless in my dingy hotel room. I got up, wandered over to the window, and looked up at the mountain through binoculars. I saw a flickering light that could have been a bonfire. I wondered if it was my associates, who could have easily reached that spot by now. But as I studied the flickering light in my binoculars, I felt that something was very wrong. I was suddenly overcome with a deep sense of foreboding. I went back to bed but, instead of falling off to sleep, I lay there trembling. Then, around midnight I heard my window break! Had it been an earth tremor or perhaps an intruder intent on taking my wallet—perhaps my life?

I grabbed a hunting knife off the nightstand and flipped

on the light. To my surprise, I found the window broken *from the inside out,* with the glass lying on the balcony just outside. I never did determine how the window could break from the inside out.

I finally fell asleep a couple of hours later. The next morning the members of my expedition team came stumbling into town, eyes bulging with fear as they told a wild story of being taken captive by terrorists, who had burned thousands of dollars worth of our supplies and equipment (the flickering bonfire I had seen in my binoculars the night before). At one point, the terrorists had put all members of the team in front of a "firing squad" but had changed their minds. Finally, they chased my associates down the mountain, firing in the air as they went.

While our expedition's plans for making the climb of Mt. Ararat were dashed, we hoped that Jim Irwin's group could still try. Irwin's expedition arrived a few days later and did start the climb, accompanied by Turkish soldiers sent along for their protection. But after getting within half a mile of the spot where aerial photos said the Ark would be, the soldiers refused to let Irwin and his group continue because it "might upset the Russians," whose border lay very close by.

I came back home feeling defeated and more than a little angry with God. Frank Minirth and I were scheduled to start a new nationally syndicated radio show, reaching a million people a day with help and advice on spiritual and emotional problems. I had wanted to start our broadcasts off with a bang by sharing my part in the discovery of Noah's Ark. The editor of *National Geographic* said that if the Ark were discovered, it would have been the greatest archaeological discovery of all time. Instead, we had become just another failed expedition, and my ego was badly bruised.

My jerk within was working overtime, and a big part of me was angry with God. The worthiness and competence legs of my self-concept were also shaky. The old feelings of "not being able to be good enough" ate at my soul. I had wanted to show my dad that his son could "really do something important."

But those weren't my only problems. While I didn't say much, I was actually frightened by the prospect of talking to a million people a day on a live call-in show. I was also worried about the financial cost. Frank and I had always maintained a policy of never accepting donations to any radio or TV program in which we were involved, but now the expenses were formidable and I couldn't see how we'd pay for everything.

We went ahead with the program and, once past the opening show jitters, everything went beautifully. We were soon getting more and more referrals and requests from people who wanted to be patients in our clinics because they had heard about us on the radio. We were able to take some of these referrals, and we also funneled as many as we could into a second Minirth-Meier Clinic that had been started in Chicago just a few months before by my sister, Nancy.

I had been back from Turkey just a few weeks, and the new radio show was going well when I got my second comeuppance, this time right in the pocketbook. The "Texas crash of '85" hit all over the state, resulting in the real estate market going into a major power dive. At the same time, the S&L crisis began and the entire Texas economy went into a recession. Several real estate investments that I had made went down to one-third of their former market value, and I was left high and dry. My net worth became a negative number, and it was all I could do to avoid bankruptcy. Restoring the family wealth would have to be put on hold.

I began feeling sorry for myself and angry with certain people who had advised me on sure-thing places to put my money. I also got angry with God—again. First, my hopes of attaining lasting glory by helping to find Noah's Ark had sunk without a trace. Now all my money had vanished as well. I wondered if He really appreciated all the sacrifices I had made for Him. Weren't righteous men supposed to be blessed? Weren't Christians supposed to experience heaven, even here on earth?

Back to Square One for My Jerk Within

By now, my thoughts were more than a little jerky, and my self-concept was in shambles. I sat around like the proverbial puppy who had been spanked for what he thought was no good reason, while my wife dealt with Federal bank examiners who were questioning my integrity (see Chapter 5). It was time for some serious introspection to try to regain a big chunk of my sense of self-worth.

Because I had been so strictly disciplined by my father as a youth, I had developed some unconscious bitterness toward authority and a certain sense of entitlement to rebel against it. At the same time, my self-worth had suffered because I had based too much of my self-concept on my parents' opinion of me. Rebelling against God was a very tempting "failure script" at this angry point in my life. It seemed to me to be a way to get vengeance on God and deliver myself from the pressures to serve Him.

Fortunately, I refused to isolate myself, turn my anger inward, and become depressed. I realized that I had to go back to Square One to deal with the jerk within, whose masochistic tendencies kept tempting him to buy friends in one way or another. I started reaching out to colleagues at the clinic who helped me get insights into my masochism, not to mention some of my own jerky attitudes about life. Even more valuable, perhaps, was that I started meeting regularly with a friend who had a background in the ministry. I shared all my emotional and spiritual pain with him. I also told him about every selfish and rebellious thought or act I could remember since my birth.

A shared burden is half a burden, and as I confessed my confusion to my good friend and other therapists on our staff, I gained a better perspective on the realities of life. For one thing, I learned that God doesn't promise wealth or fame to those living on earth. And He doesn't promise freedom from all the pains of life. But what He *does* promise is to be our Higher Power as we go *through* the pains of life. He also promises to give our lives meaning. Justice, contentment, and eternal bliss will be ours in life after death, but not now.

As my friends and counselors pointed out the errors in my thinking, I let the hot air out of my arrogance by "forgiving God"—as if He deserved my wrath in the first place. I also lowered my expectations and decided I'd let God determine how much wealth I accumulated. And once again I re-evaluated my priorities, including the parental injunctions that I had accepted since childhood. I realized I couldn't be perfect, and perhaps it wasn't God's plan for me to be rich and restore the family wealth.

I also got a better look at my own jerkiness. It was painful to realize I wasn't as holy as I had thought I was, but in doing so I learned more about genuine humility. Jan even commented that I was more "for real" than I had been in the last several years.

I decided to quit following some of the "failure scripts" that had become part of my own First-Degree jerkiness and had made me a masochist who allowed too many "friends" to take advantage of me. A typical example of a failure script for me read: "I need to risk my own finances to help others become successful financially in order to feel good about myself and to purchase their approval. If I fail financially, it will be easier to resist the pressure to 'buy friends.'"

As I removed my blinders and saw the truth, my sense of self-worth returned and I started choosing more responsible friends. I learned that "bought friends" aren't really worth having, and being rejected by jerky people who got angry because I was no longer a soft touch was not a reflection on my value as a human being. I learned that my happiness was not in the control of others who may or may not reject me. I was reminded that *happiness is always a choice*, something I had written about several years before,[7] but had never had to apply in my own life in such a dramatic way.

Most important, I decided to become my own best friend, despite my jerk within. Yes, my jerk within is still there and will be until I die. And, yes, he's still rather arrogant and selfish, but he's not as strong as he used to be.

My jerk within is sort of like a dangerous dog on a leash. At times he tries to fool me into engaging in self-pity, vengeful motives, and other selfish behavior, but the more I realize how powerless I am over him and how much I need to rely on God, family, and friends for love and "reality checks," the stronger that leash becomes.

As I keep my jerk within on a tight leash, I learn more and more about loving myself in spite of the realization that "he" is part of "me." My sense of self-worth grows stronger by the day, and I am seeing the importance of having a healthy self-concept instead of trying to be "good enough" to be approved of and accepted.

Why Self-concept Is Not a Dirty Word

The same ultraconservative critics who condemn psychologists and psychotherapy usually are very down on talking about self-concept and self-esteem. They misapply various Bible passages that speak of the dangers of self-gratification and the need to deny yourself and take up the cross daily and follow Jesus.[8] It is absolutely true that you can center too much on yourself. As our first chapter pointed out, we are all jerks of some degree because we are born with a selfish sense of entitlement. The question, however, is not whether *self-esteem* or *self-concept* are valid terms. We are all *selves*—persons who need to think of themselves neither too highly nor too lowly.

The apostle Paul's words in his letter to the Roman Christians are a perfect summation of the kind of self-concept we need to develop, not only to curb and control our jerkism, but to eradicate our masochistic attitudes and practices. Paul's advice in Romans 12:3 was not to think of ourselves more highly than we ought to think, but to think soberly, that is, with sound judgment, realizing that God has made each one of us different and has given each of us different abilities, talents, and characteristics.

In *Building Your Self-Image,* another excellent book on developing a healthy self-concept, Josh McDowell puts it well when he says: "A healthy self-image is seeing yourself as God sees you—*no more and no less.*"[9]

How Does God See Us?

Whenever two people meet for the first time, six people actually meet: the two people as they see each other, the two people as they see themselves, and the two people as God

sees them. Now if we really wanted to know the truth about
what those two people are like inside and out—their conscious and unconscious motives, and their true value and
significance as human beings—whose view would you
choose?

It's no contest! I'd take God's opinion for sure, because
God is omniscient! He sees us as we really are. And since He
created us, He's the only One who knows completely how
important we really are. All the case studies in this book
prove how poorly we as humans understand ourselves and
each other. Abused kids think they are trash. Adult children
of alcoholics marry other alcoholics, thinking they are making wise choices. Eighty-five percent of us marry someone
who on psychological testing would be very similar to our
parent of the opposite sex, yet we think we are in conscious
control of that decision.

Who are we trying to kid? God's opinion of us and our
value can only be accurately determined by Him. So let's
take a look at what God says about you and me in Psalm 139.

> *O LORD, You have searched me and known me.*

God wouldn't waste His time searching us (examining the
very thoughts and intents of our hearts) in order to know
everything about us if we weren't pretty significant, right?

> *You know my sitting down and my rising up;*
> *You understand my thought afar off.*

Wow! We are so important to God that He is paying attention to us every time we sit down or get up! He even looks
down at us from heaven and reads our thoughts! I don't
know about you, but I'd rather not have Him read *my*
thoughts. If He did, how could He possibly still love me and
think I'm worth something?

> *You comprehend my path and my lying down,*
> *And are acquainted with all my ways.*

Now I know we're in trouble. He is fully acquainted with every bit of our co-dependent jerkism and masochism. If I were God, I'd reject you *and* me, for sure!

> *For there is not a word on my tongue,*
> *But behold, O LORD, You know it altogether.*

Whatever happened to the First Amendment? God reads our thoughts, studies our behaviors, and now He even listens in on our private conversations. It all sounds pretty scary to me!

> *You have hedged me behind and before,*
> *And laid Your hand upon me.*
> *Such knowledge is too wonderful for me;*
> *It is high, I cannot attain it.*

Wait a minute. That doesn't sound like Big Brother. It sounds as if God has us surrounded by His presence, and since God is love, we are surrounded by love. But I have to agree with the psalmist, it is all way beyond me. I can't explain it, and while I appreciate it, I'm still a little frightened by it all. But what's this the psalmist is saying next? It sounds as if he'd like to get away from God. I know how he feels. There are times when I'd like to get away too:

> *Where can I go from Your Spirit?*
> *Or where can I flee from Your presence?*
> *If I ascend into heaven, You are there;*
> *If I make my bed in hell, behold, You are there;*
> *If I take the wings of the morning,*
> *And dwell in the uttermost parts of the sea,*
> *Even there Your hand shall lead me,*
> *And Your right hand shall hold me.*

It doesn't matter where we are—at the heights of spiritual ecstasy because we have really connected with God, or in a hell of our own making because of our jerkism or masochism—He's still there with us. We are so important to Him that He never lets us out of His loving sight. And while one hand holds us, His other hand guides us into the secrets of a meaningful life.

> *For You have formed my inward parts;*
> *You have covered me in my mother's womb.*
> *I will praise You, for I am fearfully and wonderfully*
>   *made;*
> *Marvelous are Your works,*
> *And that my soul knows very well.*

Amazing! God made us so wonderfully complex that our very bodies are a testimony to how valuable we are. The next time I have an identity crisis and wonder who I am, I can always say: "I am fearfully and wonderfully made—and *God don't make no junk!*" To sum it all up:

> *How precious also are Your thoughts to me, O God!*
> *How great is the sum of them!*
> *If I should count them, they would be more in number*
>   *than the sand;*
> *When I awake, I am still with You.*

I must say, I'm a bit embarrassed. For a moment there, I actually doubted God's love for me and for you, but take a look at what He's saying right here. *The Living Bible* puts these verses this way: "How precious it is, Lord, to realize you are thinking about me constantly! I can't even count how many times a day your thoughts turn towards me. And when I waken in the morning, you are still thinking of me!"[10]

The bottom line is that God thinks about you and me so many times a day, we can't even count them. His thoughts of us are like grains of sand on the seashores of the world! Do you still have even the slightest doubt that you are immensely significant in God's sight?

> *Oh, that You would slay the wicked, O God!*
> *Depart from me, therefore, you bloodthirsty men.*

For they speak against You wickedly;
Your enemies take Your name in vain.
Do I not hate them, O LORD, who hate You?
And do I not loathe those who rise up against You?
I hate them with perfect hatred;
I count them my enemies.

Hmmm, I thought I was writing the first book in history on how to deal with the predatory jerks of this world! But right here God is inspiring the psalmist to say some awfully heavy things about jerks who refuse to repent of their jerkiness, who use God's Name in vain, who destroy people, who make fun of spiritual things, who habitually and willfully sin against God.

Isn't it odd that right in the middle of some of the most beautiful and poetic verses in the whole Bible, which tell us how much God loves us and is so intimately involved in our lives, He inspires King David to write a warning against co-dependency with the sociopathic jerks of this world? Have you ever wondered why God did that? Could this be just one more strong piece of proof that He loves us? Could it be that He wants us to protect ourselves from being hurt by jerks, and the best way to do that is to literally loathe what they do and avoid being influenced by them as much as possible?

Search me, O God, and know my heart;
Try me, and know my anxieties;
And see if there is any wicked way in me,
And lead me in the way everlasting.

As he closed Psalm 139, King David asked God to reveal to him his own unconscious, innermost thoughts, feelings, and motives. Not only that, but David wanted God to point out his jerky behavior, not to put him on a guilt trip, but in order to help him learn to think, walk, and talk the way God Himself thinks, walks, and talks.

While David was still a young boy, God called him "a man after His own heart" who would replace King Saul, who had proved he was not such a man.[11] God called David a man after his own heart many years before he would sin terribly by committing adultery with Bathsheba and murdering her husband, Uriah, to keep it quiet. What counts, however, is not perfect performance, but a willing heart.

David repented. He admitted his faults publicly and apologized to God in prayer and in writing. In Psalm 51, David uses himself as an example of a repentant Nth-Degree Jerk who wants to grow up and become a mature adult. One of the most powerful kings ever to walk on Planet Earth was contrite enough to ask God to forgive him and change him.

King David Learned from His Mistakes

Psalm 139 is comforting, enlightening—even awe inspiring—but it is no magic incantation that will automatically cure a low self-concept. You and I can read Psalm 139 every day for a year, but if we keep feeding ourselves negative messages in our self-talk, we'll still have a poor self-concept and little feelings of self-worth.

In addition, there is always the danger that our "God concept" will drop as well. That's why it's always dangerous to point to certain passages of Scripture and even imply that "all you have to do is read this and everything will be fine." We may read Psalm 139, but our self-concept doesn't seem to get much better. Therefore, we erroneously deduce that God's Word doesn't work.

What does work is what David said at the end of Psalm 139. He invited God to search his heart, to even examine his anxieties to see if there were any wickedness or jerkiness in him anywhere.[12] I believe these verses aptly describe an approach to mental health called "cognitive restructuring," a fancy psychological term for improving your self-talk and learning to look at yourself and others *truthfully and realistically.*

David was willing to be taught, willing to be shown. He wasn't just sitting back waiting for God to "zap him" with the right answers. He wasn't waiting to wake up one morning and suddenly have all of his self-concept problems taken care of. David had an awful lot to answer for, but when he went through personal tragedies, he stopped and asked himself what he could learn from them to become a more mature person.

David probably did not pen the words of Psalm 119:71 (various authors wrote different psalms), but what this passage says applies perfectly to his situation and to ours as well: "It is good for me that I have been afflicted,/That I may learn Your statutes." Jesus' brother James echoed this thought many centuries later: "Consider it pure joy, my brothers, whenever you face trials of many kinds, because you know that the testing of your faith develops perseverance. Perseverance must finish its work so that you may be mature and complete, not lacking anything."[13]

As a psychiatrist, I really believe that over half the emotional pain we humans suffer in life is totally unnecessary. And a lot of this unnecessary pain is caused by our self-talk—the messages we send ourselves in our own thought processes at something like 1,500 words per minute.

How to Cure Your Negative Self-talk

If you have any tendencies toward masochism at all, it's quite likely you may be using negative self-talk on yourself. You may want to try a simple exercise we often recommend to our patients. Take a brief break from reading this book and go find a rubber band. Then put the rubber band on your wrist, where it is to remain for at least twenty-four hours. (If you are a bit embarrassed to go around wearing a rubber band on your wrist and don't want to have to explain to people what you are doing, just wear it under your wristwatch.)

For the next twenty-four hours, listen very closely to your thoughts about yourself (your self-talk). Every time you hear yourself putting yourself down, snap the rubber band on your wrist to condition yourself to be aware of those putdowns.

Over the past fifteen years or so, I have asked literally thousands of patients, seminar attenders, and seminary students to try this experiment. Most people are absolutely shocked when they realize how harshly they talk to themselves. They had no idea how painfully inferior they were making themselves feel until they started snapping and snapping and snapping. I have had seminary students come back to class the next day with black and blue wrists!

I repeat this exercise myself about once a year, with slight improvement each year, but no total cure. I recall putting on my rubber band and, during the following twenty-four-hour period, having to rush over to the seminary to give a lecture. I had been running late as I started out, but as I dashed from the parking lot to the classroom, it looked as if I would make it just in time. Suddenly I realized I had accidentally left my lecture notes back in the car! As I headed back toward the parking lot, I was furious with myself and said so: "You stupid idiot!"

Normally, that typical perfectionist's reaction would have done its damage, but gone largely unnoticed. But I remembered I had my rubber band on, so I snapped myself, and the slight sting reminded me that I was doing the very thing I advised others not to do. My thoughts reminded me that I had made a repeated pledge to be my own best friend. How would I feel if my wife, Jan, or some other good friend walking beside me at that moment had turned to me in a rage and with all sincerity shouted, "You stupid idiot!" I would have been stunned, and yet, here I was tolerating that very kind of verbal abuse from myself.

At that moment, I apologized to myself, and, as I neared the car, I looked around and noticed a rock and a tree stump near the edge of the parking strip. As I got my lecture notes out of the car, I prayed the following brief prayer:

Dear Lord, thank You for correcting my negative self-talk. Thank You that I am not a meaningless rock or tree stump. Neither object can think or feel or experience knowing You. A rock or a tree stump can't love or be loved. Thank You, Lord, for making me in Your image and giving me a loving wife and loving friends. Help me to see myself as You see me and love myself as You love me, in spite of my humanity and my many failures. Amen.

I felt so good about changing my self-talk from rage to positive strokes that I didn't even mind when I walked into the lecture room a few minutes late. After apologizing to the class for being tardy, I changed my whole lecture for that morning to a discussion on maintaining self-worth, and one of my key illustrations was my parking lot experience on the way to class.

One of the key points I made in my lecture was that here I was, a so-called expert who should have all this self-talk figured out, but I still needed to snap my own rubber band now and then to remind me of the tremendous power of my own thoughts. We must work on our self-talk the rest of our lives so we won't slip back into believing lies about ourselves.

I also emphasized, however, that improving our self-talk doesn't mean that we lie to ourselves about our sins and shortcomings. For example, if I were habitually late for appointments because I forgot my notes or just forgot what time it was, I would need to deal with myself, but I could still do it firmly but lovingly. Positive self-talk means that I quit looking at myself in black and white terms, alternating between thinking I'm all bad and should just give up, or that I am all good, which would fill me with false pride. It isn't a case of black and white. Because I am a typical human being, I fall into the gray, and that's okay. Jesus loves me anyway!

For Me, the Rat Race Is Over

Understanding this has done a great deal to help me step out of the rat race for significance that I ran in daily until I was well into my thirties. I'm still tempted to get back into the race now and then, but meditating on Psalm 139 regularly and doing the rubber band exercise at least once a year has helped immensely. For me, becoming my own best friend has meant developing new healthy experiences free of masochism or jerkiness.

For example, I've taken up golf as a spare time hobby in recent years. While I never was much of an athlete, I've taken a few lessons and learned how to hit a drive over three hundred yards. It's kind of heady stuff to drive the green on a three hundred-yard hole and then say to the foursome playing ahead of you, "Sorry, I didn't mean to come that close."

Unfortunately, however, the rest of my game isn't as impressive as my three hundred-yard drives (which don't always go where I want them to, by the way). I don't curse or throw my clubs when I hit a shot into the woods or the lake. Instead, I enjoy the companionship of friends, appreciate God's beautiful creation, and take time to smell the fairways. I don't use my golf score to reflect my own self-worth.

At play or at work, with strangers or with friends, I try to make my life a celebration of who God has made me, with no strings or garbage from the past attached!

Running the rat race for significance automatically forces you into being phony, insecure, and masochistic. You have to project an image that isn't real, and, ironically, you must base your self-worth on how others react to the phony image you are projecting. You automatically place your Certificate of Worth in the pockets of others.

The alternative is to base your worth on God's opinion of you (review Ps. 139), become your own best friend, and place your Certificate of Worth in your *own* pocket. Then you are able to quit the rat race for significance because you finally realize how insignificant it really is. You are free to become yourself instead of projecting a phony image. You are able to bond to the friends who see you as you really are and love you anyway.

Before going on, you might want to go back right now and review the masochism test in Chapter 5 to test your resolve to become your own best friend. If you truly have decided to become your own best friend, you should score quite a few points lower than you did the first time you took the test.

In addition, the same statement of self-worth that you were asked to fill out earlier in this chapter reappears below. This time, however, it is filled in with positive, healthy declarations. Read it carefully and then, as a symbol of your desire to take a crucial step toward maturity, sign your name.

My Statement of Self-worth

From this day forward, I will base my self-worth on *what God says about my worth to Him.* I will place this Certificate of Self-worth *in my own pocket* rather than in the pockets of others because I know *my best human friend is me,* and that my estimated net worth as a human being is *eternally beyond human comprehension.*

Signed: _____

CHAPTER
11

Moving on Toward Maturity

STEP SIX: Be Accountable All Your Life

So far, we have covered five of the six steps out of jerkism/masochism into maturity.

Step One encouraged us to take a look deep inside at our jerk within, particularly the defense mechanisms we use to deceive ourselves, avoid anxiety, and preserve our sagging self-esteem.

Step Two directed us to examine our family system and the role we played in that system. In addition, we were to analyze the parental injunctions taught to us all our lives by our parents, which may still deeply influence our thinking.

Step Three urged us to break the addiction cycle and grieve out the pain we feel because of our jerkiness/masochism.

Step Four suggested that we deal with the "nuclear reactor" that is within all of us—our anger—and learn how to forgive.

Step Five instructed us in how to be our own best friend, by gaining a healthy self-concept.

In these five steps lie the keys to ridding ourselves of jerky behavior and/or masochistic tendencies (continually falling into situations where we are abused by jerks). But these five steps are not enough. Just when we think we are "standing tall," we may fall back into our old patterns and habits. Psychology and psychiatry call this "regression"; the Bible calls it "backsliding." They are one and the same. That's why we need *Step Six:*

> *Develop a lifetime maintenance program that makes you accountable to significant caring others and helps you periodically reevaluate your maturity level and rate of growth toward greater maturity.*

We All Need to Be Accountable to Someone

I have vowed that I would never join a church whose pastor was not accountable to his elder board and congregation, no matter how mature and talented that pastor might be. I don't trust *any* unaccountable human being. There's too much jerkiness in each of us.

That means I don't trust an unaccountable *me* either. I have lots of good intentions. I would love to make use of my God-given talents to help as many of my brothers and sisters as possible. I would love to be a great dad and husband, a perfect, loving friend, and to die of old age, realizing I had lived one hundred years without any failures.

But that's only a fantasy. I've already failed in many ways, and I will fail again. There have been periods in my life when I tried to be "super-mature" totally on my own strength, and I fell flat on my face. At other times, I would go to the other extreme and wait around for God to make me super-mature without any effort on my part. That, of course, was "super-spiritual laziness" and, again, I fell flat on my face.

Nowadays, I try to practice the apostle Paul's advice and "do all things *through Christ* who strengthens me" (italics mine).[1] That is, I try to strike a balance between my human responsibility and an acknowledgment of my powerlessness without God's help.

Do I still fall flat on my face? Sometimes, because I'm still human and still not totally mature. When I do foul up, I follow the advice of the apostle James who said: "Confess your trespasses to one another."[2] *Sparing no area of trespassing,* I hold myself accountable to my wife and a few close friends. In particular, I have one "accountability buddy," a fellow psychiatrist, who lives at the other end of the country. Every week we get on the phone to share our successes and joys, but also to confess our faults and failures (i.e., our sins), as well as to pray for each other.

In fact, I've become so used to confessing my faults that I often make my radio producers wince as I admit my shortcomings to two million people during our Minirth-Meier Clinic broadcasts. It would be beneficial for all of us to share nearly all our faults, if all of us did it consistently, but there are still a lot of folks out there who don't realize they have any!

While I still fall flat on my face sometimes, I'm encouraged because I can see that I'm definitely less of a jerk than I used to be. It feels very good to be moving in the right direction. I take comfort in King Solomon's words: "though a righteous man falls seven times, he rises again."[3] I also like *The Living Bible* paraphrase of another proverb by King Solomon: "Don't go to war without wise guidance; there is safety in many counselors."[4]

I realize that I am definitely at war with my jerk within and I'll never conquer him, much less control him, by depending only on my own wisdom, strength, or righteousness. King Solomon knew this, perhaps better than any man. Read the book of Proverbs, written for the most part by King Solomon, and you'll see that he was very vulnerable, willing to admit his own jerk behavior and attitudes, as well as his own struggle with the meaninglessness of life. Solomon knew the value of living for and depending on God, and His counsel has never been equaled:

> Trust in the LORD with all your heart,
> And lean not on your own understanding;

> In all your ways acknowledge Him,
> And He shall direct your paths.[5]

Unfortunately, Solomon didn't always trust his own advice. He wallowed around in a lot of Second-Degree Jerk behavior most of his life, and he paid a dear price. I don't want to wind up as Solomon did. As I struggle with my own jerkiness, that struggle seems to decrease by 50 percent the moment I share it with Jan or one of my close male friends. Their empathy, their love, and their own vulnerability encourage and strengthen me, and so does their forgiveness when I admit my failures.

Develop Your Own Accountability System

As you work on your own maturity, you will want to consider having your own accountability system or network. Because each of us is unique, there is no set approach to being accountable that fits everyone. I encourage you to come up with your own plan for being accountable by getting input from mature friends and "counselors" who know you best—your mate, your pastor, and close friends.

For example, if you are an alcoholic, an Alcoholics Anonymous group would be a logical part of your accountability plan. There are also special programs for overeaters, gamblers, workaholics, co-dependents, adult children of abuse, sex addicts, and almost any other kind of addiction-related problem.

If at all possible, try to get in a support group sponsored by your local church. Unfortunately, few churches offer a wide variety of such support groups, and before joining any chapter of any group not affiliated with your church, you may have to check it out by making one or two trial visits to be sure you are comfortable with all theological viewpoints presented.

It's quite possible that you may need some therapy—short-term or long-term. People who suffer from severe chronic problems, such as bi-polar disorders and schizophrenia, probably need to stay accountable to a professional therapist for life. Many others, however, need only short-term therapy, lasting a few months or possibly a few years.

In most cases, one of the chief goals of psychotherapy is to reach a point where professional help is no longer needed in the individual's accountability system. Beware of psychiatrists and psychologists who foster their own insecurities by attempting to keep you dependent on them (and fatten their own pocketbook at the same time). Most of the psychiatrists and psychologists I have known are very conscientious, but there are jerks in every profession.

If reading this book has revealed to you that you may be a high level masochist (jerkaholic) or that you have other addiction problems, you may need as much as one to three years of therapy, followed by lifelong accountability to a good support system. In my own case, I have received professional therapy for myself and my family, which has greatly facilitated my growth and theirs. I continue to see a wise therapist periodically.

Maturity Is a Lifelong Pursuit

Being accountable is a critical part of my lifelong maintenance program, which is aimed at my emotional and spiritual development. By the word *maintenance* I don't mean that one reaches a particular level of emotional or spiritual growth and then stays there. Such an existence would be boring and life would become stagnant. The best way to travel this road toward maturity is to realize that you will *never arrive*. That is, you will never reach *total* maturity in this life.

As you seek to move to maturity, maintenance means choosing to remain your own best friend as you *maintain a course of overall progress*. You seek to continue to grow, to continue to gain insights. You learn from your daily experiences as you continue to fill your vacuums (the holes in your soul). Every day you see that you are less insecure, less in need of running the personal rat race for significance.

Our records at Minirth-Meier Clinics show that among

people who go on a crash diet and successfully lose their excess weight, thirty-five out of thirty-six will regain most or all of that weight within one year, if they don't resolve the root problems driving their food addictions, and then commit to lifelong accountability of some sort. The human denial system is strong. Negative self-talk can pull us back to the failure patterns of our past. Maintenance is a *must*, whether you are recovering from food addiction, alcoholism, workaholism, jerkiness, or masochism.

Your lifetime commitment to maintenance is your decision to be as "unjerky" and as "unaddicted" to jerks as you can. No, you can't be perfect, but you can be increasingly better at it with each passing year. The following are some helpful suggestions for developing your own lifetime maintenance plan.

1. *Recycling Through the First Five Steps*

When you work your way through Steps One through Five for the first time, it may take anywhere from a week to several months or longer, depending on a host of factors. The second time through should take only a fraction of what it took the first time. As you review the plan annually, it should take only about one day each year. Like a ship's captain checking his course, go over the first six steps, using the following questions as a guide.

Step One:
1. As I continue monitoring my jerk within, I see the following defense mechanisms as areas I must work on: _____

_____

_____

Step Two:
2. Have I completed leaving home psychologically? Negative parental injunctions that may still influence or control

me are: _____

_____

_____

Positive parental injunctions that I am adopting as my own
values and practices are: _____

_____

3. On a scale of 1 to 10, have I left home psychologically
on a total basis (10), hardly at all (1), or somewhere in between? _____

Step Three:
4. Are there still any addiction cycles in my life that I need
to break? _____

_____

5. What messages am I still hearing from the past that
cause false guilt, which leads to low self-esteem, emotional
pain, and an addictive agent? _____

_____

6. If I do have an addiction, particularly to jerks, what is
the fallout (the price I'm having to pay)? _____

_____

7. Which of my values am I still violating and why?_____

_____

8. Remnants of emotional pain that I may still need to
grieve out of my life include: _____

_____

Step Four:

9. On a scale of 1 to 10, is admitting that I am angry no problem (10), a major roadblock (1), or somewhere in between? _____

10. On a scale of 1 to 10, is dealing with anger no problem (10), one of my worst failures (1), or somewhere in between? _____

11. During the past year, has my ability to "forgive seventy times seven" improved, remained the same, or declined? _____

Step Five:

12. During the past year, has my sense of self-worth risen or dropped? _____ Reasons for this rise or fall are:

_____

13. During the past year have I been my own best friend? What specific behaviors or thought processes give me evidence that I am becoming my own best friend? _____

_____

I like to recycle through the plan annually between Christmas and New Year's Day. The Christmas season gets me more in the spirit to bond with God and loved ones, and I like to start each new year with the feeling of a fresh start. As I recycle through the plan, I forgive myself for jerky attitudes and behaviors I've shown through the past year. At the same time, I pat myself on the back because each year I seem to be a little less jerky than the year before, and less abused by jerks as well.

I do not, however, make New Year's resolutions, because I tend to get a little idealistic on New Year's Eve and make promises to myself and others I couldn't possibly keep. So now I just assess, pray, hope, and acknowledge my failures and successes, as the apostle Paul instructs us in Galatians 6:4–5:

> Each one should test his own actions. Then he can take pride in himself, without comparing himself to somebody else, for each one should carry his own load. (NIV)

When my successes outweigh my failures, I take legitimate pride in making some overall progress through cooperating with God and others in the lifelong process of becoming more mature.

2. *Meditate Daily on Scripture*

In my personal and professional opinion, Scripture meditation is the most important behavior anyone can do for the well-being of his or her body, soul, and spirit. In 1985, I wrote a short book entitled *Meditating for Success*, which summarizes the many medical, psychological, and spiritual benefits of meditation. Body, mind, and spirit work closely together, and research shows that it is possible to literally lower your blood pressure through meditating.

I strongly recommend, however, that you avoid non-Christian meditation practices, which guide you into the passive repeating of "mantras" and even calling on "spirit guides" for help. If you tend to have masochistic tendencies already, non-Christian meditation practices set you up for more and more masochism and future susceptibility to jerk abuse. If you are battling stubborn traits of jerkiness, the self-centered aspect of non-Christian meditation can make you more jerky and narcissistic.

Instead, I strongly recommend meditation on the Bible, because it is God's love letter to us. Meditating on Scripture will help you move *away* from inborn, narcissistic thinking *toward* Christlike thoughts and attitudes. It's like seeing God daily for therapy.

There are numerous ways to meditate on Scripture. Currently, I use audio cassette tapes of the *New King James Version* of the Bible, narrated by Cliff Barrows of the Billy Graham team.⁶ I listen daily, even in my car. I hear the whole Bible every few months that way, and whenever a verse really stands out and convicts or encourages me, I write it out on a 3″ x 5″ card! I carry these cards almost everywhere I go, memorizing the verses and then meditating on them.

To meditate means to "chew the cud." I like to sit in my easy chair or in other serene places, such as a secluded beach, and meditate (chew on) a scriptural phrase for twenty to thirty minutes as I focus on behavioral changes I can make to fit the principles God expresses to me in this passage. My life has been influenced, and my entire attitude and direction have been changed many times from meditating on such passages as:

"The deceitfulness of riches" (Mark 4:18–22).

"The Golden Rule" (Matt. 7:12).

Jesus' words, "My yoke is easy and My burden is light" (Matt. 11:30).

I could name dozens of other passages, not to mention hundreds of behavioral instructions and directives in the book of Proverbs, all of which have deeply affected my life.

Scripture meditation is the most positive habit I have. I spend many hours per week listening, writing, memorizing, and meditating. I also pray for God's guidance and insights. If I skip this practice more than one or two days in a row, I practically go into withdrawal and start feeling as if my best friend just moved away. If I were ever forced to spend the rest of my days on a desert island or in a concentration camp, I could survive with my Bible and my Dallas Seminary *Bible Knowledge Commentary.*

3. *Constantly Evaluate Your Self-talk*

Self-talk, the messages we send ourselves in our thoughts at around 1,500 words per minute, was discussed at length in Chapter 10. It would be a good idea to reevaluate your self-talk at least once a year but probably quite a bit more often than that. If perfectionism is a problem for you at all and you have any tendencies to put yourself down, you may need to consider reevaluating your self-talk at least once a month.

One of the best and simplest procedures for evaluating self-talk I know is the rubber band technique described in Chapter 10. Every time you put yourself down, snap that rubber band on your wrist to condition yourself to be aware of those put-downs. I have seen patients make tremendous progress in improving their self-talk by using this simple device.

Also, meditating on Scripture, discussed above, is one of the very best ways you can improve your self-talk.

4. *Monitor Your Progress Toward Maturity*

Earlier chapters contain tests and other devices to measure jerkiness and/or masochistic tendencies. Following is a test to measure how you are coming in your quest to become a mature adult.

When you take the maturity test for the first time, record the date and your score on p. 232. Then, within six months to a year, take the test again to see if you have made any improvement. Be aware that it's quite possible to sometimes regress in certain areas. Perfect maturity doesn't happen until we get to heaven. In the meantime, however, there is plenty we can do to conquer the jerk within by laying aside every weight and running the race toward maturity that has been set before us.[7]

As you take this maturity test, rate the following statements from 0 to 3, with 0 meaning "never," 1 meaning "sometimes," 2 meaning "usually," and 3 meaning "nearly always."

The Minirth-Meier
Maturity Test

I. Relational Maturity

_____ 1. I assertively but lovingly influence social situations without controlling them.

_____ 2. I assertively give my opinion on which restaurant our group may enjoy going to, but I happily go along with the majority opinion even if I don't particularly care about that kind of food.

_____ 3. I am able to appreciate the compliments of others and to say "thank you" when complimented.

_____ 4. I avoid bragging about my possessions, ability, or accomplishments.

_____ 5. When someone offends me, I forgive and do not carry a grudge.

_____ 6. I feel indignation and concern whenever I observe anyone, including myself, being victimized, but I keep my anger under control.

_____ 7. I refuse to spread gossip about anyone.

_____ 8. I refuse to listen to gossip, and I express concern about the effects of the gossip on the reputation of the person under attack.

_____ 9. When corrected for personal faults, I try to gain insight and choose to improve morally in the process.

_____ 10. I recognize the faults or failures in my children and try to help them without being overly authoritarian (too strict) or overly permissive (not strict enough).

_____ 11. I am proud of my children's successes and accomplishments because of the joy it brings to them, not to me.

_____ 12. I avoid pitting authority figures against each other.

_____ 13. I respectfully report any conflicts in which I am involved to authority figures and accept their decisions, unless they insist I do something illegal or immoral.

_____ 14. I have genuine sympathy for the poor, hungry, homeless, widows, orphans, and other human victims, and try to help them in reasonable ways.

_____ 15. I genuinely care about animals and get upset when I see them being abused or victimized.

_____ 16. I enjoy helping and protecting people who have been victimized, even if they are powerless, unpopular, or physically unattractive, and I expect nothing in return for my help.

_____ 17. I despise chauvinism in others and do my best to correct my own behavior if I become aware that I have become engaged in chauvinistic attitudes or actions.

_____ 18. When driving a vehicle, I obey the basic traffic laws of the land and practice the Golden Rule as I stay in the flow of traffic.

_____ 19. When driving a vehicle, I am concerned not only for my own safety but for the safety of others.

_____ 20. I leave for appointments in plenty of time, so I will not keep people waiting or feel rushed myself.

_____ 21. I do not knowingly drive so slowly that I block traffic.

_____ 22. I am trustworthy and dependable.

_____ 23. I tell the truth.

_____ 24. I project an image to others that is genuine.

_____ 25. I put time with my family and family responsibilities ahead of my work schedule or financial gain.

_____ 26. When I am wrong, I admit my faults.

_____ 27. When engaged in athletic events or contests of any kind, I like to win, but it is more important to me that everyone involved has a good time.

_____ 28. When I get in an argument, I am polite and fair, seeking mutual learning and cooperation, not "victory."

II. Sexual Maturity

_____ 29. I see the opposite sex as equal.

_____ 30. I will enter freely and assertively into mature conversation with members of the opposite sex, but will not compete for their time and attention.

_____ 31. I do not flirt with anyone except my own spouse.

_____ 32. I am completely committed to staying married to my mate for life.

_____ 33. During sex with my mate, I do not allow myself to fantasize about others.

_____ 34. During sex with my mate, I seek pleasure for my mate as well as for myself.

_____ 35. I let my mate know what pleases me during sex, but I do not request my mate to do anything my mate may find uncomfortable or unpleasurable.

_____ 36. I refuse to read or view hard or soft porn literature or movies because they degrade and demean women and the sanctity of marriage as well.

III. Stewardship Maturity

_____ 37. Realizing that financial crises can happen to anyone, any time, I try to save at least 10 percent of each paycheck to provide security for my family.

_____ 38. I give gifts to others out of a sense of love and generosity, expecting nothing in return.

_____ 39. When going out to eat with others at a restaurant, I pay for my fair share and leave a generous tip for good service.

_____ 40. When going out to eat with others at a restaurant, I refuse to be taken advantage of by jerks who try to manipulate me into picking up the entire bill.

_____ 41. I am honest in my business dealings, even when there is no risk of getting caught.

_____ 42. Whenever possible, I avoid borrowing money (and that includes credit cards), and I pay back loans as soon as I can, with interest.

_____ 43. I donate as generously as I can to my local church and other accountable, responsible charities, remaining as anonymous as possible, not seeking to impress anyone.

_____ 44. I am generous with our children, but try to avoid spoiling them or fostering their dependency.

IV. Emotional Maturity

_____ 45. I enjoy being part of a team and do not care about who gets the credit.

_____ 46. I truly forgive others for offenses, even if they don't apologize.

_____ 47. When offended or attacked, I refuse to seek revenge.

_____ 48. When feeling anxious or insecure, I pray, meditate on Scripture, and/or seek the counsel of others who may be able to give me insight into my anxiety.

_____ 49. I desire insight into my unconscious motives and ask God to reveal them to me as He sees fit.

_____ 50. I have control over my temper.

_____ 51. I feel genuine guilt if I hurt someone accidentally in word or deed.

_____ 52. When I become aware that I am demanding inappropriate and selfish "rights," I give them up.

_____ 53. I actively resist falling into the typical "rat race" for significance and choose to live instead for the glory of God and for others.

V. Moral Maturity

_____ 54. I feel true guilt for unconfessed sin until I confess it to God and repent (change my mind and choose to avoid that sinful behavior in the future).

_____ 55. After confessing sins and shortcomings to God, I am able to forgive myself for these sins and shortcomings.

_____ 56. I am not ashamed to get pastoral help or therapy.

_____ 57. I expect to pay the going rate for professional therapy or any other product or service I receive, and I pay at the time I receive the service or product.

_____ 58. I consider professional therapy or pastoral counseling during times of need or personal crisis a wonderful opportunity for personal or family growth. I am not too proud to ask for help.

_____ 59. I appreciate it when an honest therapist or pastoral counselor tells me the truth about my negative or selfish behavior and/or attitudes.

VI. Spiritual Maturity

_____ 60. I sincerely desire to serve God, not manipulate Him.

_____ 61. I accept personal responsibility for my own spiritual growth.

_____ 62. I admit my imperfections and resist temptations to be phony.

_____ 63. I attend church to worship God, not to be entertained.

_____ 64. I meditate on biblical principles and how they apply to my life.

_____ 65. I seek spiritual instruction to benefit myself, my family, and others.

TOTAL: _____ Date test taken: _____

Now record the date on which you took the test and add up your total score, not to rate yourself as "immature" or as "arrived," but to measure your rate of progress year after year. Your obvious goal is to score higher every time you take the test. If you get a fairly high score (above 125), perhaps one of your biggest problems could be lying to yourself. Check your answers with someone who knows you well (preferably someone you consider fairly mature) to get another opinion that may challenge or confirm your score.

We Are All on a Journey Toward Maturity

No matter where you score on the Maturity Test, keep in mind that it only marks the point at which you are today on your journey toward maturity. The purpose of this book is to set each of us free not only from being used and abused by the jerks of this world, but also from our own jerk within. This book seeks to free you from masochism (jerkaholism) and jerky behavior (jerkism) in order to learn better how to love and be loved, and to continue to live for others in a mature, healthy, nonmasochistic way.

One of the goals I have set for my own life is to gradually become more and more balanced, experiencing love, joy, peace, and meaning in my life as I dedicate each day to serving God and my fellowman. I want to follow Jesus' instructions for filling all of God's laws by obeying one simple guideline: to love God with all my heart, soul, and mind, and to love my neighbor as myself.[8]

It keeps coming up over and over again, doesn't it? *Bonding with God. Bonding with others. Loving and being loved.*

"Family values" is a lot more than a political catch phrase, but, sadly, the vast majority of mankind pursues significance and phony love in all the wrong places. They ignore the real treasure that is in bonding with God, mate, children, family, and close friends.

Another major goal of this book has been to help you examine the attitudes and traditions that have been passed down to you by your forefathers. Keep in mind that these same attitudes and traditions may be passed along to three or four generations of your descendants. Think about what family traditions (good and bad) that you have picked up automatically. Do you realize that you have the freedom and the power, with God's help, to break the bad traditions? Do you realize that you are not stuck for life with the personality your parents built into you?

You have the freedom and power to make new decisions about who you will become. You can, with God's help, choose your own dream of what you would like to be like. In psychiatry we call this a personal "ego ideal." As you optimistically but realistically pursue your ego ideal—the person you'd like to be—you can be a personality in transition. You can get rid of excess baggage (and garbage) that you picked up along life's way.

As I have pursued my own ego ideal, I have set three simple daily goals, which I believe sum up what the preacher of Ecclesiastes describes as the whole duty of man—fearing God and keeping His commandments.[9] My three daily goals are:

Goal #1: Become More Like Jesus

As a psychiatrist and as a recovering masochist and First-Degree Jerk striving to become more mature, my first goal is to become more like the One who towers over every other human being who has ever walked this planet.

Jesus, the God-man, was the essence and epitome of maturity. In fact, I believe that Jesus was the only totally mature person who ever lived. The first and major cornerstone of my ego ideal is to be like Him.

But in order to be like Him, I need to know Him through faith, and so do you. I often describe faith this way:

Right now as I am writing these paragraphs I am sitting in a chair. As you read these paragraphs, you are probably sitting in a chair also (if you aren't, please take a seat in a chair and join me in my experiment).

Now, as you are sitting in your chair, lift your legs and feet off the floor, putting your faith *completely* in the chair to hold you up. Because you are not omniscient, you can't be sure that the chair won't break; nonetheless, you are putting your imperfect faith in the chair and depending on it to hold you up. In the same way, you can put your faith in Jesus and make Him your Savior and Lord. You can believe that Jesus was God in the flesh, who died on the cross to pay for all of humankind's jerky behavior (including yours and mine), and then rose from the grave to conquer death.

The apostle Paul tells us in Ephesians 2:8–9, "For by grace you have been saved through faith, and that not of yourselves; it is the gift of God, not of works, lest anyone should boast."

When you sit on the chair, you get a "free gift" of support. In the same way, when you depend on Jesus, you are getting the free gift of eternal life. There is no work you can do. It is all a matter of faith. Just as you depend on the chair for support, depend on Jesus Christ for your salvation, and, if you have never done so before, tell Him *right now* that you are depending on Him to forgive all your past, present, and future sins and to give you eternal life.

Goal #2: Seek First the Kingdom of God

In His Sermon on the Mount, Jesus spoke again and again about quitting the rat race and joining His kingdom instead. His invitation to seek first the kingdom of God and His righteousness was one of the greatest invitations ever extended to humankind, yet most people rejected Him then and most continue to reject Him now. The lure of sex, power, and money is just too great. The black hole of inferiority and the desperate need to be significant is too strong.

Ironically, as people live for sex, power, and money, they chase the wind while true feelings of significance remain always out of reach. What is one of the chief complaints about life today? It's the same complaint the writer of Ecclesiastes voiced thousands of years ago: "Life is meaningless."[10]

Ironically, it is only when we give up sex, power, and money, and dedicate our lives to serving God's kingdom and bonding to His people that He gives us back these very things, but in a much different way.

You can have an excellent sex life with your mate, as you learn how to bond to your mate through communicating and resolving conflicts.

You can have power to overcome your jerkiness and masochistic addictions and live for things that count. Real power lies within; it isn't bestowed from without. Real power lies in the gifts God has given us, and we wield that power as we yield those gifts to Him.

And I believe you can have money, not necessarily great wealth, but material blessings. As I write this chapter, our country has just experienced a prolonged recession. Many people have been out of work, in debt, and have even lost their homes. I still believe, however, that the biblical principle holds true: When we seek first the kingdom of God and His righteousness, all the things we really need will come. Not necessarily right away, but they will come to those who have faith and patience.

At the other end of the spectrum, you may be one who is doing well financially; you may even have substantial wealth. Scripture tells you not to live for your wealth, but not to feel guilty about it either, because that would be masochism. As the preacher said: "For every man to whom God has given riches and wealth, and given him power to eat of it, to receive his heritage and rejoice in his labor—this is the gift of God."[11]

Goal #3: To Live One Day at a Time

My third goal centers on banishing worry and anxiety from my life. Worry about the past or the future is not only useless, but dangerous as well. As a physician, I can assure you that worry will ruin your health and shorten your life. Worry is likely to cause cardiovascular problems, including hardening of the arteries, which can also cause loss of brain cells at a much earlier age. The stress and anxiety that are part of worry can also cause migraine headaches, strokes, and heart attacks, not to mention lowering your resistance to all illnesses. I'm not saying that people don't have problems. I'm not claiming that I have no problems, but I like William Barclay's words when he says:

> The lesson of life is that somehow we have been en-
> abled to bear the unbearable and to do the undoable
> and to pass the breaking-point and not to break. The
> lesson of life is that worry is unnecessary.[12]

Jesus told us plainly that we are to be concerned not with yesterday or with tomorrow, but today. Immediately after He told His followers to seek first the Kingdom of God, He added: "Therefore do not worry about tomorrow, for tomorrow will worry about its own things. Sufficient for the day is its own trouble."[13]

Some Final Thoughts on the Rat Race

When Jan and I were newlywed idealistic perfectionists, we would wake up in the morning and make a list of at least twenty things we felt compelled to get done that day. By the end of most days, we might get eighteen or nineteen of them done, then fall into bed exhausted and frustrated because we *failed* to cover the whole list! Now, as recovering masochist-perfectionists, we get up in the morning, put four things on our lists, and are more than happy and satisfied that night if we get three of them done and at least two of the three were done right! We actually accomplish more worthwhile things now than we did when we were in our daily frenzy.

Is your glass half-empty or half-full? Your perspective has everything to do with it. Maybe the words I have printed on the inside cover of my daily calendar in large letters say it as well as anything:

RELATIONSHIPS ARE MORE IMPORTANT THAN THE RAT RACE!

Far too many human beings on this planet spend their lives competing in a very short, meaningless rat race. It's just too tempting to pour your time, energy, and money into proving that you are somebody (to try to fill that deep-down hole in your soul that says "you're nobody"). It is all too easy to fall into traps such as illicit sex and any number of other addictions, such as food or drugs.

In the rat race, it takes little effort to get caught up in power struggles (control issues). Oh, yes, let's not forget materialism, which sings its siren song twenty-four hours a day through every available medium.

But none of these things work, and there is one very good reason why: *You always need more.*

The solution, then, is to *need less and still be happy.* A billion-dollar treasure is waiting for you if only you are willing to bond with God, your mate, your children, your friends. The solution starts with trusting Jesus to forgive and save you, and then dedicating the rest of your life to active membership in His kingdom.

In his Gospel, Luke includes a parable Jesus told about a man who gave a great supper and invited many to attend. But when he sent out his servant to tell all those who were invited to come, they all began making excuses. So the host sent his servant out into the streets and alleyways to bring in the poor, the maimed, the lame, and the blind—anyone who would like to come in so that the master's house would be filled. (Luke 14:16–21)

While the primary interpretation of this parable concerns God's free invitation to all to come to Him for salvation, I believe it has much to say to all of us who want to learn how to survive and succeed in a world of jerks. Bonding with God is the first step, and beyond that we have the invitation and opportunity to bond with fellow members of the human race. Then we will feast on mature relationships that are free of jerkiness and masochism. Supper is ready. The table is set. *Bon appetit!*

The Masochist Manifesto

1. I am tired of pain. I'm sometimes in intense pain that I feel deep within. Pain of bitterness. Pain from being abused, neglected, lied about, and lied to. Pain from feeling alone and abandoned. Pain from a deep sense of loneliness, of insignificance. Pain from shame, guilt, and self-rejection. Pain from failures in spite of good intentions. And, oh, yes, pain from buried rage toward God because He hasn't come through for me in the ways that I asked Him.
2. I admit I cannot overcome my jerkiness/masochism in my own strength. I need help—from other people, and, above all, from God. In particular, I want to know my heavenly Father better—who He really is and what He really will and won't do for me.
3. I will endeavor to share my journey to maturity with at least one significant other—my spouse, my pastor, a good friend, a counselor, or, if necessary, a therapist. I need the objective insights that are only available from someone else who is willing to love me unconditionally.
4. My ultimate goal is to become a mature, functioning adult, whose self-worth is not dependent on what others think, someone who is not defensive and angry from being so tired of getting "jerked around." I want to learn how to deal with the jerks without who want to take advantage of me, but at the same time treat them with respect and loving-kindness and, perhaps, put them on a journey to maturity as well. And I also want to deal with my jerk within, keeping him on a tight, but loving, leash.

_____

Signed

APPENDIX

Thirty-Two Other
Defense Mechanisms

Chapter 6 focuses on eight of the more common defense mechanisms seen in counseling. Following are thirty-two others, any of which the human mind has devised to avoid facing the truth.

Acting Out: A person is unaware of his unacceptable urges (such as craving the affection of a frequently absent parent of the opposite sex) and "acts out" these urges by being sexually promiscuous or engaging in compulsive stealing.

Aim inhibition: Individuals deceive themselves about their true desires and instead accept partial or modified fulfillment of their true desires. Also called "substitution"; for example, a woman who is able to have children and desires to be a mother does not try to become pregnant because she feels ambivalent for various reasons. Instead, she becomes a school teacher without realizing her unconscious motives; through being a teacher she has contact with children and unconsciously fulfills her desire for motherhood.

Blocking: Individuals "lose their train of thought" in the middle of a sentence and when they try to consciously regain the thought, different ideas crop up, which are unrelated to the original sentence, and they begin talking about an unrelated subject less threatening to their ego.

For example, a young man who has strong, unresolved conflicts with his mother is talking to a friend about mothers, in general, and completely loses his train of thought right in the middle of a sentence.

Compartmentalization: Individuals unconsciously experience their attitudes as though they were unconnected and unrelated—in separate compartments of their brains—to hide from their conscious awareness of the conflicts between their real unacceptable feelings and motives and their idealized feelings and motives.

For example, a woman has strong repressed rage toward her father, who sexually abused her when she was a child. She has, however, compartmentalized her feelings in her brain so thoroughly that she convinces herself that she is a nearly perfect example of a "loving daughter" who has no anger toward her father at all. In addition, she has repressed only that part of her childhood involving her father's sexual abuse. This enables her to idealize her abusive father by compartmentalizing the memories of his abuse totally out of her awareness; thus she is able to see him erroneously as a truly wonderful dad, totally denying his jerkiness.

While watching a television program in which a father abuses his daughter, she develops a panic attack. Because the program is distasteful to her, she switches channels but still has no insight into the cause of the panic attack and blames it on a physical problem instead.

Compensation: Individuals attempt to make up for real or imagined personal deficiencies in physique, performance, talents, or psychological attributes. "Compensating" can become a healthy process, *if it is done consciously and with proper motives.* When used as a defense mechanism, however, compensation is an unconscious striving to make up for inferiority feelings resulting from lack of acceptance of the way God made us.

Complex formation: A certain environmental stimulus threatens to bring into conscious awareness a flood of other memories that caused a similar emotional response in the past—memories that have been repressed and kept deep in the unconscious. For example, a young woman has anxiety any time she sees a black cat, but she has no idea why. The reason is that she has forgotten (repressed) the memory of being jumped on and bitten by a large black *dog* as a small child.

In addition, she has repressed other childhood memories of traumatic events, such as the time she saw someone die in an auto accident and experienced feelings of fear, grief, and being out of control, just as she felt when the dog bit her. When she sees a black cat, it reminds her of the black dog, which triggers memories of her other traumatic experiences, thus producing her feelings of anxiety.

Condensation: Individuals react to a single word, phrase, or idea with all of the emotions that they unconsciously associate with a complex group of ideas. When a catchy advertising slogan doubles the sale of a product, it is often because condensation is at work in a large number of people who are hearing or seeing the slogan.

Controlling: Insecure individuals who are relatively unaware of their severe feelings of powerlessness (and inadequacy to perform up to their superego's standards), develop strong urges to think for and control other individuals, thus causing themselves to feel more powerful. It is common for a controlling person to marry a passive, pleasing, overly dependent person in order to feel more powerful and secure.

Defensive devaluation: Individuals are continually critical of others to convince themselves that they are better than others. Related to Phariseeism and projection, both discussed in Chapter 6.

Delusional projection: The more severe, psychotic version of primary projection, which was discussed in Chapter 6. An individual becomes so paranoid and fearful of his own feelings (anger or lust, for example) that he projects those feelings onto someone else and then convinces himself that the other person actually has those feelings and is plotting to harm him in some serious or even terrible way.

Dissociation: Individuals dissociate or detach emotional significance from an idea, situation, or object. For example, a youth director is strong on emphasizing sexual purity to his group of teenagers, but is unconsciously seductive with girls in the group as he dissociates his sexual feelings from his actions—and remains unaware that he is being a hypocrite.

Distortion: Individuals grossly reshape external reality to suit their own inner needs, often suffering delusions, such as "voices from God." For example, a young man is flunking out of law school, but he convinces himself he will soon become student body president, because God has told him, perhaps even in an "audible voice," that He wants him to be a Supreme Court justice someday, even though he has no law degree.

Externalization: Individuals with a weak ego experience their inner thought processes and feelings as if they were occurring outside themselves. They go through life experiencing themselves in and through others vicariously. Their idealized self is also externalized so that their identity becomes intertwined with another individual, usually of the same sex, who is perceived temporarily as an "ideal" companion. Externalization can even lead to homosexual behavior as a result of severe inferiority feelings and the idealization of a same sex friend.

Hypochondriasis: Individuals convince themselves that they are physically ill when they really aren't, or else exaggerate in their own minds the severity of the illness they actually do have. A common term for someone using this defense mechanism is *hypochondriac.*

Hysterical (histrionic) conversion reaction: Unacceptable feelings (such as anger) or motives (such as vengeance) result in symbolic loss of function of a part of the body innervated by sensory or motor nerves.

For example, one of my patients was a college girl with a B+ average whose mother had abused her through neglect and having multiple affairs, which became a public embarrassment to the daughter. When the mother called to tell the daughter that she was dying of cancer within six months and wanted her to quit college and come home and take care of her until her death, it was the "final straw." The girl was suddenly "struck blind." Neurologists could find no organic explanation for her blindness, and she was referred to me for psychiatric treatment. After three weeks of daily therapy focusing on her love-hate feelings toward her mother, the girl fully regained her sight.

Incorporation: Symbolic representations of a person or parts of a person are figuratively ingested by someone who feels inferior for some reason. For example, a young boy feels inferior to his father because his father has larger, stronger legs. Whenever Mother serves fried chicken, the boy always wants drumsticks. Consciously he thinks it is only because he likes dark meat but unconsciously he wants to eat a lot of chicken legs to make his own legs larger and stronger than Dad's.

Idealization: Individuals overestimate the admired attributes of another person. This frequently happens when members of the congregation put the pastor on a high pedestal because he seems "so perfect." When the pastor proves to be quite human, these same members are the first to become disenchanted.

Intellectualization: Individuals deal with severe inferiority feelings and other unconscious conflicts through the excessive use of a very large vocabulary, as well as getting into heavy discussions of philosophy, for example. The college philosophy major who talks in multisyllabic words and is bored with anything but a high level discussion of complex ideas and issues may well be intellectualizing to hide the unconscious inferiority feelings he has because he felt so conditionally accepted by his parents while growing up.

He also may be "emotionally disabled," meaning that he has very little insight into his emotions, not knowing what emotion he is experiencing, and often not even realizing that he is experiencing the emotion at all.

Introjection: Individuals symbolically redirect toward themselves the feelings they have toward someone else, or even the feelings of another person. Introjection is the opposite of projection. An example would be a teenage girl who feels very angry at her father, but to avoid guilt feelings she unconsciously redirects the anger back toward herself, saying she never does anything right and is a failure.

Isolation: Various unacceptable emotions (such as jealousy, greed, or lust) are split off from conscious thoughts and isolated in the unconscious, even though the individuals may have good insights into other more acceptable emotions. Isolation of specific emotions is very close to repression, which is a more general process. Isolation can be seen, for example, in the person who mistakenly thinks all anger is sin. He isolates his anger to relieve his own false guilt.

Magical thinking: A very common defense mechanism whereby individuals compensate for inferiority feelings by believing they have subtle, supernatural powers. People who open the Bible at random to put their finger on "just the right verse" to get directions are usually using magical thinking. So is an eight-year-old child who becomes very angry at her father and fleetingly wishes he would die. That night she has a nightmare about her father dying, and the next day he does die in an auto accident. The little girl believes her anger "magically" caused her father's death, and may be overwhelmed by false guilt, which could turn into severe depression.

A common, and usually harmless, form of magical thinking involves sports fans who watch athletic events on television and scream encouragement, advice, or criticism to the players or coaches on their favorite teams. Somehow they believe that their audible groans and/or cheers really make a difference in the game, and they feel "magically" proud of themselves when their opinion is "proven correct" by the result of a particular play.

Reaction formation: Individuals adopt attitudes and behavior that are the opposite of their true conscious or unconscious impulses. Reaction formation could have been part of the problem for the pastors described in Chapter 3, who would disproportionately focus their preaching on the terrible results of extramarital sex and then fall repeatedly into sexual affairs with women in their congregations.

People who focus a great deal of their time, money, and energy to crusade against a single area of "injustice" often have strong unconscious temptations to do whatever it is that they are crusading against. The true purpose of their crusade is to hide the truth about their own impulses from their awareness. James 1:26 speaks of the consequences of reaction formation.

Regression: Individuals faced with stress or conflict return to an earlier stage of emotional immaturity where they felt more protected from life's pressures. Three- and four-year-olds who are toilet trained may regress back to bed wetting, baby talk, soiling their pants, and temper tantrums when a new baby arrives in the family, because these were the things that they did back when they were the center of attention and felt more secure.

Adults can also regress to variable extents during times of stress (such as moving to a new community, changing jobs, having a first child, physical illness, or death of a loved one) by going back to the behaviors they engaged in at the age when they felt most important and secure.

Sarcasm: Individuals with repressed hostility toward themselves, another individual, or a group ventilate that hostility without even being aware of it by making critical jokes about themselves or others. An example would be a young man who grows up with repressed hostility toward his mother and women in general. He can't understand why people are offended by his constant critical jokes about women, and claims that he is "only joking." Not all sarcasm has underlying hostility, however, and a "friendly roast" can be a lot of fun.

Schizoid fantasy: Individuals who find reality painful escape the pain of reality through excessive daydreaming. An example would be a young girl who daydreams constantly about the "perfect romance" but refuses to date boys because she is very shy and fearful of intimacy. She may still be single at seventy, but she will still be going through her bride magazines to "pick out her trousseau."

Somatization: A defense used excessively by hypochondriacs. Unacceptable, unconscious feelings (such as anger) or motives (such as vengeance) come out through genuine physical symptoms (such as headaches, diarrhea, or heartburn) in parts of the body innervated by the autonomic nervous system. Such persons are thus able to keep their minds on their physical symptoms to avoid being aware of their true feelings and motives.

For example, a student is reprimanded in class by his professor and becomes angry, but he stuffs his anger because he doesn't want to get in trouble and jeopardize his grade. His body responds almost immediately with tightness in the lower back muscles. In a few days he is immobilized by severe back pains and has to see a doctor.

Psychosomatic illness is a broader description that includes real illness brought on by somatization or imagined illness brought on by hysterical conversion reaction. The term *psychosomatic* was coined by Johann Heinroth, a Christian psychiatrist who lived one hundred years before Freud.

Symbolization: A single act or object represents a complex group of acts or objects, some of which are unacceptable to the ego (a form of complex formation and condensation). For example, a young man is reared in a home where sex is looked upon as dirty and ungodly. He tries to deny his sexual impulses and yearnings, but nevertheless is heavily influenced to purchase products whose TV advertisements include subtle, or not so subtle, sexual symbols: a car described by the phrase "I love what you do for me," or aftershave lotion sold by a beautiful blonde saying, "My men wear this or they wear nothing at all."

Undoing: Individuals carry out unconscious acts or verbal communication to negate (or "undo") a previous mistake, thus making themselves think the mistake never occurred. For example, a woman criticizes a friend behind her back and feels such strong unconscious guilt that the next day she goes out of her way to compliment this person, even though she doesn't really remember making the criticism, nor does she know why she's being so complimentary.

Unhealthy identification: Individuals model their attitudes and behavior after another person without even knowing that they are doing so. This defense mechanism can happen as a child watches a violent "hero" on TV, a teenager watches steamy sex scenes in R-rated movies, or an employee observes underhanded business methods being used by his employer.

Unhealthy sublimation: Unacceptable emotions (such as hostility or lust) are acceptably channeled without the individual ever becoming aware of these emotions, which lie deep within his unconscious.

For example, a boy grows up in a strict religious family that preaches love, but is really cold, critical, or hostile. The boy develops strong hostile drives himself, but because these aren't "acceptable," he becomes an excellent athlete and wins a college football scholarship due to his "killer instincts" as a linebacker. He goes to seminary and eventually becomes a successful preacher noted for pointing out the "godless errors" of psychology and the "spiritual dangers" in trying to get help through psychotherapy.

Unhealthy suppression: The only defense mechanism used "on purpose," whereby individuals indefinitely postpone dealing with a conflict of which they are fully aware. They consciously suppress the truth by fooling themselves into thinking they will deal with this later, but "later" never comes.

For example, in Chapter 6, I mentioned that I had been using denial to avoid confronting an abusive employee. When friends called this to my attention, I planned to deal with the employee at an opportune time. I did so within a week, but if I had kept putting it off, saying I would deal with it later, and then forgotten about it completely, I would have been using unhealthy suppression.

Withdrawal: Individuals deceive themselves about the existence of tension-producing conflicts by removing themselves from the situation. For example, a young man fears intimacy but won't admit it to himself. He gets engaged to three different women, but withdraws from each relationship when the wedding date draws near, blaming the break-ups on minor imperfections he finds in each of the women.

Another example would be a single young woman who desires marriage but who unconsciously has a strong fear that she will "act out" sexually (engage in premarital sex). She asks God to send her a mate, but unconsciously withdraws from all social situations where she might actually meet a man. Then she may even become angry with God for not answering her prayers and sending her a husband.

NOTES

Chapter 1

1. Larry Crabb, *Inside Out* (Colorado Springs: NavPress, 1988), p. 20.

Chapter 4

1. The details of Saddam Hussein's life come from a compilation of numerous news reports, including "Saddam Hussein's Three-Ring Circus," *U.S. News and World Report*, September 10, 1990, pp. 29–40.

2. See Romans 12:19.

3. Alexander Pope, *Essay on Criticism* (University Press, 1896).

Chapter 5

1. For a thorough discussion of the shame base and how false guilt drives away the feeling of having rights to good and basic things, see Robert Hemfelt, Frank Minirth, and Paul Meier, *We Are Driven* (Nashville: Thomas Nelson Publishers, 1991), chapter 7.

2. See Robert Hemfelt, Frank Minirth, and Paul Meier, *Love Is a Choice* (Nashville: Thomas Nelson Publishers, 1989), p. 11.

Chapter 6

1. Jeremiah 17:9–10.

2. Charles Morris, *Psychology: An Introduction* (Englewood Cliffs, N.J.: Prentice Hall, 1973), pp. 439–40.

3. See Meg Sullivan, "Hey, Baby . . . Sexual Harassment Haunts Women in Non-Traditional Jobs," *The Daily News*, August 30, 1992, "Women" section, p. 1.

4. Proverbs 14:8.

Chapter 7

1. See Exodus 34:7; Numbers 14:18.

2. John Bradshaw, *Bradshaw On: The Family* (Deerfield Beach, Fla: Health Communications, Inc., 1988), p. 27.

Chapter 8
1. 2 Timothy 1:7.
2. For a more detailed discussion of food addiction, see Frank Minirth, Paul Meier, Robert Hemfelt, and Sharon Sneed, *Love Hunger* (Nashville: Thomas Nelson Publishers, 1990), Part I, pp. 11–52.
3. *We Are Driven,* p. 248.
4. Adapted from *We Are Driven,* pp. 249–250, 252.
5. See Proverbs 1:7.

Chapter 9
1. Ephesians 4:26.
2. See Romans 12:19.
3. For a thorough discussion of depression, see Frank Minirth and Paul Meier, *Happiness Is a Choice* (Grand Rapids: Baker Book House, 1978). Part I, Chapters 1–4, discusses what is depression. Part II discusses the causes of depression, and Part III discusses how to overcome it. Pages 124–28 list 101 signs or personality traits commonly seen in depressed individuals.
4. James 1:20 NIV.
5. See, for example, the account of Jesus cleansing the Temple, John 2:13–25.
6. Matthew 5:48 NIV.
7. Proverbs 19:5 NIV.
8. See Ephesians 4:15–16.
9. Lewis B. Smedes, "Forgiveness: Healing the Hurts We Don't Deserve," *Family Life Today,* January 1985, p. 25.
10. Ephesians 4:26-27 TLB.
11. 2 Timothy 4:14–15.
12. Romans 5:5.
13. Corrie ten Boom, *Jesus Is Victor* (Old Tappan, N.J.: Fleming H. Revell Company, Power Books, 1985), p. 95.

Chapter 10
1. See Matthew 7:3-5.
2. Maurice Wagner, *The Sensation of Being Somebody* (Grand Rapids: Zondervan Publishing House, 1975), p. 32.
3. Ibid, p. 34.
4. Ibid, p. 35.
5. Ibid, p. 36.
6. See Matthew 11:30.

7. See Frank Minirth and Paul Meier, *Happiness Is a Choice* (Grand Rapids: Baker Book House, 1978).

8. See Matthew 10:38; 16:24; also Romans 2:8; Philippians 2:3; James 3:14–16.

9. Josh McDowell, *Building Your Self-Image* (Wheaton: Living Books Division, Tyndale House Publishers, Inc., 1988), p. 39. Italics added.

10. Psalm 139:17-18 TLB.

11. 1 Samuel 13:14.

12. Psalm 139:23-24.

13. James 1:2-4 NIV.

Chapter 11

1. See Philippians 4:13.

2. James 5:16.

3. Proverbs 24:16 NIV.

4. Proverbs 24:6 TLB.

5. Proverbs 3:5-6.

6. Thomas Nelson Publishers, 1989.

7. See Hebrews 12:1-2.

8. See Matthew 22:37.

9. See Ecclesiastes 12:13-14.

10. See, for example, Ecclesiastes 1 NIV.

11. Ecclesiastes 5:19.

12. William Barclay, *The Daily Study Bible: Gospel of Matthew*, vol. 1 (Edinburgh: St. Andrew Press, 1956), p. 263.

13. Matthew 6:34.

ABOUT THE AUTHOR

Paul Meier, M.D., is co-founder of the Minirth Meier New Life Clinics. He received an M.S. in cardiovascular physiology from Michigan State University and his M.D. from the University of Arkansas College of Medicine. He completed his psychiatric residency at Duke University Medical School. He also received an M.A. in Biblical Studies from Dallas Theological Seminary and has taught pastoral counseling in seminary.

Dr. Meier has written or co-authored more than forty books, including *Love Is a Choice*, *Worry-Free Living*, *Love Hunger*, and *The Third Millennium*. He resides in Richardson, Texas, with his wife and family.